occy

the rise and fall
and rise of Mark Occhilupo

occy

the rise and fall and rise of Mark Occhilupo

by **Mark Occhilupo** & **Tim Baker**

EBURY
PRESS

All internal photos courtesy Paul Sargeant unless otherwise noted.

An Ebury Press book
Published by Random House Australia Pty Ltd
Level 3, 100 Pacific Highway, North Sydney NSW 2060
www.randomhouse.com.au

First published by Ebury Press in 2008

Addresses for companies within the Random House Group can be found at www.randomhouse.com.au/offices

National Library of Australia
Cataloguing-in-Publication Entry

Occhilupo, Mark, 1966–.
Occy: the rise and fall and rise of Mark Occhilupo.

ISBN 978 1 74166 643 4 (pbk).

Occhilupo, Mark, 1966–.
Surfers – Australia – Biography.

Other Authors/Contributors: Baker, Tim, 1965–.

797.32092

Inside front cover: A timeless line – Occy leans into a solid Pipe bottom turn,
              looking for the tunnel. Photo: Sarge.
Inside back cover: Occy's trademark hook in the pocket at one of his favourite
              places in the world – Rocky Point lefts, Hawaii. Photo: Sarge.
Cover and internal design by Adam Yazxhi/MAXCO
Typeset by Midland Typesetters, Australia
Printed and bound by Griffin Press, South Australia

Random House Australia uses papers that are natural, renewable and recyclable products and made from wood grown in sustainable forests. The logging and manufacturing processes are expected to conform to the environmental regulations of the country of origin.

10 9 8 7

To my beautiful family, Luciano, Pam, Shanla, Alex, Fleur, Mae, Jay, Jonah and Rainer, for all their love and support.

And in memory of all those loved ones we've lost along the way: Luciano, Beatrice, Ronnie Burns, Mark Pripic, Mark Sainsbury, Peter Whittaker, Andrew Ferguson, Adam Daley, Randall and Carol Kim, Peter Crawford, Dan Nakasoni, Richard Herbert, Joe Engel, Sean Fanning, Joel Green and Midget Smith.

Contents

Introduction

Junior profile: Mark Occhilupo – sixteen years old, lives in Cronulla and comes out of the classic 'surf nazi' mould. Goofy-footer with heaps of ambition and talent to match. Cheeky little bugger, but very entertaining. Considering such a short time as a competitive surfer, his results are excellent. Definitely one of the hottest juniors in the country, but whatever you do, don't tell him that.

Kelly Slater: Occy was always a missile going hyperspeed, about to blow up at any moment. It's true of so many highly intelligent or gifted people. He was having a hard time containing himself and understanding things in his world, which he got to the top of pretty easily. All of his passion was put into his surfing.

Mick Lowe: When he was seventeen, eighteen, he was the reason I started surfing; he was the guy I saw on the TV and went, *far out*.

Gerry Lopez: He's really in the moment and that's why his surfing is so beautiful. He's right there. When you watch him do it you just go, *wow*. He's like a jazz musician or a blues musician more than a rock star up there going through the motions. He's really, really feeling it – so heart, body and soul – in that moment . . . It really becomes an example for a lot of people.

Bruce Irons: He has a really unique style that no-one has, real stylish and lays down the heaviest carves, real soulful deep bottom turns, long arcing turns frontside or backside. No-one draws lines like that – real stumpy legs, real low gravity. He feels the wave – it's pretty crazy.

Joel Parkinson: He's got a stepmum in Mundaka who's classic. She speaks not one word of English but they just understand each other. Every year she just comes out of nowhere and goes, 'Occy, I love you, my son.' When I first met her I thought she was a nut case and he goes, 'Nah, she's been coming there for fifteen years.' She's been like that since they first met. She's got photos of him everywhere; she just loves him. Every year she gets a paper signed by him. She's, like, sixty, but she just idolises him.

Kelly Slater: Occy's a child trapped in a man's body just going out there doing his thing.

Occy (from *Tracks*, December 1985): There is a park near where I live, and I sometimes go for walks in it. There are these birds in it, and they go, 'Ark, Ark.' And I reckon it sounds like they are saying 'Mark'. I reckon they're saying it for me.

By any measure, Mark Occhilupo has had a remarkable career. The numbers alone are incredible enough. Occy is such an enigma, with such a mythology around him, that it is probably helpful to first consider the bald statistics to begin to understand his achievements.

Occy has enjoyed two distinct careers, separated by an almost ten-year gap, and either one would have been enough to satisfy most pro surfers.

He qualified for the ASP World Championship Tour at his first attempt, rated sixteenth in the world in 1983, leapt to third in '84, then fourth in '85, third again in '86, and dropped to ninth in '87. Then, in a shock move, he quit the tour mid-1988, publicly citing frustration with poor waves, but privately suffering an awful psychological burnout. In that brief five-year stint, he made eleven finals and won nine of them. Out of 247 heats surfed, he won 189, a 76 per cent success rate. At the time, only Mark Richards and Tom Curren had higher winning percentages.

All that would have been enough to cement a place in history. But his remarkable comeback, after ten years in the surfing wilderness, was simply beyond comprehension – and completely unprecedented. At age thirty, when most pro surfers were planning for retirement, he went through the arduous World Qualifying Series and earnt a place on the World Championship Tour in 1997. Against a whole new generation of surfers, some almost young enough to be his offspring, he proceeded to finish second in '97, seventh in '98, and first in '99 for his long-awaited world title. In 2000 he dropped to twentieth, his mission and fairytale comeback seemingly complete. Yet, just when we might have expected him to drop off the radar altogether, he rose to second again in 2001, tenth in 2002, and sixteenth in 2003 – the same rating he held when he first qualified twenty years earlier. Again, when we might have imagined he was done, he climbed back to twelfth in 2004. When he announced his retirement in 2005 there was outright revolt among his friends on tour, who convinced him to continue until his ultimate retirement at the 2007 Pipeline Masters at the age of forty-one, a full twenty-three years after he first entered the event.

All this is even more remarkable when you consider that the years he spent *off* tour, from the age of twenty-two to thirty, normally constitute the prime of a pro surfer's career.

But of course statistics alone only tell part of the story. It is the way he has done all this that has endeared him to surfers, friends and fans all over the world. From the heaviest Hawaiian locals, to the women who work at Namotu Island in Fiji and catch boats out to cheer him on from the channel at Cloudbreak, to elderly Spanish grandmothers who have adopted him in Mundaka, Occy has been the people's champion – cutting across cultural and generational divides.

As anyone who knows him will tell you, Occy is a fascinating character, completely unique, with an uncanny knack for narrowly averting disaster on land and weaving magic in the ocean. His troubled relationship with motor cars is the stuff of legend. He's accidentally rolled them down driveways, reversed them through shopfronts, ridden into the back of one on a 'borrowed' Harley Davidson, punctured all four tyres driving over spikes while trying to exit through the entrance of a car rental lot, filled diesel cars with petrol (twice). The lists goes on.

This should probably come as no surprise. Occy and cars are polar opposites. Cars operate on mechanics and physics, pure and simple – predictable, measurable, repeatable. Occy runs on emotion, 'the feeling', and when it isn't there you may as well pack up and go home – as he has done more than once in his long and tumultuous career. When the feeling is there, when the elements align, the energy is right and the vibe is good, anything is possible.

This has been vividly made clear to me in the process of documenting that astounding career in this book. When Occ wasn't feeling it, I may as well have been pulling teeth, or it would become virtually impossible to pin him down to a time and place. When we were in the flow, the stories would pour forth in a torrent, tumbling over one another.

I went to his apartment one afternoon, boarding the lift at the ground floor, only to be greeted by him already in the lift, a case of beer under his arm, ascending from the basement garage. He likes that kind of synchronicity. 'Looks like we're going to have a good session,' he said, grinning. And so it proved to be, as we sipped VB Midstrengths on the balcony of his high-rise apartment, enjoying sweeping views over Coolangatta's famed Superbank as his wife,

Mae, valiantly entertained the kids inside. Another time, we met on the top of Duranbah Hill, and Occ held court for an hour nonstop with wild tales from his '80s heyday in California to the time he fed a cameraman betel nut on location in Indonesia during the filming of *Green Iguana*. At the conclusion, spent and almost giddy with the reminiscences, Occy declared, 'This is our spot', as if the hill and view of the surf provided the geocentric energy lines compatible with good storytelling.

Occy, I've come to realise, operates energetically. He assesses and responds to almost any situation on a purely energetic level, requires the necessary 'vibe' to produce his best surfing, craves real human connection with the people around him, and can come a spectacular cropper when he misreads or ignores this tried-and-tested approach to life. In the water it is easy, feeling, reading and responding to the pulses of pure energy the ocean sends. It is more difficult on land, where people's motives can be obscure and the swirling play of energy less easily observed. These qualities are often described as 'childlike', but in reality it is a highly evolved state, perfectly suited to successfully negotiating your path through a pitching sea. It is perhaps less well-adapted to life on land in the modern, Western world of capitalism and consumerism, where pitfalls are plenty and currents difficult to read. That Occy has prevailed without compromising that approach is testament to his resilience and the protective instincts of those around him.

At times it can be almost impossible to tell whether he is being deliberately humorous or unwittingly naive. Once when discussing the chemical plant near his childhood home in Kurnell, I recalled seeing a news report about a toxic plume spreading underground from the site, which was in danger of leaching into Botany Bay. 'And it makes all the local people weird?' he asked, deadpan, before exploding into laughter, as if some scientific explanation of his extraordinary life's path would almost come as a relief.

His is a uniquely Australian story, begun at the birthplace of white Australia, where Captain Cook's ship *Endeavour* dropped anchor in 1770, at the interface of modern Sydney's city, suburbs, industry and ocean. It's the story of the son of an Italian migrant, who defied the strict academic expectations of a stern father while fulfilling the sporting dreams and enthusiasms of a doting mother. It's the story of an Australian beach scene that offered suburban kids a long shot at stardom, wealth and world travel based on their skill, reflexes and dedication to dancing over ocean waves.

Ultimately, I'd contend, it's a story tailor-made for a world that sometimes needs reminding about the power of pursuing one's bliss, the therapeutic properties of a good lie down, and the importance of never, ever giving up.

– Tim Baker

Occy

For a sleepy hamlet of just over 2000 people, Kurnell looms large in Australian history. It is where, on 29 April 1770, Captain James Cook first set foot on Australian soil after anchoring his ship *Endeavour* in Botany Bay. At the end of his historic exploration of the South Pacific, and in the midst of surveying some 3200 kilometres of the previously uncharted east coast of Australia, Cook sought safe harbour in what he dubbed Botany Bay and came ashore at Kurnell Peninsula.

Communication with the local Gweagal people proved difficult. Cook offered them trinkets – beads, nails and the like, 'which they took up and seem'd not ill pleased with,' Cook wrote in his journal. He thought they beckoned him ashore, but he was mistaken. As Cook's party landed the few men on shore grew threatening, and Cook fired a musket between them. One retaliated by throwing a rock. Cook fired again, hitting one of them, 'yet it had no other effect than to make him lay hold of a Shield or target to defend himself.' Cook's first steps on Australian soil were thus met with a volley of spears. So began British settlement of the Great Southern Land.

Almost 200 years later, Italian migrant Luciano Occhilupo chose to settle his young family a few hundred metres from Cook's first landfall. 'He kind of created Italy at home,' remembers Occy. 'He worked for an Italian firm, they all spoke Italian at work, they'd

book one

In the Beginning

have wine with lunch, just like Italy.' On weekends, Italian friends visited, spoke Italian, listened to Italian music, while Luciano prepared Italian food. But despite his best efforts, Luciano's children showed no interest in learning his native language and distanced themselves from his culture for fear of being labelled 'wogs'. While the grown-ups enjoyed Luciano's risotto, his New Zealand-born wife, Pam, would cook chops and vege for the kids.

The son of that Italian migrant, Marco Jay Luciano Occhilupo, took to the national pasttime of wave-riding with a talent and enthusiasm that would carry him to the top of the surfing world. The culturally neutral 'Occy' became his moniker, easy off the tongue and immediately identifiable to surfers throughout the world. His surfing spoke an international language too: wild, unrestrained, boundlessly creative, breathtaking.

That small peninsula between Botany Bay and the Pacific Ocean provided young Marco with what he remembers as an idyllic childhood – parental conflicts and his father's disapproval of his surfing aside. Its beaches and reefs held sport that captivated him. He developed an intuitive sense of how the interplay of wind, swell and tide produced the most favourable surfing conditions, and happily gorged on this aquatic playground.

In 2004, Kurnell Peninsula was added to Australia's National Heritage List, as a place of special cultural significance, along with the MCG, the Opera House and Uluru. Surfers might argue that honour was warranted even if Cook had never gone near the place.

– T. B.

Occy

Chapter One

Kurnell Days

Pam Occhilupo (Mark's mother): Mark was different, even in the womb. I was three months pregnant when I went water skiing in New Zealand and had a very heavy fall. That afternoon as I waited with my mother at her medical centre I felt a rush of something I feared was blood. Sure enough, as I rose from the creamy couch it was soaked with a spreading red stain. In great embarrassment I slunk out of the crowded waiting room and mother carted me off to a GP and then a gynecologist – both confirmed I had miscarried. Strangely enough, I went on growing and six months later produced a lusty, healthy boy on June 16, 1966. No-one ever gave me an explanation for this strange event, though my theory is that I was carrying twins, one miscarried and the other, Mark, clung on. So, you see, he was tenacious even before he was born!

My earliest memory is nearly drowning on a fishing trip with my family when I was three, near our home at Kurnell. At low tide a big finger of sand would stick out, and my dad would fish off the end of it. That was the place to catch whiting. I used to hang with him and loved it when he'd pull a fish from the water thrashing and writhing. He must have walked in to shore with a fish or to get more bait or something, and the tide was coming in. Because it was just a narrow sandbar, it used to disappear pretty quickly on the incoming tide, and I got bowled over by a tidal surge and can remember the water going over my head and seeing bubbles. It was a beautiful sunny day and I was looking up through this clear blue-green water and thinking, *someone's going to come and get me.* I was so young I don't remember being scared. It was kind of a pleasant sensation. And I was just waiting for someone to come and scoop me out. I'd been playing around the ocean all my life and was pretty used to getting scooped out. But I can also remember that I was a long way away from anyone – maybe 500 metres from the beach – and just hoping that someone would come. Eventually it was my sister Alex who scooped me out, but I wasn't scared. There was something about being swept up and taken under by the ocean that I quite liked.

We lived at 41 Captain Cook Drive, Kurnell, on the edge of Botany Bay, a stone's throw from where Cook's ship, *Endeavour*, first dropped anchor in what would become Sydney. Kurnell's a funny place, a little country town in the middle of Australia's biggest city, surrounded by this huge industrial area. Maybe having the oil refinery and chemical plants as neighbours is what has saved it from development. People used to joke that the locals at Kurnell had two heads, but we loved growing up there.

I was the youngest of four children, and the only boy. With three older sisters, my mum reckons I took a bit of an interest in girls' clothing. In fact, when I was four or five, I was a full-on crossdresser. I remember wearing a dress a lot and my sisters putting make-up on me.

> **Pam Occhilupo:** It wasn't enough that he was dressed up in tutus for the girls' plays, or in bunny outfits when it was Easter and time to deliver eggs to the neighbourhood: No, I had to make him a kilt so that he could be like the girls all the time. Admittedly, he did look very cute in it at four years old. It was just as well he got cross-dressing out of his system by the

time he was ready for school or it might have created some problems.

Fleur Occhilupo (Mark's sister): Mark once asked me when he was going to turn into a woman. He actually thought he was a girl, and we said, 'Actually, no, we're just dressing you up.'

Kurnell was a great place to grow up. We had a fruit shop right next door, with a big concrete parking area. That was where me and all my friends would meet up to ride our skateboards. Right in front of my house we had an area of grass as big as a football field, with no trees, so there was room for touch footy and everything. It was all happening in front of my house; there was always stuff to do. My best mate, Richard Maurer, lived up the road on Polo Street, and there was always a gang of mates to play with.

The milk truck would pull up while we were playing footy or skating, and we always made sure we had fifty cents to buy a strawberry Moove, a little carton of flavoured milk. They just tasted all-time, and they'd keep you going for another hour. Out the front of the fruit shop was a big green electrical box, about four-feet wide and eight-feet across. We called it 'the green box', and on cold days we'd lie on the top, because it was always warm, and watch the cars go by.

Right across the road was the national park and Captain Cook's anchor. There was a little booth where you had to pay money to get into the park. You could only go in when the man was in the booth to take your money, otherwise the gates would be locked. I got to know the guy in the booth, and he let me sit in the box and take the money I loved that. The road up through the national park was really steep, and we used to skateboard it a lot. We also had a pool in our backyard, and we would climb onto the roof of the fruit shop next door and jump in the pool.

Me and Richard and Beaver and Darcy and Joey Morgan, we

used to hang out a lot and all go to Kurnell Primary School, and ride our bikes everywhere. There was hardly any traffic because Kurnell was the end of the road, it wasn't on the way to anywhere, so you could let your kids run around. It wasn't a worry, apart from the local larrikins driving 100 miles an hour.

> **Pam Occhilupo:** Mark was a loveable child – naughty, yes, but able to charm the birds out of trees, as the saying goes. On the frequent times he would try my patience and I would start laying down the law, he would answer with a 'Yes, Your Maj' [short for Majesty], which would take the wind out of my sails and I would collapse in giggles. At this time we were building a new house and pool, living in a little cottage at the back. Luciano refused to fill the pool until Mark could swim, so he tenaciously applied himself and was swimming in two days flat.

I remember watching guys surf at Botany Bay. The biggest the surf would ever get in the bay was only four or five foot, and that was only a few times a year, but when you're four years old it looked huge. I remember guys shooting the pier at Kurnell, and a couple of guys got nailed trying to do it. I used to love to go and watch when there were waves in the bay. It was this amazing spectacle. The town would light up and we'd all go down to watch.

When I first learnt to surf, it was right there at Botany Bay, and I think it was my sister Alex's boyfriend who taught me, but Fleur reckons it was her boyfriend . . . The waves were one to two foot, and Kurnell Point was breaking. I remember the board was called a Woodstock, with red rails. I got pushed into a little wave, and it wasn't an easy board to ride, seven or eight foot, but I was really light so I was straight up on it. Like my kids their first time on a board, I just stood up and rode it all the way to the beach. I was probably six or seven and instantly hooked.

Pam Occhilupo: The boy next door, Colin Rowland, threw out his old surfboard on the rubbish heap. Mark went and got it, and then Alex took him down to the beach. When Alex first pushed him on tiny little waves, he just stood up straightaway. But there's always an argument between his sisters about who took him first . . .

Alex Occhilupo (from Jack McCoy's *The Occumentary*): I dragged him down the boatshed so that I could meet this guy that I was in love with at the time in primary school.

Fleur Occhiupo: They have those rubbish days, and Mark and I went off walking down the road and we found this blue board with a star on the nose, dings on it everywhere, so we would take it and push each other on. It would fill up with water and we'd have to dry it out before you could use it again. We always liked to do the same things because I was a bit of a tomboy.

We started off at the boatshed, which were like little, gentle, Waikiki rollers, and then we graduated to Kurnell Point itself. We used to surf Kurnell Point a lot – well, every time it broke at least. Even if it was one foot, me and Richard Maurer were out there, but we were so small it didn't matter. When we were on our way to and from school and we'd see waves and we knew Kurnell Point was pumping, we'd get off school as fast as we could. We'd run or ride or get someone to pick us up and be straight down there.

Kurnell Point's actually a pretty gnarly wave. When we were young we'd hang on the side of it, because it was too shallow for us. At low tide you can't even surf it. At mid to high tide you can fully backdoor it, and it spits nearly every time. Once you come out of the barrel you get a wall that wraps right around towards you, and you can do the best cutties off the wash and a little turn on the wall. But when we were young we used to watch guys pull into the barrel and hope they fell off, so we could drop in on the shoulder and do snaps on the wall – and it might even barrel again at one or two foot. It's a really good wave, but it just doesn't break that often.

I don't know if we didn't have enough money for legropes, but we would cut bicycle tubes up to make our own leggies. I remember one night we knew it was going to be good the next day – we must have seen it that afternoon when it was pumping – and we were going to Kurnell Point early the next morning. We were probably eight years old, cutting up these bike tyres, with a bit of rope for a leash, and tying that through a hole in the base of the single fin. There were no legrope plugs, and we'd use socks for the ankle strap. We were out there the next day in the most old-school wetties. It was the biggest we'd ever seen it. We paddled out way down the beach and saw these older guys getting so shacked. We barely even caught the shoulders, maybe three or four waves from morning to lunchtime. We were just scratching over the biggest sets, watching guys get barrelled, and we'd be sitting all together in a pack, wide-eyed and terrified. In between sets one of us would catch a little one on the side, and we'd all be screaming. It was an epic day.

> **Richard Maurer:** I remember heaps of times surfing out Kurnell Point when it was one or two foot, just learning how to surf, learning reef breaks and watching the older guys when it did get bigger, like Ross Marshall, or older Kurnell guys like Tony Austin, who was about six foot four and played for the Cronulla Sharks at the time. He was sort of like the big guy that nobody dropped in on, nobody fucked with. At that stage me and Occ were going to nippers, under-13s, and we knew Kurnell Point was breaking so we finished nippers at twelve o'clock, sprinted to the point. There was Tony Austin, right on the point where you jump off, smoking a cigarette as he normally did, surfboard under his arm. And we walked up to

him and he goes, 'Where have you two little cunts been?' And we said, 'We've been to nippers.'

'Nippers?' he said. 'Geez, if you two blokes came out to save me I'd swim out further.' I thought, *hang on, that's a payout*. I was sort of stoked because he was the coolest guy. He'd see a set coming in, put the cigarette out, paddle out; just before the set came he'd turn around, catch the wave, get barrelled, come in on the point and light up again. He was the legend guy.

My dad really wasn't too sure about this whole surfing business. Dad was from Italy and came to Australia after the Second World War. He was a civil engineer, and people with those sorts of qualifications were offered the chance to emigrate to Australia – engineers and doctors and people like that – so he got on this boat to Australia. Mum was from New Zealand and going on her first big overseas trip when they met up. We even lived in New Zealand for a year or two, when I was really little, but eventually settled back in Sydney.

I remember Dad as a really good man, definitely really strict and he didn't take much shit. My mum and dad used to fight a bit and it was pretty radical as a kid, but I think it was pretty common, because my mates' parents had big fights too.

Dad was a sensational cook. I always remember him cooking risotto with seafood. It smelt better than anything. He'd cook it on a Sunday afternoon for hours. I used to sneak up and take spoonfuls of it when no-one was looking. But I'd always end up with my mum's chops and vegies. He didn't think we'd be interested in his traditional Italian food. But he'd cook up some amazing dishes. His Italian friend Tulio and his wife, Joyce, would come over every weekend. They'd drink KB Lager and talk Italian and listen to Italian music, while me and all my mates played in the pool, jumping off the roof of the fruit shop. There was a big tree in the backyard with a swing hanging from it, and we had a little cricket pitch where we played cricket. They are some of my favourite memories of summertime in Sydney.

Pam Occhilupo: Luciano was a civil engineer and he came out to Australia. He was actually thinking of going to South America, to Brazil, but for some reason he came to Australia instead. I think it was because after the war there weren't many opportunities in Italy, but he was always torn between the two countries. He worked for an Italian firm out here and he kept going back. Around the same time, I set out on a working holiday from New Zealand where I worked as a nurse. I got as far as Cairns and met Luciano, and that was the end of my working holiday.

I was waitressing in Gino's Café, and Luciano used to come in every day and stare at me. Gino was his best friend and said, 'Well, Luciano wants to go out with you.' So I sort of said, 'Well, he can ask me himself.' Gino replied, 'I'll sack you if you don't go out with Luciano. That's it.'

One day, Luciano came in by himself and asked me out, so I thought, *okay*. I was going to go on travelling, but we fell madly in love and that was it . . . I'd been married before, and my daughter, Shan, was in New Zealand with my family. Luciano said, 'You've got to get her to come over', and when I went back he just bombarded me with phone calls and letters until I came back again with Shan. They had an instant rapport. He adored Shan, and she him. I had Alex and Fleur up in Cairns, then Luciano was transferred down to Sydney. We built a house in Kurnell and Mark was born in Sutherland Hospital.

I used to have bad dreams about the oil refinery catching on fire, because a few times it did, and I still have the dream today. I still have most of the dreams I had as a kid – I don't know why. We had to be evacuated because Kurnell's so close to it. It was always a worry when we heard the local fire station alarm go off, because we had so much national park nearby. If that caught on fire, it was so close to the refinery. You had to drive through all that industrial area, right past the oil refinery, to get in and out of Kurnell. These radical dreams were about evacuating, and you'd want to run because it was going to blow up, and you couldn't run. Your legs would just be going on the spot, but you weren't getting anywhere.

But the refinery also provided us with a bit of sport. You used to be able to walk along the oil pipes that ran along parts of the coast, and fish off them, even though you weren't allowed to. We'd climb through a hole in this little cage and walk along the pipes, and they were always warm from the oil pumping through them. We used to walk way out on the pipes, and every time a car would come we'd hide. And we would fish out there and catch good fish.

Me and my mates would go on these long walks along the cliffs. If the swell wasn't too big and tide wasn't too high, you could walk all the way to that wave the Bra Boys now call 'Ours'. We never dreamt of surfing it. It looked way too heavy and too close to the rocks, so we'd just sit and watch it. We'd play in the caves up there and jump in the rock pools.

One hot summer's day, at low tide, we decided to walk round the cliffs to the rock pools. We always seemed to know what the tides were doing, and they governed our activities. We found these little rock pools and jumped in and, because it was so hot, they were as warm as bathwater. We were just hanging in the pools when one by one we all started scratching and screaming. There were some kind of weird lice in the water, and we ran screaming all the way home. We all broke out in this burning hot rash and could not stop scratching ourselves. We had welts all over us, and a couple of the boys had to go to the doctor. Our mums smothered us in calamine lotion, and we got a couple of days off school. We always talk about that one.

There were all these wooden forts in the school playground that we loved playing in. We used to go mad on the monkey bars and swing from them until our hands were covered in the biggest calluses. We'd play handball and marbles for hours. It was a great school. Richard and I can still sing the Kurnell Public School song.

Joey Morgan was from a family of professional fishermen and the wildest kid in school. He used to do some radical things and was always getting the cane. His home backed onto the school, and every time he'd get in trouble all he had to do was jump the fence and run down this little track past the swamp and he'd be home. We'd hang out in his backyard a lot. They were a full-on fishing family and used to fish in Botany Bay when it was still full of fish. I seemed to be attracted to troublemakers, and I got my share of the cane too.

Richard Maurer: We took a couple of days off school and surfed Kurnell Point in the morning. Then it was too big for Kurnell, so we went round to Joey Morgan's, who was always up for a day off. Around lunchtime it was low tide, Joey decided to get in his boat and row out just at Kurnell. We all jumped in too and got about 200 yards out. A set came in, Joey turned it around and caught the wave of the day. We were all on it. Occy jumped off after twenty metres on the wave, I stayed on a bit longer, and Joey decided to ride it straight towards the groyne, all the way to the beach. We were out the back, going, 'How good's this day?' And then the vice-principal drove past and stopped right in front of us and we're going, *errr, we're in trouble now*. And the next day we went to school, walked in, sat down and he's gone, 'Occhilupo, Maurer, Morgan, good to see you here. Have a good day yesterday?' We went, 'Yes, sir' and he went, 'Good.' And that's all we heard about it. Our parents didn't hear about it, so we were stoked.

A couple of times a year my mum would take us down to the snow to go skiing, because she loved skiing. Dad's attitude to skiing was about the same as surfing – a waste of time – and he never joined us. But Mum worked really hard to afford those trips, because it wasn't cheap to take a bunch of kids to the snow. She was one of the fastest shorthand secretaries in Sydney, and she had some good jobs, but my favourite was when she worked for Toyworld. She would bring home toys from work every night for us to test out. But she put all her spare money aside to take us on those skiing trips.

I immediately fell in love with the snow and the speed and exhilaration of skiing. I used to hang out for those trips to the snow – it was even more exciting to me than surfing, because it was such a special occasion. Mum would drive us to the snow in her silver Celica, and we'd stay at this place in Cooma that we called 'Smelly Lodge', but it was all we could afford. You could see the snow way off in the distance from Cooma, but it was still a two-hour drive away. That first afternoon we had to just drive out and see it, not all the way to the ski fields but just until we reached snow on the side of the road. We got out and skied down these little hills. We got back to our place at Cooma, and that night I slept in my boots and ski gear. I didn't want to get out of them, even though they were too tight. The next day we hit the slopes at Smiggins and there was no stopping me.

I used to ski pretty well and I'd meet people on the T-bar and put on an Austrian accent and try and tell them I was from Austria. I'd make up all these stories about how I skied over there in the northern winter and then came and skied here in the southern winter. People must have been going, *who is this kid?* Maybe I was pulling it off, but I don't think so. I really wanted to be a ski instructor, and that's where I'd got the accent from, because most of those guys were Austrian.

Pam Occhilupo: We were so excited that we'd often set off at midnight to drive through the night so we could get there when the lifts first started . . . We skied all day and only stopped when the last chairlift closed down. At night we stayed at an awful old bedsit in Cooma. Our room at Ivy Lodge, or 'Smelly Lodge' as Mark called it for obvious reasons, had two narrow single beds with mattresses that dipped almost to the floor. He was so in love with his ski equipment that he slept in it, the clothes and the boots – fortunately the skis wouldn't fit in the bed. The next day we were up there again, at first light, driving back to Sydney when the last lift closed, tired but so happy. That year I took a job purely to enable us to ski, and we went five times in all, sometimes taking the girls but mostly ourselves. On occasion, when I didn't have much money, we would sleep in my small car, moving every so often to heat up the engine when we started to freeze. Each year we would drive down as often as we could afford, and that was Mark's passion for the next few years until surfing took over.

When I was really getting into surfing, I started going with Jason Marsh, because he was already surfing, and then his younger brother, Richard, got into it. We started going through the sandhills and discovering all the beachbreaks at the northern end of Cronulla. When the sandhills were still really big, we used to get a lift halfway to Cronulla, and there was a track through the dunes. They seemed to be miles high, before they mined them all. It's a shame. I think half of Sydney is built out of sand from those dunes. Back then we used to stumble upon major movie productions going on in the sandhills, because it looked like the Sahara Desert.

One of our mums used to drop us off early in the morning, and Jason would tell us classic stories to get us psyched as we trudged through the sand dunes. It always seemed to be freezing in those dunes in the mornings. We'd have tracksuits on and two jumpers. But by the time we walked back after a surf it would be baking hot, and all I'd wear was my shoes and my wettie, pulled down to my waist. I was so lazy I couldn't be bothered carrying all my clothes home. I'd just leave them lying in the dunes, and Jason would grab them – that's where he got most of his clothes. It used to drive my poor mum crazy.

We were like our own little clan: me, Richard Maurer, Richard and Jason Marsh, Beaver, Dave D'Arcy, Joey Morgan and a few others. We started a little Kurnell Boardriders Club, and we used to walk all the way through the sandhills to have our own little club contests. I think I might have even won one. Because there were only about six of us, sooner or later there was a good chance you'd win.

The south swells would get right up there into the corner, and we'd have these little beachbreaks all to ourselves. We just called it 'Hills'. I can remember a grey day, and we walked over the hills and there were good little waves. We had a camp fire, and we had the flags and everything for our contest. We didn't have a tent but we had a couple of clipboards, and we held our own little contest – me and Richard Marsh already going at it like maniacs.

Richard 'Dog' Marsh: We first met at preschool – our mums car-pooled. Mark picked surfing up before me, probably a good year before me. His mum was into it – I think his mum's old boyfriend was a surfer – so Occ had a board, and he started before all our group. We'd leave our boards at Occ's; it was close to the beach and boards were heavy back then. It was a big deal to get your board to the beach. Surfing the boatshed is my earliest memory of surfing together, and then we were surfing a lot. We were both hooked and surfed every day. There was a bunch of us, probably ten kids, and every day, between us, we'd talk our mums into driving us or ride our pushies or walk through the sandhills. We'd find a way.

I've always been pretty keen on cars – it just seems like cars aren't too keen on me. I've had a long history of automotive mishaps, and it started early. One day I was round at the Marshes' and started fooling around with their dad Lenny's car. They had a really steep driveway, and then the road at the bottom had a small cliff at the other side that dropped off into bushes. Somehow I flicked the handbrake off and, sure enough, the car started rolling down the driveway really fast. I was terrified and just managed to jump out as the car hit the road, right before it launched off the cliff into the bushes below.

Did I ever get my arse kicked! I was sent home squealing like a dog. It was the first of many similar incidents, and somehow I've managed to survive them all.

As we got a little older we started to realise there was a bigger playground to explore than just Kurnell. We used to walk from Kurnell to Voodoo, a classic left-hand reef just on the edge of the industrial area that handled really big swells. I remember one time I walked out there by myself – it was a good forty-minute walk, or a twenty-minute ride on a pushie. I remember it was a rainy day and the waves were really big, and the wind was nor'-east so Kurnell was onshore. I was already right into what the winds were doing and what breaks worked best on different winds, and I knew Voodoo would be offshore. So I walked out to Voodoo and it was at least fifteen feet, the biggest I'd ever seen it. There was only one guy out and it was Jim Banks, a hot Cronulla surfer. I don't think I'd ever met him, but I was just in awe that there was one guy out charging it on his own. I walked away feeling pretty rattled. I talked to him later about it and he still remembers that day.

Chapter Two

Discovering Cronulla

When I was around nine or ten we started to discover the world of waves and wild characters just up that long stretch of beach to the south at Cronulla. A few of us joined Cronulla Junior Boardriders, which my mate Richard James's dad used to run, and that was a good club. You had to be a good surfer to be in the club. We had some great surfers, like Rod Schaffer, Eddie Noodle and Scott Topper, and we used to have really good contests. I think I even won a contest or two, but not many because the competition was pretty fierce.

Cronulla was a whole other world to Kurnell. We'd heard of Cronulla Boardriders and Windansea Boardriders, but those guys were almost like surf stars to us, like Ross Marshall and Craig Naylor, really good surfers. There were distinct areas to the Cronulla surf scene – the Alley, Elouera and Wanda – and they each had their own clubs and we'd surf against each other. Our little crew all used to hang out at Wanda at my mate's shop, the Top Shop. I remember surfing Elouera one day; the surf was really good and I got my first real barrel. It seemed about a six-foot day to me, but it might have only been four foot. I remember coming out going, *that was epic*.

The heaviest crew were the guys who surfed Cronulla Point and Shark Island. There was Gerry Manion, a little guy who charged huge barrels and who was also a racing car driver. Or Richard Herbert, who also went by the stage name Dick Bent in his band the Bentniks. There was Jim Banks, who already had a burgeoning pro career and a reputation as a serious charger, Grant Coulter and a host of others.

The Coca-Cola Surfabout was held at Cronulla a couple of times, and I remember us all heading in to check it out. I met Buzzy Kerbox, the great Hawaiian surfer, and he had his own stickers and gave us some and was nice enough to talk to us. We were stoked. I think Rabbit Bartholomew won it both times, and we'd come and watch the whole thing. There were so many great surfers just in Cronulla. At that stage I didn't dare believe I'd ever be a pro surfer. I had my work cut out for me just trying to be one of the better surfers at my local beach.

> **Richard Maurer:** When we started surfing Cronulla Point, Jason and Richard Marsh's mum would take us out there early in the morning, before school and stuff. I remember in second form Occy started going in Cronulla Boardriders, that was a year before me, and just how good some of the surfers were in the club – this Jim Banks guy and Ross Marshall and Craig Naylor and Pete Smith. He went, 'I wish I could surf as good as them.' I went, 'Mate, I didn't know you had any aspiration.' I didn't have an aspiration to surf better than anybody else. Just going surfing was fine.

Once we started at high school, the full-on beach rat lifestyle took hold. The school was right over the hill from the surf, and we were surfing all the time. There'd be me and Richie Maurer and Beaver and D'Arcy, and Jacko would let us all leave our boards at his place, so we could surf before school and we could surf after school and sometimes we'd even rack off at lunch for a surf. It was all-time. On the weekends we'd hang at the Top Shop – Darren Paxton's mum owned it – and it was the perfect hang, right on the beachfront. That's how I came to surf so well, because we surfed so much. We had a full clan. We'd all just hang out together every weekend, surfing, eating hamburgers, living the life. It was so much fun. Wanda was right there, and we had Voodoo, Cronulla Point, the Island. We were loving life – lying in the sun in front of the shop between surfs, checking out the chicks and trying to hook up or whatever. You wished days like that would never end.

I actually made a brief cameo in *Puberty Blues*, which came out in '81, depicting the Cronulla beach scene in a not-too-favourable light. That whole film production took over Cronulla for weeks while it was being made. I'm one of the grommets walking past on the beach, writing the two chicks off when they go for a surf. 'Chicks can't surf' was my big line. I just yelled it out on the spur of the moment, and the director asked me to do it again, and they ended up using it in the movie.

> **Brett 'Beaver' Schweickle:** These local guys, Jacko and Packo, made him his first board, a little pintail. Jacko shaped it, Packo glassed it. He left it in the rocks at the Alley one day and someone snapped it clean in half. It was pretty heavy at the Alley. People would say, 'Give us a lend of your board', and if you didn't they'd punch you in the head and take it anyway. He hid his board in the bushes, and when he came back someone had snapped it in half. We came back and we were shattered. Then Herbie made him one at G & S, a short little stubby thing. That's when he started weaving his magic. When Occy went into pro surfing I didn't even know what pro surfing was.

A lot of the Cronulla guys used to work in the G & S Surfboard Factory at Taren Point, which was the biggest surfboard label in town. There was this one older guy who was really nice, but people used to say he had a foot fetish. He'd want to check out everyone's feet, and some of the young guys were a bit freaked out by it – but he never did it to me. But then I've got pretty ugly feet, so I don't blame him. I used to work there after school, doing the till, and I loved it. Eventually they offered to sponsor me and made me a board at a special discount price – this little marbled red twin fin. I loved that board, I really did. I was only about eleven or twelve, but by then I kind of knew I wanted to be a pro surfer. There were just so many guys better than me that I didn't really think it would happen.

G & S stocked Peak wetsuits, and so the Peak sales rep, Dougall Walker, came to Cronulla a lot, and then the owner, John Howitt, came down talent-scouting. I met him at the surf shop and he was really cool, and they started giving me wetsuits. I went and stayed with John at Newport a couple of times and met a few of the Newport crew, like Tom Carroll and the pack of great Newport surfers who were around at the time, which was great for my surfing.

> **John Howitt (Peak wetsuits):** You could just see that he had so much potential it was ridiculous. He just knew what he wanted to do in life – he just wanted to be a pro surfer. As soon as I saw him I had this instant feeling that this kid was going to do anything he wanted to do. He had this belief in himself, even at that age, even though he hadn't done any-thing. And he had the natural ability to go and do it. But he had this crazy side to him too. My ex-wife was a school teacher, and she thought he was the most delinquent kid she'd ever come across, and I'd go, 'Nah, he's unreal.' I broke up with her and not Occy. He had this spontaneous personality that was great.

> **Tom Carroll:** I remember watching him surf for the first time at the Peak. John Howitt had brought him over to surf. I

remember seeing how low he was to the board, just ripping the top off the Peak. I just went, 'How's this guy? He's just a kid.' I was pretty astounded.

Barton Lynch: I first met him at Lovers Rock, Duranbah, in a little north-east wind swell, both up there for holidays, about ten or twelve years old, surfing together. I remember being surprised and amazed at how good he was. We walked from Duranbah to the Coolangatta pie shop together, two little groms talking, going, 'What are you going to be?' I said, 'I'm going to be a pro surfer.' And he goes, 'Yeah, me too. I'm going to be a pro surfer too.'

A little later another shop, Cronulla Surf Design, started sponsoring me. That's where I first met the owners of Billabong, Gordon and Rena Merchant. I was hanging round the shop like I usually did and the owner, Mark Aprilovic, introduced me to Gordon and Rena, who were showing him their latest range. Mark just introduced me as a little local ripper and I remember saying, 'Hi Gordon, hi Rena' in my high-pitched voice. They were really nice to me. It was in the really early days of Billabong, because they were still travelling around showing their ranges themselves.

Mark Aprilovic: He was just a grommet in our boardriders, Cronulla Boardriders. At the time all the locals used to be pretty tight, and the club was strong and very parochial, and we used to head off to a few contests. And we tried to foster some of the young guys and take them away with us. Whether we were helping them or leading them astray I don't know! But it was really great.

In the early '80s we'd been to a few contests and Mark was really standing out, a real talented surfer, and we went to the Capricorn at Taree, at Old Bar, and it was the biggest pro-am event at the time. There was, like, 250 competitors or something, and we all camped out, stayed at Saltwater Point there.

Occ did really well and was getting through all his heats. And the Saturday night here's this fourteen-year-old going around different camp fires and telling hard, seasoned pros like Greg Day, 'I'm going to kick your arse tomorrow.' He'd let 'em know, 'I'm coming to kick your arse' and they'd look at him like, *who's this kid?* And the next day he'd fucking do it, and you'd shake your head and go, *wow*. This brash young bloke. And he did, he made the final, and here's this kid, fourteen years old, not carrying his board because he couldn't get his arm round it, but holding the nose and dragging it behind him. And he's made the final of the biggest pro-am event in Australia. He got fourth in the final. I think Glen Winton won it.

We came back to Sydney, and later on I had Gordon and Rena Merchant dropping in to show us their range. I had this little hole-in-the-wall surf shop down a back alley, Cronulla Surf Design. Gordon and Rena are sitting on the doorstep just showing us some boardies, pretty relaxed, they've got this big bag of stuff. And Occ sauntered in. I had a little filing cabinet and he jumped up and sat on that, and I went to Gordon, 'You better get on to this young bloke. He's really going to go places.' Years previously when I was growing up, I was at Broken Head in the early '70s or late '60s, and Geoff McCoy turned up. He had a young grommet with him, Mark Richards, and he got out and he just blitzed the surf. And it was similar, seeing the same talent appearing again. And I said to Gordon, 'You want to get on to this young bloke.' And Gordon went, 'Yeah, yeah, yeah, when you're up in Queensland come and see me. I'll give you a couple of pairs of boardshorts', and left it there. Anyway, a bit later the Straight Talk Tyres contest was on and Occ made the semifinals and Gordon was right on the phone.

Occy

Gordon Merchant: I was down there and I had my little range of board shorts and I was showing him and he said, 'I've got Occy here to meet you.' And this kid pops out from behind the counter. He wasn't much taller than the counter. So that was kind of the start of it. I didn't think too much of it. I believed Mark [Aprilovic] and I thought he would be a good little surfer. And so this sponsorship was very simple. Maybe it was just clothing at the time.

Wayne 'Rabbit' Bartholomew: I remember the very first time Gordon mentioned Occy, this kid, and he said, 'I've never seen anything like it.' Just the way he said, 'There's never been anything like him.' The fact is it's true, because those tree-trunk legs of his and that natural build he's got, he's the sort of guy you'd go, 'Never spend a day in the gym. You are already full to the brim of everything you need.' And I think that augured well for his longevity. It's a natural thing, the perfect surfer physique.

Nick Carroll: The Mattara was an APSA [Australian Professional Surfing Association] contest and Occ went in it, he must have been thirteen, riding his Jim Banks twinny in the open division. It was so bold of him. I just remember how bold he was, having a dig. He didn't seem to think he was out of place – his eyes were really wide open to learn how it all worked. He wasn't fazed by it. He made the final of one of the bigger pro-am contests in the country. It was really memorable: messy six foot, difficult to surf, onshore – he was still having a full-on go at it.

When I was about fourteen I entered a few APSA contests, which was the Australian pro-am circuit. I did all right and made a couple of finals against much older surfers. This created a bit of interest as these guys were already established pro surfers and I was just a kid.

At the same time, I was surfing in a little local junior circuit called the Mooving On series, against other up-and-coming juniors like Damien Hardman and Todd Ingham. I thought Todd Ingham was even better than Damien back then – he was this little blond-haired kid riding a Geoff McCoy shaped, Cheyne Horan model Lazor Zap and was just ripping. He was the guy to beat in our generation, but I don't know what happened to him. He kind of faded off the contest scene.

I was still playing a bit of football, with Cronulla–Carringbah, at lock or second row, and even went to try out for the New South Wales junior squad. I didn't get in because there was a guy called Barry Russell, who was a really good footballer, and he got the spot. I was pretty disappointed because the coach had told me I had a good chance, but the very next day there were tryouts for rugby union and they encouraged me to give that a go. I didn't even know what I was doing, but I got picked for the team. I was reserve but I got to play, and I was playing in this really important game without even knowing what I was doing. Union wasn't that popular back then in juniors. I was about fifteen and some of the guys were getting really big. I turned up the following year just to play in the regular club competition and the guys were getting so big I just went, 'Nah, I want to surf.' Back then, you were either a footballer or a surfer, because you got pounded playing footy and then you wouldn't be able to surf. I went, 'I'm over it, I'm just going to surf.'

Pam Occhilupo: I was all for sport, that was my focus, so wherever he wanted to go I'd take him. He was good at everything. He was good at football. The coaches would come out and pick him up, they were so eager to have him playing. He joined Cronulla Boardriders and one day he came home and said, 'Oh Mum, I came third or something' and the phone started ringing with people wanting to sponsor him, and I realised something had happened. The first time I went to watch him I thought the first guy that got to the beach was the winner. I didn't know a thing about it . . . Naturally all of this surfing took precedence over his studies. Luciano, being an academic himself, decided Mark needed to go to a private college where the emphasis was on academia.

We settled on St Andrews, in the heart of the city. It was close to Luciano's office and they could travel together, but it did mean a long day for him. No chance of surfing now. Admittedly, Mark looked very cute in his uniform – trim grey suit, blue striped tie, long socks and straw boater – but he absolutely loathed it and would lie on the floor of the car as we drove through Kurnell and Cronulla so none of his friends would see him. Mark endured purgatory for three weeks before declaring he wasn't going back and stamping on his boater. No amount of persuasion would move Mark, and he went happily back to his friends at Cronulla High School, within sight and sound of the rolling surf. It had literally been like taking a fish out of water.

Robbie Page: I was only a grommet. He'd won the Newcastle Opens or Juniors, or something. He was only fifteen, and he came down with Cronulla Boardriders to surf against Woonona. Obviously, I'm telling everybody, 'He's not that fucking good. Look how slow he's going. He's fucking slow, this guy. Those turns look good but he's fucking slow.' And I went out in my heat and I didn't realise but the whole area was covered with seaweed. I could hardly get through a wave but, with those big legs of his, he could cut through the seaweed.

Unlike a lot of the top surfers, I didn't have a great amateur career. I did all right – I won a New South Wales schoolboys title but never won an Australian title, and I think that just made me more impatient to turn pro. I made the New South Wales state team, along with guys like Paul Burnett, Damien Hardman and Todd Ingham, and we went on this trip to WA. It was mobile all around the Margaret River area. One day it was at Margarets and it was big, and I had my little marbled red twinny, riding a 5'10" at twelve-foot Margarets. The bigger kids were into it but we were all on the shoulder. I think I did all right that day, considering I was hanging on the shoulder. I think I won my division, but it was a round robin competition and I didn't end up winning overall. I remember, when we pulled up at Margarets on the big day, there was a guy out there they called 'the Maestro', Tony Hardy. He was the only one out in twelve- to fifteen-foot surf and absolutely ripping. I just went, *oh my goodness*. I was in awe of him.

But I was frustrated with the long-winded amateur system and decided I wanted to get on tour as soon as possible.

Pam Occhilupo: Paul Sargeant was captain of Cronulla Boardriders and could see Mark's potential. He became Mark's mentor, taking him away on surf safaris, paying his competition entry fees, etc, though he could ill afford it. Paul was a freelance photojournalist and had just won a prestigious award for his photographic work with *The Sydney Morning Herald*. He shot a lot of film about Mark, naturally, and when his photo of Mark appeared in *Tracks* it was a first for both of them. From then on his stories and photographs appeared regularly in *Tracks* and many other magazines and publications. Paul would take Mark to surf competitions. Now that Mark was getting older, trailing around with Mum was a bit demeaning. One day they went to a competition at a beach in Kiama, sleeping in the car for the weekend. Neither of them had any money and couldn't afford to buy food, but even on an empty stomach Mark won that competition.

Paul Sargeant: I moved into a house full of surfers, including Ratso, who's now a judge, and John Veage, who ended up being my first apprentice. Twenty-four Judd Street, a very infamous house in Cronulla's history. Occy used to come around occasionally. Veagey used to shape in those days in the back shed. One night they all came home from their board-riders club meeting, and I said, 'How was the meeting, boys?' And they were like, 'No good. The president's resigned, no-one wants to do it, and the club is probably going to fall apart.' And I said, 'Well, I just ran Wanda surf club for four years, I can probably give you a hand.'

A month later I was club president, and that lasted for eleven years. One of the things I organised was inter-club events, and one of the first ones was at Broulee. And I don't remember Occy actually being in my car on the way down, but somehow on the way back he was in the back seat. He was about fourteen, possibly fifteen, and he was riding a red-and-blue striped deck board.

Driving back from Broulee, this little squeaky voice came from the back seat: 'Let's go to Pipe. It's nor'-east, it's south swell, let's go to Pipe.' And I went, 'What's Pipe?' And he went, 'It's this place, you turn off here.' I just remember going and going, wondering, *when are we going to get there?* And it was like head-high and perfect shape. By that stage I'd started shooting him, and a photo from that session I sent to Kirk Willcox at *Tracks*. He used it on the letters page. It was the July '82 issue and, anyway, it just kind of went from there.

THE ROAD TO BLACK ROCK

Paul Sargeant: Pam used to give him that car from when he was fourteen. I'll never forget going out to Kurnell to see him one day. There's this big sweeping right-hand bend as you go past Cronulla High into a big long straight, and then there's this right bend as you come into the stretch between the marshes and the sand dunes. Next minute – beep, beep – there's Occy overtaking me, on the wrong side of the road, completely blind corner, going, 'G'day, Sarge.'

When the surfing obsession really took hold, I used to steal my mum and dad's cars to go down the coast chasing waves. I got a key cut for my dad's car, and when he parked at the train station in the morning on his way to work I'd take it and go down the coast – and then try and park it back in the same spot. I was driving at thirteen, and I was driving sweet, all the way down to south coast Pipe sometimes, but mainly Garie, Thirroul or Sandon Point. But if south coast Pipe was on I'd charge it down in the morning and come back before Dad got home from work in the afternoon. I'd be sure to put the right amount of petrol in it. I wouldn't fill it up – just back to where it was – and park as close to the same place as I could. He never found out, or at least he never let on. And I used to do it with Mum's car too, and she let me take it. I'd get my older mates to drive, but once we got down the road I'd tell my mate to get out and I'd drive it.

I got pulled up one time and I think someone was smoking a joint in the back, so I jumped out of the car before the cop came up to us so he wouldn't smell it. He said, 'Where are you going?' I went, 'South coast Pipe' in my squeaky little voice. He said, 'What's the hurry?' And I said, 'We've got to get there for the right tide.' He said, 'You're kidding. Have you got a licence?'

Somehow he didn't book me and just made one of the older guys who had a licence drive, and let us go. I'd return the car at the end of the day and be circling the car park as people came home from work, waiting for the right spot to become vacant. A couple of times, Dad was walking out of the station as I parked the car and bolted.

They were some really special times, going down to Pipe. We used to do it a lot, me and Dog especially. Every time there was a little south swell, and the wind was nor'-east, we'd jam down there.

Cronulla only had to be two or three foot from the south, and we'd go down to Pipe and it was six foot and we'd score. You come back and no-one else has surfed. For a two-hour drive, that's not too bad a deal. There's something almost magical about roaring down the coast chasing surf along all that beautiful south coast bushland. We used to stop at this health food store and get those apricot delights and a block of carob and just eat that all the way down. We'd have the music blaring – David Bowie or Talking Heads or Devo. There's nothing better.

If I hadn't had a chance to nick Dad's car, Sarge would drive us down a lot of the time. When he was young, Sarge smoked a lot of mull and drove really fast, and he'd be pulling cones while he drove. I'll never forget him going round a corner, a dangerous kind, at 120 to 130 K, with a bong in one hand pulling it, someone lighting it and him just going *shoooooo*. He didn't even miss a beat, straight through gears and everything – unbelievable. He was a really fast driver, but he was a really good driver too, so he never really freaked me out. He was into motor racing and he'd done courses and stuff. He probably could have been a racing car driver, but it was still pretty crazy.

All that time chasing waves and in the water was starting to pay off, and I could feel my surfing progressing. I was getting a few photos in magazines and a bit more attention, and learnt how to attack a contest heat. Finding the best waves on any given day and winning a heat felt like puzzles I had to work out, and I was starting to get the hang of it. I started to feel like this whole pro surfing dream – just to keep on surfing and get paid for it – was actually within reach.

Richard 'Dog' Marsh: Your friends can drag you along in a certain direction, and Mark was so good for all us guys. We were best mates, we had so many fun times. We'd just surf every day. This place is such a cool place to live when you're surfing every day. It was such a good time. It was a bummer things had to get serious. The next few years when he was semi-competing, I was trying to be competitive – that was fun, man. We just surfed and ratted around, just kids with a new game. Then things get a bit faster and sponsors came and expectations, and that was the next phase in Mark's life.

Robbie Page: We had a lot of great surfs at south coast Pipe. Terry Richo was holding down the line and then there was Occy and Greeny and Dog, the goofies, and myself, and the Aboriginal surfer Todd Roberts from the camp. We were all running together and probably helping each other surf it good. I remember one time Occy came to pick me up to go surfing, and he tied his tracksuit pants to the middle of the steering wheel. As he was driving, whenever he turned the steering wheel he'd start climbing up the walls of the car, going, *ohh-hhh, whooaaa*. He'd be climbing up onto his feet on the seat, his arse out the window. I'm going, 'Untie the things, man!' I think it was him and Richard James, they were just laughing. I got out and said, 'I'm going to drive my car.'

Barton Lynch (from Jack McCoy's *The Occumentary*): At the JJJ Junior we had a three-set final. I was, like, eighteen and he was sixteen, and I paddled to his inside for about the thirtieth or fortieth time, and he just looked at me and tears started rolling down his face and he said, 'You always do that to me', and just started crying. And I remember feeling abso-lutely no guilt at all and just going, 'That's right.' . . . He used to try and compete with integrity and let his surfing do the talking, and consequently he became so incredibly good.

Hugh McLeod (photographer/former publisher of *Surfing World*): What impressed us was Occy was already a surf star at sixteen, but we'd go to pick him up to go to Black Rock and he'd just have a board, a wetsuit and a towel. He'd jump in and we'd go surfing for the day and drop him home that night. There was no pretension or drama. He was just a kid stoked to be going for a surf.

Occy rose to prominence as part of a concerted Cronulla push – the leading edge of a wedge of local talent including Sean Charters, Craig Naylor, Ross Marshall, Gary Green, Richard Marsh and transplanted Kiwi, Iain 'Ratso' Buchanan, to name a few. In 1983, five Cronulla surfers made it through the trials into the main event of the Coke Classic, the biggest surf contest in the country. Cronulla had long produced great surfers, but only a few had gone on to success on the world stage. Something about the 'Nulla seemed to hold surfers captive, as if their beloved Shire was simply too comfortable to stray too far from.

Cronulla has always been a melting pot of Australian society – the one Sydney beach with a train station, delivering the inland masses to the coast. The Cronulla beach scene of the time was captured vividly in the classic Australian film *Puberty Blues*. Based on a largely autobiographical novel of the same name by two disillusioned, teenage 'surfie chicks', Kathy Lette and Gabrielle Carey, it was shot in just six weeks around Cronulla in 1980 by acclaimed director Bruce Beresford. *Puberty Blues* shocked parents with its raw exposé of a world of teen angst, surfing, drugs, sex and peer pressure. It also hinted at the simmering cultural tensions that led to the infamous Cronulla riots of 2005.

'There were three main sections of Cronulla Beach: South Cronulla, North Cronulla and Greenhills.

book two

The Rise

Everyone was trying to make it to Greenhills. That's where the top surfie gangs hung out – prettiest girls from school and the best surfers on the beach,' explains the film's central character, Debbie Vickers. 'Bad surfers on their "L" plates, the Italian family groups and the uncool kids from Bankstown swarmed to South Cronulla ... Dickheadland.'

While a young Occy made a brief cameo in the film, by 1983 he already appeared set to soar above this world, breaking free of the gravitational pull of its aimless pleasure-seeking. His was a talent that lifted him above any of the cultural or ethnic distinctions that otherwise divided the beach.

'Leading the charge like a bull is a raging nugget of potential called Mark Occhilupo. Followers of the contest scene will have already mastered the correct pronunciation and spelling of the name, so familiar is it already,' *Tracks* magazine gushed in February 1983. 'Occy's style can be likened to nobody's. Suffice to say he is a goofy that is equally at home in twelve-inch slop or smokin' six-foot Pipe. He has zilch respect for waves – he smashes, slashes and carves them to pieces. His cutbacks defy comprehension. He is here to stay!'

Within a few months, he was on the pro tour, a citizen of the world at sixteen. When he discovered the magic foil for his bullish style, in Californian shaper Rusty Preisendorfer's blocky angular surfboards, 'something just happened', according to ex-pro surfer Derek Hynd. A phenomenon had been set in motion, and the pro surfing world would never be the same.

– T. B.

Chapter Three

Tomorrow the World

In the space of a year I'd quit school, moved out of home and decided to have a go at the pro contest scene full-on. My circles were widening, and I was also discovering some of the attractions of having a big city on your doorstep. When there wasn't any surf we'd venture out into some of Sydney's more colourful districts in search of entertainment. We used to go to the Strand Arcade every Saturday night, because they'd have theatre and the gay people used to come up and do a poem or mime a favourite musician. It all seemed pretty exotic for young lads from Kurnell.

This singer called Marilyn tried to crack onto me there once. There was Boy George and there was another one called Marilyn, who was a guy who looked like a girl. And he came up to me, and went, 'Gee, you've got nice muscles, do you want to hang with me?' I went, 'Ah, no thanks' and bailed.

But the nocturnal adventures weren't going to distract me from the main game, which was trying to somehow get myself sponsored and on the pro tour.

Richard Maurer: From thirteen to fifteen he progressed from surfing with all of us to surfing in Cronulla Boardriders to competing on the APSA circuit, at fifteen, so it was a really quick rise. And then from fifteen to sixteen he won the Pro Junior, and then he was on the tour.

Me and him moved out together when we were sixteen. We had a lot of good times then, hanging out up the surf club; I was doing a carpentry apprenticeship. We were going to the Strand Arcade in town. Occ had been there once or twice before, and I was going, 'There's a couple of nice girls here.' And then there's this girl with heaps of make-up and big hair doing a stage show, and I'm going, 'Wow, she's gorgeous.' Occ goes, 'He's a guy.' It was the first time I'd seen transvestites. I went, 'What are we doing here?' And he goes, 'The chicks come here.' I went, 'I know, I know.'

Nick Carroll (from 'The Best of the New Breed', *Tracks*, **March 1983):** After bombing out in the second round of the Pro Junior, all Mark Occhilupo could say was 'Fuck!' It's easy to see why when you consider that Occhilupo was one of the pre-event favourites. For his age (16), 'Occy' is certainly one of Oz's finest contest surfers, ranking a close second to Glen Winton on the APSA Pro-am list and a threat to any surfer in the world in small waves, where he excels. His big strong frame, combined with more than enough slop practice in the Cronulla beachbreaks where he dwells, has helped develop a formidable and explosive goofy-foot attack with more than a splash of individuality. Occy has recently changed to Jim Banks' equipment after a stint at Gordon & Smith, and says that Banks shapes 'unreal boards' (although Banks later claimed to have 'closed his eyes' while shaping said equipment). Once he overcomes what he calls 'my main problem in contests' – wave selection – he'll be well on the way to being a hit-pick of the future.

In 1983 I entered the trials for the Australian leg of the tour, the so-called Grand Slam. As luck would have it, the first event was the Straight Talk Tyres and me and my mates were so stoked to have the pro tour and all our heroes come to town. I remember walking over the hill and Tom Curren was out there at Wanda. It was about six foot and he was the only one out and he was surfing unbelievably. The waves were cranking, and Curren was riding this six channel, Channel Islands surfboard. It was a trippy-looking board. It had this thin glass at the end of the tail, wafer-thin, right at the end there was no foam, with a clinker tail – he surfed on it so good it was amazing. He was so fast and so smooth.

The day before the trials me and Richard Maurer were mucking around and I jumped this fence. I'm so clumsy I've almost always got a stubbed toe. I've had one for years. We were running after each other to get home to get our boards to go for a surf. I was psyched because I was in the trials and slipped and went straight into the fence and cut my knee pretty deep. I freaked, going, 'Oh no, I'm in the trials.' But nothing was going to stop me. I still surfed in the trials, at the Alley. It hurt, but once I was in the heat of the moment I didn't even think about it. I got fifth in the trials, riding a Jim Banks board, and had a great heat against Tom Carroll in the first round of the main event. He beat me pretty clearly, but I'd got a taste for top-level competition and wanted more.

Jim Banks: He was kind of coming through as I was stepping off the tour because I'd opened up a surf shop and I was getting back into going to the desert and going to Bali and just going surfing. I was heading in another direction. He appeared and I think there was a little buzz started around Cronulla. Guys were saying, 'Occy's ripping', and I noticed him in the surf and he was good. He was riding twinnies and he didn't really have the carve in his turns, so I made him these thrusters that forced him to carve. My boards are always built for speed and drive, and you couldn't just flick them around. I was getting into riding barrels and I wasn't really into making boards for turns.

He got into the trials of the Straight Talk Tyres and didn't have a great heat. He was losing, but he got this one wave and he did this one turn and it just made everyone pay attention. It was one of those moves that made everyone go, 'Did you see that?' He came off the bottom on a close out and did this upside-down carve under the lip – such a gutsy, powerful move – and everyone went, 'Okay, that kid can surf.' During the whole day there was definitely no other move that came close to it.

Tom Curren: The first thing I remember is he had an orange-and-blue board. He just looked like he was really fast, and I remember seeing him at Burleigh. I just remember he was really fast and he had a pretty exciting style. The style wasn't as polished as it was a year later. A year went by and all of a sudden he got a lot more coordinated. Over that year I saw him, he was definitely a stand-out that grabbed your attention already, but his style came together in the phase when he started riding Rusty's boards. Then I saw him at Ocean Beach [California] and he was surfing really good. I surfed against him several times and he won almost all of them that first year when he started to do really well. We had some close heats, but I think he won most of them.

Tom Curren won a car that contest but he left straight after, and I can remember driving it down to Black Rock soon after – this little red station wagon that he'd just kind of left in Cronulla. This guy called Steve Core used to film us a lot down at Black Rock, and we drove down in Curren's car and picked up Terry Richardson on the way. I still didn't have a licence, but we knew it was going to be pumping and I was psyched. We got some good Pipe back in those days.

The next event was the Rip Curl Pro at Bells Beach, and I entered the trials and came seventeenth and missed out on the main event. Joe Engel won the trials and the main event, which was pretty awesome, and showed me that it was possible to come through the trials and beat the best in the world. Joe was a real character and we became good friends later, when we travelled together for Billabong, and he was definitely different, to say the least. He had a real mysto presence at that Bells event, and he was so shy I think he hardly wanted to talk to anyone. But he surfed so good and really attacked the wave. He took a real different approach and it seemed to work for him at that event.

He always had a bit of a wild look in his eye, and you could never tell if he was just trying to freak you out or if he was a bit crazy. I'll always remember a shot of him in a Billabong ad charging Inside Sunset from behind the peak, and he'd apparently made a huge impression on the local crew in Hawaii.

> **John Howitt (Peak wetsuits):** We used to have a team bus, and the first time we took Mark to Bells he would have been fifteen or sixteen. I can remember he was in the trials, and he got through to the third round and the swell got really big. He was sitting in the bus and you could see he was going, *shit*. This was probably the biggest surf he'd ever been in, a solid eight feet. And Ken Davidson said, 'You don't have to go out there', and he just went, 'You're kidding. Of course I've got to go out.' And everyone was just blown away by this gutsy approach and the way he charged these waves.

From Bells it was up to Narrabeen for the Coke Surfabout. I won the trials, or the Lightning Bolt Eliminations as they were known, and it was a pretty epic event for Cronulla surfers. My mate Iain 'Ratso'

Buchanan, a Kiwi but an adopted Cronulla local, came second, Sean Charters came fourth, Gary Green came fifth and Craig Naylor came ninth. We were all through to the main event and I was psyched. The Cronulla boys were storming the barricades and I was ready to go in over the top.

I came up against Shaun Tomson in the main event, who'd been world champ in 1977 and was still a world title contender, but I fancied my chances. I thought I surfed a good heat. I was pretty sure I'd won, and a lot of people on the beach were telling me I'd won, but the judges gave it to Shaun on a split decision, 3–2. I was devastated. It was a rough introduction to the world of pro surfing, where it seemed ratings and reputation could count for more than performance.

> **Shaun Tomson:** I surfed against Occy, I think it might have been his very first pro event, and it was at Narrabeen, the Coke, and it must have been early '80s. I'd seen him surf at Cronulla in the shorey. They had this little contest for grommets and I remember paddling out. They called it the Alley, and I remember seeing this stumpy little kid swing round on this dumping little four- to five-foot shorey. I remember him swinging round and making this impossible take-off and I went, *wow, who's this kid?* And I paddled out and I asked him who he was. Then a couple of weeks later I ended up in this heat against him at Narrabeen, and it was a really close heat. I actually thought he beat me, and in those days it was five judges and it was a split decision. I won it narrowly on a 3–2 split decision.
>
> It was Occy's first big chance, he had all his mates there; he thought he'd won so he was super buoyed up, and when he heard the result I saw that he was crying. I felt so bad for the kid. I remember going up to him and going, 'Don't worry, Occy, there's going to be plenty more', and someone took a

picture. He's there crying and I'm consoling him. It was obviously so important to him that he was crying. At that young age, that's how much it meant to him. He has that sort of aura and that type of personality where you want to stick up for him. He's that sort of guy. He's like a big kid and he's never lost that. I think that's why people like him so much. He's kind of maintained that innocence in a way.

Nick Carroll: That Coke contest, it was really a big moment in some ways. One of the things that really struck me watching him in that contest – having such a duel with Shaun especially and being so emotionally committed to winning it even at such a young age – was that he was the sort of guy who really had an idea of how good he was going to be. It didn't seem a mystery to him. He was very sure of himself. You could tell he was a real showman. The media gave him the nickname 'the Raging Bull'. He was like a little raging bull. He was certain he could win and angry when he didn't. He really put everything into it.

Graham Cassidy (journalist, newspaper editor, former director of the ASP): In Cronulla it had been a long time between drinks for having a major local surf star. I had a close association with Sarge back then. When I was writing for the *Sun*, I'd have Sarge telling me there was this new guy emerging. Early on it became very obvious that there was a virtuoso on the horizon. I was running Sandshoes Boardriders even back then. Occy was a member for about two weeks, we put him in a couple of contests, then he drifted back to Cronulla. I saw him at the state titles and that sort of stuff: one of his early Coke Classics, his big breakthrough when he was up against Shaun [Tomson]. You could see that sort of robust squat-style. He had every manoeuvre, the whole combination of manoeuvres coming together. You just had to go, *this is the real McCoy*. I came up with the nickname 'the Raging Bull', that was the De Niro movie, because he's Italian. The whole idea and the subject of that movie was the pugnacious Italian boxer who was hitting above his weight and had that 'crash-through or crash' approach. All of the various components made it a good tag for Occy.

Paul Sargeant: I went up to him and I said, 'You're really impressing people. This could be your turning point. Be polite to people and listen to what they've got to say, but don't agree to anything and, whatever you do, don't sign anything.' And he was like, 'Yeah, yeah, no worries . . .' And the next morning he's bouncing up and down on the end of my bed, at about seven o'clock in the morning, going, 'Sarge, Sarge, I've got to tell you something. I've got a deal, I've got a deal.' I said, 'You didn't sign anything, did you?' He said, 'Yeah, I got this incredible deal from Terry Fitzgerald.' I was just like, 'Oh, what?' He said, 'This year I get $3000, next year I get $4000, and the third year I get five grand. Can you believe that? Five grand!'

He was just stoked off his head. I said, 'You're off your head. And you signed it? You fucking idiot. What, for clothes and boards?' 'Yeah, for clothes and boards.' I got out of bed, rang his dad, and he just blew up on the phone. So Luciano then rang Terry Fitzgerald and told him to stick his contract up his arse – Mark was only sixteen years old and he wasn't legal to sign anything! And so then I rang Banksy, and Banksy got onto Gordon and that's when Gordon said, 'Okay, I'll put him on the tour.'

After getting some good results in the Australian Grand Slam, I got picked up by a manager called Brian Walsh, who also worked for 2SM. He and his partner, Graham McNeice, had a management company and both went on to pretty senior positions in the media.

I remember being with Brian Walsh, and maybe Banksy, in Brian's office overlooking Sydney Harbour. We'd decided we were going to try and get me a sponsor to go on tour. The first guy we were going to ask was Gordon Merchant at Billabong. So Brian called up Gordon and I could just hear his voice on the other end of the line, exactly the way he still talks today. Brian went, 'I've got this young guy Mark Occhilupo' and Gordon went, 'Yeah, I've met him.'

He just knew there was something coming and his whole tone was saying, *what do you want?* Brian went, 'Everyone says he's ripping, and he wants to go on the tour.' And the phone went silent on the other end for a while. Then Gordon said, 'Okay, how much do you guys need? I'll do it.' It was a lot of money back then. Brian told him, 'I think he'll need forty grand to do the whole tour, so he's safe and travelling well, because he's just a young kid and he doesn't want to be grovelling.' And Gordon said yes.

Just imagine how happy I was driving back to Cronulla that day, jumping out of my skin. I kept repeating, 'I'm going on tour, I'm going on tour . . .' I couldn't believe it.

I was only sixteen when I went to my first overseas pro event.

ON TOUR – FIRST STOP: SOUTH AFRICA

Once I actually found myself on tour, at age sixteen, travelling with all my boyhood heroes, I was just in awe really. I just missed out on the Mark Richards era by one year. But all the older guys were really cool to me. Rabbit took me under his wing. Shaun Tomson was always really nice to me. Michael Ho and I became great friends, and I immediately felt like I could relate to the Hawaiians. I was a bit shocked, though, to see another young goofy-footer absolutely ripping, who bore an uncanny resemblance to Michael. His younger brother, Derek, was just doing the trials like me, and I can remember us checking each other out as the new young goofy-footers on tour. We both seemed to be thinking, *who's that guy?* I'd be checking out his surfing and he'd be looking at me with that intimidating Hawaiian stare, as if to say, *what are you looking at?* I was trying to rip in front of him, as if to say, *don't you know me? I'm the new kid on the block.* And he'd be looking at me, *nah, never heard of ya.* It was like this full mind game. Eventually Michael pulled me aside and went, 'This is my brother. Wha'sup?' It was almost like that movie *North Shore*, when you meet Vince, the head local. He was giving me the Hawaiian handshake and I didn't really know how to do it, and if you blow it you look like such a kook. They just look at you like, *this guy hasn't got a clue.* But I ended up hanging out with Derek and Mike a lot, because I could relate to them and we liked the same kind of things, and they were great to surf with.

That first year I also travelled a lot with Greg Day, a success-ful pro surfer from Sydney's northern beaches. We headed to Durban for the Gunston 500 and stayed at this little old bed-and-breakfast called Windermere. The surf got really big and I caught a really bad flu. I had a fever and was sweating and hallucinating. My first time away on tour and I was out of it. I somehow managed to make it through the trials to the main event, but I came up against the great Hawaiian surfer Dane Kealoha in the first round and didn't stand a chance. Coming up against Dane as a young trialist was so intimidating. We all knew the rules when it came to Dane. I hadn't even been to Hawaii, but I just knew not to even look at him in case he went, 'What are you looking at?' He was an incredible surfer and had just been stripped of his points by the ASP for competing in some unsanctioned Hawaiian events, and it probably cost him a world title. So he was understandably pretty angry at the world. So I kept my head down. He just had this aura around him.

In the next event, the Renault Sport, also in Durban, I got as far as the second round and was bundled out by one of my travelling companions, Gary Timperley, a big strong natural-footer from Byron Bay.

From there we headed down to the legendary Jeffreys Bay. We stayed at a cheap little bed-and-breakfast called Kitchen Windows, right on the point. I had to share a double bed with Timpo, and we slept head-to-toe, while G'Day was on this little single bed.

I felt instantly at home at J-Bay. I met a local lady, Cheron Kraak, who ran a clothing company called Country Feeling, which sponsored the contest. She later became the local licensee for Billabong and a great friend, who always took good care of us in J-Bay. As soon as I walked into Cheron's house on the point I just thought, *this is where I want to be*. I kept on going back there a lot and staying at her house. I did okay in the contest, finishing eighth, but I knew it was somewhere I could do really well, and in my free-surfs I really started to click into the place.

> **Pam Occhilupo:** On one occasion we were watching him being interviewed on TV in South Africa. By this time Mark was halfway through his first year on the tour, and when the reporter questioned Mark he had to look at the hotel towel he was carrying to see where he was. 'We're here in . . . [looking at towel] Durban.' Poor darling – maybe it was too much too soon.

SURFING USA

From South Africa we went to Atlantic City, on the east coast of the US, and it was a real shock after J-Bay. It was basically a massive city right on the beach with terrible waves. But I was just stoked to be on the tour and took it all in my stride. I'll never forget going to Los Angeles for the first time; I could tell the California lifestyle was going to agree with me. Everything was new and fast and super-exciting: the place was full of larger-than-life characters and beautiful girls and wild parties.

One of the top Californian pros at the time, Dave Parmenter, was just radical. If he won an event he used to get up and grab the microphone and say, 'I'm going to rule the world! I was always going to win. You guys are nothing.' It was crazy. The tour was wild in those days, with twenty-four or twenty-five events a year, so you were in a different city – sometimes a different country – every two weeks. With the fairly hectic partying that went along with the tour in those days, it quickly became a bit of a blur. Everywhere you went there was a local crew keen to show the visiting pros a good time, and it was easy to get swept up in it all.

California was also fateful for me because it was where I met shaper Rusty Preisendorfer. I remember getting the first board from Rusty, and it was just the all-time board. Nothing against the boards I'd been riding, but the Rusty just suited me so good, and something clicked. I got this one magic 6'0" from him and I felt my surfing take off. At that point I felt things were starting to roll for me and I was going to do really well.

In October that year we went to Chiba, Japan, and I hopped on my new Rusty and it all just seemed to come together for me. I kept getting through heats and felt unstoppable, but then disaster struck. I snapped the nose off the Rusty and I was devastated. I tried riding another board but it just didn't feel the same, so I jumped back on the Rusty – even with five inches of the nose missing – and made it all the way to the semifinals. I beat Shaun Tomson in the quarters, who was the man to beat at the time because he was so polished, and eventually lost to Curren in the semis for a third-place finish, which was my best result to date. Curren went on to beat Derek Ho in the final and marked himself as the new pacesetter, but I definitely put myself in the picture with that third, and I could tell people

Occy

were starting to take notice. I got the Rusty fixed and kept riding it because it was just the magic board.

There's footage of me somewhere at the Charity Classic in Cronulla riding a Rusty, and that's the board. There were so many good surfers on tour and I was doing all right, but not good enough to be a top pro surfer. But when I jumped on that board, that's when it all finally kind of clicked . . . I was probably a bit of late bloomer. Some kids get really good when they're eleven or twelve, but I wasn't like that. I had a bit of a weird style and I'd only just got it all sorted out.

Paul Sargeant: There was this whole new brand of surfing that nobody had seen and he was just surfing rings around people, with power that made people go, 'How do you do that?' He just became a sensation, a phenomenon. With those Rustys he came alive. It was a magic combination. I think Occy was blown away as much as everybody else. The Rustys were when the turbo jets were fired up and it was just massive.

Rusty Preisendorfer: I watched him at a contest in Ocean Beach, California. It was the equivalent to a modern WQS. I saw a young, powerful, goofy-foot forcing his board through turns. He was using more energy to recover and compensate for a board that wasn't right, instead of just uncorking it and cutting loose.

As a surfer and a shaper, I always placed a premium on speed and power. I felt these were the elements and foundation to great, radical, innovative surfing. At sixteen, Occy already embodied these traits, and the way he was trying to surf was a natural fit for where I was trying to take my designs. His surfing validated my design ideas at that time.

I was going in my own direction with flatter decks; thinner boards; boxy, angular rails; rockers with lower or longer arcs and more drive. With Occy, Tom Carroll and a few other power surfers, I had different hull designs and fin positioning that helped them surf the way they wanted to. From a design standpoint, they may have appeared crude because everyone else was still on the crowned deck, pinched rails. I was on my own little tangent: I was trying to keep the volume in the boards, so I made them thinner in the middle but pushed volume out to the rails. People used the description 'boxy', but they weren't really boxy. They were steep and angular – and the angular bit was key. The bottom part of the rail had a smaller radius, and as the curve travelled up to the deck it straightened out a little bit. If you were to take a cross-section, it would appear that there was almost a flat spot mid-rail between the apex [outermost part of rail] and the crown. The crown is the top of the rail, which was more defined because of the flatness of the deck. This flat band helped the rail set and lock into its arc. I made the deck in the tail section very flat, and behind the front fins the rails were essentially square.

In my mind, this helped the three-fin design by keeping it running up and on its rail and not having the tail anchored so deep in the water. It also provided a tremendous amount of release. Also, going thinner meant the deckline followed the rail-line [rail rocker] more closely. It's funny, because at the time I thought they were fairly thin boards – 2¼", maybe 2⁵⁄₁₆" – but because of the volume being carried out to the rail I think this is what some people looked at as 'crude'.

Rabbit Bartholomew: The very first time I saw Occy, I hadn't heard his name or anything. I was down in Cronulla for a charity event and someone pointed him out to me. And there was this little guy out on a tiny red board, and I was just like, 'Wow, he is amazing.' He was a little guy, like about twelve, and really busy on a wave, but you could see that he had natural power and connectivity of his moves. But a few years later I went back again. It was probably 1983 and I was actually leading the world rankings, and I went down for this charity event. We all made the final and there was Occy and Gary Green and myself, and Occy won the event. It was pretty classic in a way. It was a fun event for me – it wasn't a big serious event – and I was happy to make the final and do my bit. But Occy put on a show in that final, and it was just so meteoric from that point on.

Chapter Four

Nineteen eighty-four was a big year for me when I look back on it from start to finish. In January I won the Pro Junior in small beach-breaks at Narrabeen – the biggest junior contest in Australia. By December I was surfing ten- to fifteen-foot waves in the final of the Pipeline Masters on the first day I'd surfed the place. In between, I'd surfed all over the world, won events in Lacanau, France, and Jeffreys Bay, South Africa, and lived a lifetime of experiences in a year.

The Pro Junior was a big deal back then, the first contest to offer real prize money to my generation of grommets, but it was like I was already looking beyond it. Don't get me wrong, I was stoked to win it – and it was a tough 2–1 victory in the three-set final against Mitch Thorson. But the banners and scaffolding at North Narrabeen were really a leaping-off point for me to attack the world stage.

> **Nick Carroll:** The Pro Junior was such a big thing, but it didn't seem like a big thing to him. He somersaulted right by it. I remember the first one: he beat Damien Hardman in a heat, and it was such a brutal beating – he beat Damien so badly, with such an arrogant display of skills. He blew Damien out of the water. Damien was entitled to think he had a shot at it, but he so didn't.

Robbie Page: I had this heat in the Pro Junior – I had this wave at the beginning of the heat and I let it go and he got it and found his Occy rhythm and just annihilated me. And he left the water and got in his car and drove away. I'm sitting in the water at Narrabeen and he's gone . . . I wanted to paddle around the back of Narrabeen to Little Narrabeen, but I had to walk up the beach and give my singlet back, like, *oh yeah, the guy who beat me's already gone home*. There was fucking ten minutes left in the heat.

THE TOP SIXTEEN

The Australian leg in autumn would decide the end-of-year ratings and the world title race. The tour at the time didn't operate on a calendar year but finished in Australia in March/April, rather than Hawaii, and then the new season would kick off in May. I'd had a good first year to date, but the goal was to finish in the top sixteen and earn an automatic seed into the main events of all the contests the following year. It was a big ask in your first year as a trialist, but anything less would have been a disappointment.

At the Stubbies at Burleigh Heads I lost in the first round to Joey Buran, and Tom Carroll beat Rabbit in the final to tighten his grip on the world title. At what was then called the Beaurepaires, back in Cronulla, I started to hit my stride, winning the trials, defeating my hero Tom Curren in the first round and making it all the way to the semis. Barton Lynch beat me, but a third was a great result for a young trialist and I was stoked. I didn't make the main event at Bells, but I'd just done enough to finish sixteenth with total prize money earnings for the season of US$7500, which would have barely covered my airfares. But I was over the moon. I was on tour with a top-sixteen seed and living the dream.

I thought Martin Potter and Tom Curren were going to be two

of my biggest rivals. We were kind of the new guard. Curren was the best surfer in the world for me back then, for sure. And he was the full mysto guy. I used to wonder, *is he pissed off with me or is he just introverted?* I thought he was too cool for school, but later I realised he was just really shy. Pottz was the new kid from South Africa, who went on tour at sixteen, like me, and wanted to absolutely destroy every wave he caught. I knew we were going to have some great showdowns in the months and years ahead.

HAWAII FOR THE FIRST TIME

Around this time Gordon Merchant suggested that going to Hawaii would be good experience for me and help my development as a surfer. It was great advice, and that first trip in the late season made an indelible mark, leaving me in no doubt where my destiny ultimately lay. I went over with Gordon and we stayed with Billabong's Hawaii rep, Buddy McCray, right on Sunset Point. The flights from Australia used to get in at midnight, and I crashed on the couch at Buddy's, woke up about seven o'clock, sat up, looked out the window and saw the most beautiful eight-foot wave breaking on the west peak. That was my introduction to Hawaii. I just opened my eyes and went, 'Oh . . . my . . . goodness.' I had tingles and butterflies and goose bumps and everything. It was such an amazing sight. Gordon was like, 'What do you reckon? You're out there.' And I just went, 'Oh, I guess so.'

Gordon was telling me what size board to ride, and Buddy was tying my leash string for me. Buddy's an amazing character, a really good kneeboarder, who lost an arm to cancer when he was quite young. But there was nothing Buddy couldn't do with one arm. He did a better job tying my leash string than I would have done in my state. He could even roll a joint with one hand. So I ventured out at Sunset for my first Hawaiian surf, nervous and excited. It was the start of an unforgettable day.

I went to Hawaii with no expectations of surfing big waves. I was just going to check it out. But as I paddled out at Sunset that morning I discovered I was actually more excited than scared. You always seem to remember it better than it was, but it made a big impression on me – in more ways than one.

On one of my first waves, Sunset lifeguard Darrick Doerner dropped in on me, and I kept on riding behind him on the inside bowl, keeping up with him. We flicked out together and he came up and slapped me in the face and said, 'Do you know who I am? The waves are coming up. I'm the lifeguard here. What's your name? Do you know what you're doing out here?' I was like, *fuck, this place is radical.* He didn't send me in, but it was more like, 'Are you right out here? Do you know what you're doing?' And I was like, 'Not really.' I was just trying to be humble and respectful, so he didn't send me in. And we kind of got talking and laughing because I hadn't completely burst out crying.

That afternoon Ken Bradshaw bit a chunk out of the rail of my board. I'm not sure why, to this day. He might have seen me get a good wave, I was having a good surf that afternoon. I was riding a big board and I was loving taking those west peaks for the first time. And then out of the blue Ken paddles up to me and bites a chunk out of my rail and then looks at me and goes, 'Do you know who I am?' I decided to paddle in after that, just thinking, *who was that guy with the big beard? And why did he bite my surfboard?* It was apparently important to know who people were out in the surf here. I don't know if I was getting too many waves or he noticed I could surf okay and he just wanted to let me know who he was. But it was a bit of a wake-up call.

I went in and one of the head locals, Eddie Rothman, was at Buddy's place, trying to sell him some land up on Comsat Hill, over-looking the North Shore. I said to Buddy, 'You'll never guess what just happened . . . This big guy with a beard just bit my board and sent me in.' They immediately knew who it was and Eddie just went, 'Get back out there and, if he says anything, you tell him Eddie sent you back out.'

I'd been surfing all day by then and didn't really want to go back out, but I figured I'd better do what he said. I didn't really want to say anything to Ken, so I just kind of hid from him out there. I didn't want to have to say, 'Eddie told me to come back out', because I didn't know what he might do. He might bite my nose off this time, my real nose, not my surfboard's. So I kind of skulked around the outskirts of the line-up till he went in. I've had some classic run-ins with Ken over the years. He's just so passionate and he loves surfing that much, and we've become really good friends since. But that was my first day in Hawaii, and I realised pretty quickly it was not a place to be taken lightly.

Buddy McCray: I didn't have a clue beforehand. I didn't know who he was. They told me he was this kid coming out of Australia, a junior pro and all this stuff.

Very few people show up here and surf really well, right off the bat. And Occy was one, Tom Carroll was one, Joe Engel was one . . . He surfed like he was made for it. We had a really nice spring and had really good surf everywhere we went. After the first couple of times watching him surf I could see that he was dialled.

We were on a pretty good mission. My girlfriend at the time was a really good cook and would prepare all these vegetarian meals. We were doing yoga and surfing and eating good . . . There was actually a little bit too much cleaning up after him. Mrs Occhilupo could have potty-trained him a little better. He was definitely focused on what he wanted to do, but not the other stuff, like cleaning up after himself!

Mike Latronic: We had a blast surfing together that first year in Hawaii. He used to froth like a dog, sticking his head out the window at oversized windblown Rocky Point. He spoke so loud when he surfed but he was a pretty humble, quiet, boyish kid – and turns up doing things no man had ever done.

THE NEW SEASON 1984–85 – GETTING ON A ROLL

I was fit and focused after Hawaii. I started the new season well, with a second to Pottz in Japan, and it felt like there was a bit of a new era dawning on tour with a bunch of young surfers shaking things up. In South Africa I got a ninth at the Spur Steak Ranch Pro in Capetown, losing to big Simon Anderson, but there was no disgrace in that. The guy was and is an absolute legend who rips in any size surf. But my free-surfing was feeling great and I felt sure the results would follow.

Mitch Thorson: In '84 he did the entire South African and European legs in a pair of tight red tracksuit pants, black pointy shoes and a range of Billabong T-shirts. We went to this very ritzy civic reception in Durban, with the mayor and all these dignitaries. Shaun Tomson was on a first-name basis with whoever was running the country. I'm sitting there, and Occy's seventeen, getting restless and bored. The next thing I know he's lying on the floor at my feet. He used to fall asleep like a cat. He just curled up on the ground. It came time to go and Derek [Hynd] or someone's gone, 'Come on, Occ, let's go.' And in my natural big brotherly mode, I had a quick look down to where he'd been lying and there was his passport and about $200. So I picked it up and put it in my pocket and gave it to him later. He was just like a little kid.

We flew down to Capetown, surfed all over for a while,

scored really good waves at Outer Kom, Crayfish Factory, and some of the stuff that he was doing . . . I remember just going, *holy fuck, how the fuck am I going to beat this guy?* I saw him doing some shit at Outer Kom – I still haven't seen people doing that. It was incomprehensible.

JEFFREYS BAY

Going back to Jeffreys Bay, I had a feeling something special was in the air. I already loved the place and couldn't wait to get back there on my new boards and test them out on those big, fast J-Bay walls.

They didn't have time to wait for waves in those days, they just ran the contest straight through. As it happened, from the first blast of the hooter on the first day, there were fifteen or twenty waves stacked all the way to the horizon, and they just kept coming. I was smoking a chillum with some older local guys in the sand dunes, who seemed quite amused by the prospect of getting a young visiting pro stoned to the gills right before a heat. They'd make you bust the chillum, and you'd get so clubbed because you had to get it to glow red-hot. I wasn't sure this was a good contest strategy, but I was already determined to get on well with the local crew – wherever I went – and this was one sure-fire way to break the ice. As they blew the hooter we were laughing our heads off, and this set that seemed about fifty-waves long just roared down the point. I felt like I was in a dream.

From my first heat, I had a great run on my Rusty. It was going so good and I was treating it like a baby. The surf was eight to ten feet and I was riding a 6'0", but it had the biggest, blockiest rails, so it just handled it. Tom Carroll already had a bit of a reputation for dropping in, but there was one wave at J-Bay that year during a free-surf when I didn't mind a bit. People still talk about it. I'd be doing my bottom turn, looking up at him doing the wickedest snap, and then we'd cross over and I'd do the same – and we did it about eight or ten times, all the way down the point, in complete synchronisation. We came in and people were just babbling about it.

Wes Laine and Willy Morris always seemed to have the inside and get some of the best waves out there, and Shaun Tomson was ruling, riding the deepest barrels. And somehow I made the final. I wore booties the whole time, and I normally hate booties, but I couldn't do a thing wrong that event. The surf dropped for the final day and it just all came together for me. The Rusty went so well and my backhand surfing felt really in tune with the wave. I couldn't believe it. I'd won the Country Feeling Classic, my first pro win, and I was away. After J-Bay I scored a fifth in the Gunston 500 in Durban and was looking pretty good for my first year in the top sixteen – and growing in confidence all the time.

> **Shaun Tomson:** I was there at J-Bay in '84 when he made his first big impact. I always thought of Occy as this kid from Cronulla who didn't really have the chops to cut it in bigger, more powerful surf, but that day was a pivotal moment. He went on to win the event, but it wasn't so much his performance in the contest on the last day because the surf was shithouse, but the previous day the surf had come up, six to eight feet, and he put on a brilliant performance. Before then the ultimate goofy-footers at J-Bay had been Wayne Lynch in 1970 and Tom Carroll in '81, and Occy kind of raised the bar. It was nice to be on the beach.
>
> It was an afternoon session and I didn't go out. I remember sitting and watching and thinking, *this kid's going to go places* . . . He had that really square bottom turn and really square off the top, and he got a lot of projection out of that turn. Occy's manoeuvres were always very clearly defined, which was great. A lot of people sort of change rails and adjust, but with Occy there was always that commitment,

on the rail, and I always thought the true test of a surfer was how hard he carves, not how high he goes in the air. Occy's a carver, he just carves it, power on all the time, which is sort of the antithesis of modern surfing, which is power on, power off, power on, power off. He's just full-on power, old school, and I've always admired that. He's a carver, a natural born carver.

Cheron Kraak (owner of Country Feeling): It was eight feet and probably the best surf we'd had for an event. Suddenly there was this kid, this blond-headed kid with a squeaky voice, and he was absolutely amazing. He was levels ahead of anyone here – his backhand surfing at Supers, doing these incredible carves. He won the event. I think he was seventeen.

Then I met Gordon and we were all talking. Occy came around to the house and made himself immediately at home. Then he said to me, would I mind if he came back and stayed here. I said to him, tongue in cheek, 'If you win the Gunston, you can come back and stay.' The next year I get a call saying, 'I won the Gunston, can I come back and stay with you?' And that was the beginning of a very long, real relationship with Occy. He's almost like one of my own children.

Mitch Thorson: He was incredibly clumsy. The number of times I was with him and surfing J-Bay and he'd stub half his foot off and just go, 'Ooooh' and make these funny little noises and stick his chin out and go, 'Mitch, do you think it will be okay?' And I'd just go, 'Yeah, just get it in the water', and he'd just keep going. A lot of people used to say they didn't think he was that bright, because he didn't used to talk much. I think he did a lot more observing than talking. I don't know if it was naivety or cunning, but he used to say really funny things that embarrassed himself, and that made it even funnier. But I used to have conversations with him and think, *this guy is borderline genius.*

VIVE LA FRANCE

My first time in France, I'd heard so much about it and it was all true. We got to Lacanau and we had such good waves that year. There were good banks and we were getting shacked off our heads, with nude people on the beach. We were tripping on it, and the whole French way of life: the food, the culture, the nightlife. A top local surfer, Thierry Dominich, befriended us and was really cool. There was a little local grommet, Jean Michel, who later became a really good friend, and his parents had a little shop in the main street. It was one of the first major pro contests in France, surfing was still pretty new there, and everyone seemed stoked to have us in town. It was so uncrowded and we used to stay at this hotel like Fawlty Towers, right on the beach at Lacanau.

I just seemed to get on a roll, beating Curren, Shaun and Glen Winton along the way, and ended up winning the contest in a close final with Tom Carroll.

I quickly discovered I loved surfing man-on-man. I've never been a good paddler, so for me four-man heats were always a hassle. I'm only good when the waves come straight to me, and in man-on-man it's easy to do that. Because I've got short arms and everyone else has got long ones, they can paddle over the top of me, so the man-on-man format really suited me. It clicked really quick. And with the way the judges are, even to this day, if one guy is ripping he gets through a lot of heats because he's the flavour of the month – you get on a roll.

Rabbit Bartholomew: The other event that really stands out is the Lacanau final with him and Tom Carroll. That was the best of three sets and Occy won. It was unbelievable, this kid beat Carroll at his best. The final was just outrageous, beautiful surfing.

Paul Sargeant: It was magic, magic, magic waves – four to six foot. I remember Michael and Derek Ho coming back from the beach, going, 'Man, these beachbreaks are like Pipeline', and they were for those couple of days. And Occy became the darling of the French as well. They loved him to death. They'd follow him into the water, he'd kick off a wave and they'd be waist deep, waiting for autographs: 'Occy, Occy!'

Rusty Preisendorfer: I was already making boards for many good surfers of the day: PT, Ian, Shaun, Dave Parmenter, Greg Day, Mike Burness, Wes Laine, to name a few. But Occy was the one that captured everyone's imagination. Soon after he embarked on his rampage on the first boards I built him, twelve of the top sixteen were coming to me for boards. Some out of curiosity, some simply because they felt the only way they could beat him was to get into his head.

Tom Carroll: It was a big challenge for me, a real affront to my ego. I had to try to use every part of me to take it on board and try to learn from it. My ego didn't really want to do that – like, *I'm Tom Carroll*. The fact of the matter was I could see something in him that was very, very special, and I had to try and learn from that. I really liked his style of surfing. While I was the world champion at the time, Occy was leading the ratings in '84 in the first part of the year, and they were calling him the world number one because he was the ratings leader. I was having a hard time with that.

I was quite clear about it in my head that I needed to improve my surfing in a bunch of different areas. It was a real challenge. I loved watching Occy surf. It was clear he was head and shoulders above a bunch of us. He had the freedom and the style. I'd look at his boards and the way he was standing and try and figure it out. When he surfed J-Bay in '84 I watched that closely, and that's where I wanted to be with my backside surfing.

It was obvious he had a really unique body intelligence. He's a super-sensitive character, highly aware and tuned in, especially when he was in the surf; very expressive. His nervous system was allowing him to be loose, he wasn't attached to a hard-wired nervousness. Kong [Gary Elkerton] for instance, at that time, had a hard-wired nervousness. I think I had a very edgy forcefulness, a little bit nervous in its origins. I used to use a lot of force. What I got from Occy was to try and free that up, and I got that from Curren as well. Getting down lower and tighter inside the section of the wave. When Rusty made those boards for him, I went and got one made because I went, *that board is sitting into the wave so well*. That lifted my game immeasurably. You could see Occy was able to freely express himself on a wave.

That year I started travelling with Cheyne Horan, and he had a huge influence on me. Cheyne was considered a bit of an out-there character at the time, right into his yoga, vegetarianism and Eastern mysticism, like I Ching, which involves throwing three coins to predict your future or seek guidance. When I started travelling with Cheyne it was considered an extreme move, and there were a lot of people going, 'Oh no, what's going to happen to Occy?'

I went seriously vegetarian and learnt Hatha yoga, and we religiously did it morning and night for hours. The best thing about it was it got my body real loose, because I've always had a stiff kind of body. So my surfing loved it but my energy levels didn't. We were smoking a lot of mull too, which probably didn't help my energy levels. I'm not condoning pot, but it was an interesting time for me, getting right into yoga and I suppose a kind of spiritualism, because Cheyne was a very spiritual guy. He was a great guy to travel with, because he was always training and eating well. Throughout my career, no matter what's happened, I was always in my best frame of mind when I was either doing yoga or training and eating really good food, and they're the things I picked up from Cheyne. You've got to pick the best out of everything. But in the end I felt like I didn't have enough energy, because I wasn't eating meat. I almost felt sometimes like I was floating, like I wasn't grounded – and it wasn't just from all the joints. I seriously felt my energy levels were out of whack.

I was doing yoga one early morning with Cheyne at Oceanside, in California, and there was this one backbend we did, where you lean over backwards as far as you can, like a back arch, and all the blood rushed to my head and I nearly passed out. I was thinking, *maybe I am getting too into this.* It was kind of a bit scary. Cheyne was really into awakening your kundalini, or your enlightened spirit, and when you do that you can kind of go a bit crazy. That's what a lot of yogis are working towards, but if you don't know how to harness that energy you can kind of lose it. And we were getting close, and I was getting a bit freaked out by it.

Cheyne loved to fast too. He'd eat nothing but grapes for four or five days, which I don't think is really that good for you, because you're just eating sugar really. You're drinking a lot of water, and it does clean you out, but I was doing a grape fast during this event in Oceanside and I just had no energy. I was in the water in a heat and I deadset felt like I was anemic. It was a wake-up call. Fasting is good, but you can't be doing lots of exercise at the same time, not in the middle of a contest.

Eventually I figured it was all going too far for me, and I pulled back and started doing my own thing, keeping what worked and leaving the rest. But I'd never regret that time I spent with Cheyne because I learnt a lot. With my diet these days, I eat a bit of everything but I like to eat health food mostly. Once in a while I'll snack out on junk food. And I kept on doing yoga throughout my career, but just not as intense and not with the incense and music and chanting and mantras. Cheyne's much more normal these days too. He's got his surf school at Surfers Paradise. He's a great coach, and he'll even have a beer. He would never have drunk beer back then. I've heard it said that going off on that tangent with Cheyne cost me a world title in '84, but I've got no regrets. I don't think I could have won the world title that year anyway – I always felt like the two Toms, Carroll and Curren, had my measure at that point in my career and they had the world title sewn up between them.

Cheyne Horan: There were no preservatives, no additives, everything was natural food – 100 per cent natural. We were doing yoga in the morning, surfing all day long, living on carrot juice, brown rice, beans. Occ wanted to get involved in the cooking, but he didn't know how to cook, so I'd get him to pitch in with the brown rice. And Occ used to make this dessert at night which was all-time: sultanas with the rice and some soy milk with it, like a rice pudding. And for how we were eating, it tasted fantastic. We were so regimented about it, and we were separated from the tour in a way, because everyone was eating meat pies and McDonald's and drinking Coca-Cola, and we were making our own food, or we'd eat at health food restaurants, but we'd always make sure it was pure.

Paul Sargeant: Cheyne was totally into it at the time and he wanted to share it. Like when you've found God, you want your mates to find God and you may be a bit of a pain in the arse, pushing the point. But that's what you want – it's only their good you're looking out for – and I think Cheyne was like that.

Occy was so into it and I remember coming back from the Stubbies once sitting next to him on the plane, an early-morning flight in the days when they used to serve you a proper breakfast. So off came the alfoil after the stewardess put the trays down and Occy said, 'What is it?' And she said, 'Egg and hash brown and a sausage' and he goes, 'No, I'll just have a glass of water.' So I started eating it and he was like, 'Yuck, I don't know how you can eat that.' I'm eating it and the next thing I know I hear this, *mmm, mmmm,* and I turn around and he's got these green bubbles coming out of his mouth, all foamy. I go, 'What are you doing?' And he's like, *mmm, mmmm.* He'd thought the hostess would bring the water back straightaway, so he's thrown these spirulina capsules in his mouth, and there was green everywhere, foaming out of his mouth. And the chick came back with the glass of water and was like, 'Oh my God, are you all right?'

At one stage he had all these tablets and bottles he was taking every day, and he fully got into it. He was very lean – very lean – and probably I think still looked the cleanest he ever looked, in my opinion. I don't know how much he was smoking at the time, but he looked young, clean, fresh, full of energy.

SURF INTO SUMMER

Billabong held an event at Duranbah late in the year, and it produced a moment that guys still want to talk to me about. Aerials were still a really new thing then and Gordon decided to hold an aerial expression session. I'd already been knocked out of the contest, so

I was keen to make amends. No-one had really mastered aerials at the time and guys were falling off everywhere. I was on my favourite Rusty and this perfect peak came to me, the lip just presented itself like a perfect ramp. I boosted an air pretty high but also way out into the flats and landed backwards. I was concentrating so hard and holding my rail and I landed in the flats, and I was so determined I somehow pulled it. That wave ended up in a movie called *Blazing Boards* and I still have all those Santa Cruz guys, who are the full aerial masters, come up and go, 'Dude, that wave in *Blazing Boards* inspired me to try and do airs.' It's weird, because I can hardly do an air now to save my life.

THE 1984 PIPE MASTERS

I'd had a great run through '84, but Hawaii loomed as my big challenge. I got invited to the Pipeline Masters without ever having surfed Pipe before, when it was still an invitational. I'd won a couple of events and was kind of the new kid on the block, so they thought they'd put me out at Pipe. It wasn't so much me thinking, *I've got to go to Hawaii and prove myself.* It was more them going, 'You've got to come to Hawaii and prove yourself.'

It's funny, Hawaii is such a second home now but back then I was pretty overawed. I guess I'd always felt a calling. I'd seen a photo of Gerry Lopez doing his bottom turn at Pipe, and you could see the likeness of a Polynesian goddess in the depths of the barrel behind him. It was a pretty amazing photo and it made a big impression. The photographer was Denjiro Sato, and that guy has the gift. There's another photo he took of Waimea shorebreak, and you can make out a turtle in the whitewater. It's amazing. I can see that stuff sometimes in the whitewash. You've only got to look for it.

I went in the Sunkist World Cup at Sunset and did all right, got a fifth. Michael Ho won it. Pipe wasn't a rated event, it was still a one-day specialty event, and it was quite an honour to make the list. Of the twenty-four invitees, fourteen were local Hawaiian surfers, and most of the rest were well-established pros and good Pipe surfers.

I remember the first day of my first Pipe Masters quite vividly, because I was staying at Buddy McCray's house at Sunset and contest director Randy Rarick lived close by. I was surfing a lot with Rod Kirsop at the time, a doctor and big-wave charger from Sydney. We looked at the surf and it was really big, about fifteen foot. Sunset was pretty out of control. And then we saw Randy pulling out of his driveway and he said, 'Pipe is on at nine o'clock.' I said, 'Are you kidding me?' I asked Randy what board to ride and he said a 7'10". So Rod and I grabbed our 7'10"s to go down there. We used to ride longer boards back then.

We pulled up at Pipe and the right of way there at Gerry Lopez's house was packed. We had to squeeze through and we came out the other end on the beach, and there was no-one out there. Everyone was looking at us. We were the guinea pigs and I'd never surfed Pipe before. I was looking at Rod and he was looking at me, and we were like, *I guess we're out there.* So we charged out, and just made it through Ehukai, like a ten-foot shorebreak. We got out there and were floating on the second reef, and there was a massive crowd on the beach before the contest.

I remember I got my first wave right off the second reef, and Rod got the one behind it. There's a photo of me on that wave, with my hands above my head. When I took off, my eyes were as big as golf balls, and my heart was in my throat, but I really got over a hurdle right there. And the waves settled down that day and got so perfect and we all got really good barrels. Pipe was run in one day, on the best Pipe day of the season, with an invite list packed with all the Pipe heavyweights. I managed to get past Tim Fritz and Dane Kealoha in the quarters, and Brian Bulkley and Allan Byrne in the semis. I ended up getting second to Joey Buran in my first effort at Pipe and won $2500, so I was over the moon. I knew Hawaii was somewhere that was going to play a big part in my career, and my life.

Nick Carroll (from _Tracks_, February 1985): Two figures – Occy and Kirsop, looking very alone – were sitting on the second reef, a quarter mile out. Every twenty minutes or so, something truly insane happened – first, the cloudbreak erupted, then the lines of swell marched into the base of Pipe's lava reef, the huge lips falling in frighteningly slow arcs, peeling across the entire length of the beach to Ehukai. It almost looked like big Narrabeen, but then a surfer was scratching – it was Occy, paddling like a bastard to overcome the sudden rush of wind up the face, paddling, paddling (you could see his tiny arms spinning through the spray), and – yes! – his board broke away from the feathering lip and he took the longest, fastest drop he'd ever taken, and as he pulled it cautiously through the inside, arms held high with that ecstasy of relief and victory . . . Good God! Not Narrabeen.

Rod Kirsop: We were already in our wetsuits and we ran down that little track and there were people everywhere. We looked out and there was no-one in the surf, and everyone was looking at us because we were in our wetsuits with our boards under our arms. We didn't have leggies, but there was a lull so we paddled out. I'd surfed it like that a couple of years before, so I had a bit of an idea. Occ was a bit further on the inside and a set came through. He got the first one and I got the second one. We shook hands afterwards and then everyone else started paddling out – half an hour later it was crowded.

We used to hang out and go surfing together a lot. He was into yoga and that. He was in a fairly healthy phase at that time. He was keen to surf big waves and stoked to surf Pipe that day. What I remember is just the purity of his surfing and him wanting to get as involved in the spirit of it as he could and just really loving going surfing.

Gerry Lopez: Occy showed up and charged right into it. Everyone here, all the local guys who surfed the place, always eased into it. It's a pretty terrifying place, and that was normally how everybody came into the place. It was always intriguing to me that these guys would come over – and there were a bunch of them who did it: Terry Richo, Al Byrne, Banksy. They all came and they didn't have that luxury of being able to be here and ease into the situation. They had to go straight into it, so I always had my eye on those guys . . . Then Occy came along and, oh man, he impressed the shit of me.

Randy Rarick (Triple Crown director): I think he was typical when he was young – totally oblivious and not really well-aware of what the scene was. And sometimes that works in your favour. When you have naivety and innocence, you just go into it not knowing what to expect . . . It was just like, 'Let's go out and give it a go', and that was to his advantage. Not having preconceived notions of what to do and what not to do, just go out and charge it.

Buddy McCray: I remember one of the Pipe contests he got his bell rung pretty bad. He stayed out and finished the contest, but his skull smacked the reef and his ears were ringing for months and months afterwards. He finally ended up going to a herbalist, a Chinese guy in town. He tried everything. I remember one morning waking up and looking outside, and he was sitting there almost crying, going, 'My ears keep ringing and ringing.' He hadn't complained about it. It was weeks after and his ear hadn't stopped ringing.

Tom Carroll: He was really made for Pipe, in many ways, just the way his style was, how low he is on the drop. The lower to your board you are on the drop the better. He was just made for that, those driving big bottom turns. There was something about Pipe, though; he seemed a little bit intimidated by Pipe. He's not the absolute gung-ho crazy guy – he's actually quite calculating. I think he was better at Sunset, because of his heel bottom turns. I loved watching Occy at Sunset and Haleiwa.

THE WILD WEST DAYS

I only just caught the tail end of the real Wild West days on the North Shore. They reckon it was way more radical in the 70s, but it was still plenty wild enough for me. Later that season I was checking Rocky Point one day, just minding my own business, and 'Fast Eddie' Rothman pulled up – the head of the local surfers club, Da Hui, or 'the Black Shorts', as they were known. Then these guys pulled up behind him in their car, because that road at Rocky Point is only narrow. Eddie goes, 'Hey, move your car' and the guys are like, 'No worries, just a minute, we've just got our boards under the trees. We're just going to grab them.' And he goes, 'Hey, move your fucking car *now*.' And they go, 'Nah, it's sweet, we'll just grab our boards.' I was going, *oh no, is this seriously happening*?

Before I knew it, he knocked one of them out. There were about five of them and they all just jumped on him, and I was the only guy around. I was only eighteen, it was only my second time in Hawaii, so what do I do? Walk away, and Eddie knows I didn't come to his aid? Or jump in and get my arse kicked too?

Eddie broke free and one of them spun around and gave him a blind kick to the head, and they all jumped on him. I figured I'd better help out, so I was trying to pull them off, going, in my squeaky voice, 'You don't know who you're fucking with! You don't know who you're fucking with!' Then out of nowhere these big Hawaiians appeared and just waded in and sorted the guys out. They were holding these guys while Eddie dealt it to them. It was a big fight and the stone wall there at Rocky's started collapsing under the strain.

I saw Eddie the next day and I was like, 'Fuck, how heavy was that? What did you do with those guys?' He's like, 'I thought they were Brazilian but they were Israeli, and my mum's Israeli, so they're all staying at my house.' I couldn't believe it. I thought, *this place is way too heavy*.

Another time, I was surfing Rocky Point and dropped in on this girl. She'd paddled inside me and I didn't think too much about it. I didn't even look, just took off and faded to get in the barrel, and she just cleaned me up. We both went over the falls. I came up spewing and went, 'What the fuck are you doing?' and kind of sent her in, which wasn't really the right thing to do but it seemed to be the way things were done over there.

About an hour later I was still out and I saw Ken Bradshaw paddling out. This was strange because I'd only ever seen him surf Sunset before. I said, 'Hey Ken, what are you doing out here?' He went, 'Hey Mark, you know that girl you dropped in on? That's my fucking girlfriend.' And he just kind of roared and came charging at me. He didn't hit me, but he grabbed me and put me underwater for a while. I came up and I was like, 'Fuck, fuck – sorry, I didn't know.' He stormed off and I went in pretty freaked out. I must have already made a few friends over there because I mentioned it to one of the local crew and that night all Ken's furniture and white goods and TV got stolen.

That's just the way things worked on the North Shore.

I was lucky I became friends with another one of the main local guys, Brian Surratt, really early on. He was full-on back then, but he's mellowed out now. If you didn't come and see him, he'd be looking for you. I think a lot of people misread the locals there. What they really want is to be your friend, and then they get pissed off because people are intimidated. They interpret your intimidation as being stuck up. It's like, 'You come to our place and you don't even talk to us?' I've always been a big believer, everywhere I've travelled around the world, in meeting the locals and respecting them. You're not respecting them if you just don't want to know them, and keep away from them. If you're genuine and respectful, you'll get on fine. Back in the day, Brian and Eddie were like the head locals, and from then on I got to meet everyone. Any time I had a problem, if someone was after me, I'd go and see Brian. I used to hang out with Mickey Neilson a lot too, and got to know all the local crew. I used to know truck drivers. I'd be at Sunset and a big loader truck would come by, going, *beep, beep* – 'Hey Occy!' And people would go, 'How do you know him?'

I've stayed out at the Turtle Bay Hilton, what used to be the Kui Lima, a few times. But Turtle Bay is nothing like the North Shore. You really feel like a haole when you're staying out there. When you stay out there, every time you drive to the North Shore you get those butterflies that you get on the plane when you're first flying in. You might spend a day surfing and then you go back to Turtle Bay, and the next day you drive to the North Shore you get those butterflies again every time, because you're not staying in the thick of it.

THE BAY

I was keen to get into surfing Waimea Bay, the premier big-wave spot on the North Shore. All the guys would show me around out there, but I was never the deep guy. I was on the shoulder. They'd say, 'Come on, paddle in here', but I'd just go, 'I'll be sweet here, thanks all the same.'

Me and Mike Latronic tried to go out there one big day. I was wanting to get into it, I really was. I'd been surfing it a bit, but the thing that freaked me out was when that big left came through and cleaned everyone up in January '85. I was going to go out there that day. Owl made me a board and he always told me where to surf – go to Waimea, or go to Pipe, or go to Sunset. I used to hang out with him a fair bit. Owl made me this 9'6", this big red board, especially for Waimea. Me and Mike were going to go out that day, and Mike's mum, Dolly, was freaking out, crying. Mike only had an 8'6", and that day was so radical.

We were watching it, and Bradshaw was out there and Mark Foo. Ken lost his board and it was already like twenty-five to thirty feet, and he had to swim in. He didn't make it in the first time – he was getting sucked towards the rocks and he had to swim all the way round the bay again. The second time he didn't make it, and then the third time he made it. And he'd been swimming for an hour and a half. He got to the beach and he kissed the sand. I was going, 'Mike, Mike, we've got to go check it out.' And Dolly's crying. So we walk down and run into Owl and Roger Erickson, and they go, 'Nah, you're not going out there.' Especially Mike, because he only had an 8'6", and they said, 'It's getting bigger every set.' And we're going, 'Nah, we're not going to take off, we're just going to sit in the channel and look at it.' And they said, 'But there *is* no channel.'

So we tied our boards on the roof to go back to Sunset and have a look and, I promise you, they reckon it was about fifteen minutes after we left that that big left came through and cleaned everyone up. And our boards got blown off the roof of the car on the way up to Sunset at the same time. I know it was the same time. Maybe it was a sign, I don't know, but those guys got cleaned up and they had to get rescued by a helicopter. And I thought, *whoa, I was going to be paddling out right then.* And that's when I thought maybe Waimea's not my cup of tea.

Randy Rarick: I remember surfing Waimea with him, and a lot of people don't even remember that. We were surfing Waimea on about an eighteen-foot day, and he was really good, really charging backside. It was a pretty fun day, it was about fifteen to eighteen foot, and there were a few twenty-foot sets. It wasn't killer Waimea, but it was definitely exciting. I was quite impressed that he was such a young guy and he never got any accolades for that.

Chapter Five

Into the Stratosphere

'It makes me feel so high, I feel so stoked! Especially 'cause it's my home beach. You heard all the people cheering for me . . . It just makes me feel so high.' *Tracks*, May 1985.

THE 1985 BEAUREPAIRES

I was so stoked to compete back in front of my home crowd at the Beaurepaires in '85. The local support was amazing. I was going back to Mum's house in Kurnell between heats, and Mum was really good, making sure I was rested and fed and watered, looking after me. It was televised live and I was watching it on TV when I wasn't actually surfing. I knew exactly when my heats were coming up and I could leave just before I had to surf. It was a beautiful sunny day for the finals. I was getting massages from a Chinese doctor at the event and getting right into my yoga.

There were still a lot of the old guard on tour, the first generation of pro surfers like Shaun Tomson and Rabbit. I was definitely new school, and that event felt like the changing of the guard. It definitely felt like I was accepted by the judges. For the first time, I felt like I had an advantage. The judges were really looking for something new. When you first enter pro contests, like at that heat with

Shaun Tomson at Narrabeen two years earlier, you kind of know you've won, but you're not winning because you're still new and you haven't paid your dues yet. Or you're against the world champion or someone like Shaun, so the judges just aren't ready to give you the heat. But at the Beaurepaires I felt like it was our time.

I had a lot of local support in Cronulla and a lot of media attention as the new young guy coming on strong. My dad came down to watch me compete for the first time, and I was stoked to have him there – even if he was getting around in a pair of green budgie smugglers. He'd worn his favourite red tracksuit, but he got so hot he had to strip down to his sluggoes, which was an interesting look. He'd promised me if I made the final he'd come and watch, and I really wanted to impress him. It was a hot summer's day, nor'-east wind, with these little two-foot lefts and a massive crowd. They didn't have competitors' parking back then, and it was really hard to get a parking spot, the full Sydney summer beach scene. It was like a football crowd, and most of them were cheering for me.

I got that feeling of not being able to put a foot wrong and made it all the way to the final. I came up against Tom Carroll, the reigning world champ, in a best of three sets marathon, and won it two sets to one. Winning in front of my home crowd, with my dad there, was the best feeling in the world. It's funny the little things you remember looking back on it. I had an Astrodeck tail patch in that event too and, I don't know why, I never used one again for the rest of my career. I think they were really good, but I just kind of forgot about them. I'm famous for doing things like that. I'll probably start using them now that I've finished my career.

It's weird, too, back in 1985 I won $30,000 plus a new car for winning the Beaurepaires. These days you still only get $30,000 for first place – and no car. Thirty grand was a lot of money back then. I bought a beachfront apartment in Cronulla a couple of years later for about seventy grand, so that puts it in perspective. It'd be nice if you could win half the price of a beachfront apartment for winning a surf contest these days. That'd be about five hundred grand!

Dad gave me a pat on the back when we got home and told me not to party too hard. You could tell he was kind of stoked but kind of worried at the same time about the direction my life was taking, like he could see me about to get swept along in a current, not sure where it would take me. He was really strict and not one for dishing out praise lightly, but I think deep down he was really proud. We had a pretty big party at the leagues club that night and, not for the first or last time, I pretty thoroughly ignored Dad's advice.

Pam Occhilupo: Luciano was more of an academic, and he really thought Mark was wasting his time. Mark would come home and say, 'I came second, Dad', and he'd say, 'Why didn't you come first?' The first time he ever went to the beach to watch Mark compete was when he was in the Beaurepaires and he ended up winning it. That was the first time Luciano ever went. And he said, 'I'll only come if you win.'

Paul Sargeant: One of my clearest memories of that event is on the final day, standing next to Luciano. The bloke was near blind as a proverbial bat and wore Coke-bottle glasses. Every time somebody took off, Luciano would say, 'Is that Mark?' 'No, no, he's the one in red.' He had no idea who he was looking at, let alone 'what' he was looking at. Fact is, he was *so* proud of his young charge that he probably couldn't see over his puffed-up Italian chest.

Fleur Occhilupo: In between heats Mum wanted to drive Mark home for a rest, and we forgot Dad, who was in his red tracksuit that he always wore, on the beach, thinking, *where have they gone?* We were driving home and I went, 'Mum, where's Dad?' And she went, 'We haven't got time. We'll go home and then we'll come back.' That's why he never went to

Occy

another surfing competition again, because he was stuck on the beach in his red tracksuit in forty degrees.

Paul Sargeant: Luciano was such a strict man. It was left to Pam, the raising of the kids . . . I remember going there for dinner, and Luciano would sit at the table and have a glass of red with ice cubes in it, eating his soup, this full noisy slurping. And I remember Pam telling us beforehand, 'No talking at dinner tonight.' So we all sat there in silence . . . Then he'd stand up and sit right in front of the TV, a couple of feet away, in his red tracksuit with his Coke-bottle glasses on. He'd watch the news and then go downstairs to his study, where he had this big draftboard with all his drawings on it. He'd light up a cigar and one by one the kids would file down and say goodnight, and he'd give them a kiss on the forehead and away they'd go.

Pam Occhilupo: My mother was in a nursing home overlooking the beach, and she was beside herself with excitement, quite the most popular person in the hospital, especially when Mark brought her the trophy after the presentation and she could proudly display it on top of her locker. Mother was rather naughty and spoilt and gave the nurses' a terrible time. She was the only person I had ever known to be expelled from a nursing home, and this happened not once but four times. I was running out of nursing homes by this time and feeling quite frantic.

Added to this stress was worry about Mark. The day before the Beaurepaires finals, Mark and I were sitting on the beach together in between heats and Mark opened up to me about how he had been smoking dope – and God only knows what else – but was trying to get off it. He was going through withdrawals and was even more thrilled at his success because he was clean. I was so thankful that he had shared this with me but still felt distraught and worried for my boy and the difficult path he had to negotiate. A couple of months after this I went to visit Mother – in another nursing home by the way, as she had been expelled once more. She was surprisingly sympathetic for someone who had always been rather selfish and told me to spend the next day taking Mark down the coast for a surf and having a good talk to him and not to worry about visiting her.

Mark and I had a wonderful day, talking on the long drive down and back and surfing in the meantime. When we got home that afternoon the phone was ringing. It was the nursing home to say that Mother had died a few hours ago. It was as if she had given us her blessing. 'Go and get close to your son, and don't worry about me anymore.'

Dougall Walker: Greeny, Dog and Occy were all with Peak and all with Billabong, so they were the trifecta, and they travelled a lot together and were all from Cronulla. It's amazing how much your peers can help create a champion. There was a lot of competition between Occy and Dog and Greeny for a long time. Occy went on to do bigger and greater things, but they helped get him there.

Richard 'Dog' Marsh: Occ did so much for us. He was just good. He was a natural. He was brilliant. He'd go in contests when I didn't even know what a contest was. He was amazing. He was winning contests, and all of us got a bit more contest savvy then because he went in 'em and did well, and we all went, 'Shit, that's what we should do.' It fired us all up. One of your best mates coming from a small town is just a rock star, winning contests. It was unreal. It just opened us up to travel and moved our small-town mentality a bit. Friends can take you to new places, and he did for us.

HELL'S BELLS

Rabbit had stayed with me at Kurnell, and we drove down to Bells together in his little Mazda RX7. We were psyched. I'd just won the Beaurepaires, we were listening to David Bowie all the way down there and we were kind of feeding off each other's energy. We stayed at this little motel in Torquay, right next door to Claw Warbrick, the co-founder of Rip Curl. And it was radical because as soon as we got there Rabbit got dropped by his sponsor, Quiksilver. He was so upset he barely left the motel room, and I was really upset for him. He was heartbroken. I thought he'd done so much for that company, and I couldn't understand why they dropped him. I was just embarking on a pro career and I thought, *if this is the way it works, I don't like it at all.* Rabbit lost early in the contest and it was just a real bummer, because we'd been driving down there so psyched. He was feeding off me and I was feeding off him, and then there was nothing to feed off. The only feeding I was doing was bringing him food to the motel room because he wasn't leaving it. It was heavy.

He'd finished second the year before. They wanted him to take an office job, and maybe in hindsight he should have – he could have ruled and been a millionaire right now. But it's hard to imagine Rab in an office job, especially back then. He's doing it now with the ASP, but he still surfs as much as possible. I see him in the water all the time. He's either in the water or going for massive walks around Coolangatta. He's such a walker. That's one thing I learnt from Rab, because I love walking now too, especially when I'm overseas. I love walking around new places. Rab always loved to walk, and he taught me so much when I did the tour with him. He told me, 'When you walk you can think.' And it's so true, because when you walk the mind slows down to the pace you're walking. You can think about things and they come more into focus and you can make sense out of stuff, rather than just rushing around trying to sort things out in your head. It's good exercise too, good for the mind and body.

> **Rabbit Bartholomew:** The year before, I ended up number two and Occy made the top sixteen for the first time, in sixteenth. And the next year, I was fifteenth and he got third, so it was really a revolving door for me. The next year I was mucking up and not serious about it because I wasn't a contender, and I didn't enjoy making up the numbers. He was coming on and his star was on the rise. And it also coincided with me leaving Quiksilver, and Occy was the one who encouraged me to go and see Gordon [Merchant]. Occy kind of helped broker that, so that's how I joined Billabong. When the tour started in the middle of the year, in '85–'86, Occy was a contender and Gordon didn't want me going on the tour. But I wanted to go on the tour because I was enjoying spending time with Occy, and what else was I going to do? That's what I did: I went on tours. Obviously there would have been some fear, and I had that extra purpose of working in Occy's camp, because I was now officially with Billabong and he was their top guy.

BOAT WAKES AND WAVE POOLS

I'd finished the year in third position and had led the ratings for much of the first half of the season – in only my first year in the top sixteen. At that point, I probably thought a world title was only a matter of time – but I had no idea then just how much time, or how many challenges the tour lifestyle would throw at me. We had some pretty weird conditions to contend with too.

That year we had an event called the Wave Wizards Pro, at Jensen Beach, Florida, and it seemed to epitomise pro surf contests at the time. The waves were so tiny, at one point they drove a motor boat up and down the beach to try and generate little wake waves, but the boat was too small and it didn't work. We were left to try and ride this six-inch shorebreak. Florida surfer Matt Kechele had a novel approach, actually pushing off with one foot on the sand like a skateboard as he tried to squeeze in one more turn.

One of the weirdest events on tour in '85 was the Allentown, Pennsylvania, wave pool event, or 'the World Inland Championships' as they were called. The waves were tiny, weak, one-foot dribblers spluttering out of this mechanised wave pool. It was completely surreal. Rabbit got knocked out early, and it's always hard travelling with a mate when they get knocked out early. They're all bummed and you're still psyching. Rabbit would just stick his head in the newspaper, but I didn't mind. I'd just go and do some yoga or go for a walk.

The weird thing about Allentown was that you couldn't just go for a surf to prepare for your heat. I remember sitting by this freeway with my Walkman on, listening to David Bowie and watching the traffic fly by. I'm psyching for my heat but it's miles from the coast with no ocean in sight. I was thinking, *this is so trippy*, trying to psych up for my heat and waiting for the wave pool to open. That was the first time I ever rode an epoxy, which Rusty Preisendorfer made for me, and it worked really well. It was nice and floaty, but the waves were so small, it was just a joke. They could have turned it up a bit higher, but the locals were spewing because they were in the midst of a serious drought – every time the waves went spilling over the sides of the pool the local community would freak out. Tom Carroll won in those little board shorts of his, which must have helped.

I brought my own unique fashion sense to the tour. I had this pair of pointy black shoes I wore everywhere, without socks. I was quite into fashion and I used to wear these pants that were the fashion back then – tight all the way to the bottom, stovepipe pants –

and these pointy shoes. I travelled the whole year in them without socks, and they smelt so bad. Every hotel I went to I had to leave them outside the window. I wore them for years, and if I ever took them off on planes it would become a major incident.

> **Rabbit Bartholomew:** We used to go down to this place in Byron to buy shoes, and they were very stylish shoes you'd wear to nightclubs, and we were into nightclubs. Occy wore them to nightclubs, wore them everywhere actually, these black pointy shoes. And there was this one flight Occy and I got on, sat down, and he's taken his shoes off. You've never come across a reek like it. I actually went, 'Oh shit, what is that? What is that fucking *stench*? There's something really, really bad going on here. I've got to get off the plane, it's that bad.' I looked over and people are deadset having a reaction up and down the aisles. I'm seeing people having major reactions and calling attendants, and they've gone searching for the stench. And they finally came up to him. I'm ready to chew my arm off and dive under the seat and get to another part of the plane. And they've ordered him to put the shoes back on. He's gone, 'Ah nah, I'll be right', and the senior steward's come down and gone, 'Put the shoes back on.' I was going, 'Get them on, man. Get them on.' It was so heavy. The thing is, if you wear shoes and you don't wear socks, it doesn't take long for them to stink up.

GUNSTON 500, DURBAN, SOUTH AFRICA

I was stoked to get back to J-Bay that year, and Cheron had promised me if I won the Gunston I could stay at her house. That was all the motivation I needed. I loved everything about J-Bay and especially Cheron's place on the point. It would get really cold and

Above: Me, Mum and Fleur. (*Photos on this page courtesy Pam Occhilupo*)

Right: A beach boy from the start – me and Alex.

Bottom left: Me in my kilt – and not looking too sure about it.

Bottom centre: Dad and me at his graduation for his Masters degree.

Bottom right: Now *that's* what I call a haircut.

From November 1979

No	Date	Contest	Placing
1	NOV 1979	NSW TITLES SCHOOLBOYS U15 - NARRABEEN	4th
2	DEC	AUSTRALIAN TITLES SCHOOLBOYS U15- N/CSTLE	9th
3	FEB 1980	CRONULLA MOOVIN ON 13 YR	1st
4	MAR	NSW MOOVIN ON 13 YR - NARRABEEN	2nd
5	AUG	CRONULLA BOARDRIDERS OPEN	2nd
6	SEP	CRONULLA BOARDRIDERS OPEN	2nd
7	NOV	CRONULLA ELIMANTIONS NSW SCHOOLBOYS UK5	1st
8	NOV	NSW SCHOOLBOYS U15 - AVOCA	1st
9	NOV	CRONULLA ELIMANTIONS NSW JUNIOR TITLES U19	1st
10	DEC	AUSTRALIAN TITLES SCHOOLBOYS U15 - PERTH	3rd
11	JAN 1981	CRONULLA OPEN - HANIMEX SURFOUT	1st
12	JAN	SUN SURFOUT - CUE COLA PRO JUNIOR	12th
13	JAN	CAPRICORN PRO AM OPEN - TAREE	4th
14	FEB	CRONULLA BOARDRIDERS OPEN	1st
15	AUG	NSW SCHOOLBOYS U17 - KIAMA	1st
16	AUG	CRONULLA CHARITY CLASSIC OPEN ·	4th
17	SEP	O'NEILL NEWCASTLE CLASSIC JUNIOR	1st
18	DEC	AUSTRALIAN SCHOLASTIC TITLES QLD U17	2nd
19	JAN 1982	CAPRICORN PROAM OPEN - TAREE	7th
20	JAN	CAPRICORN PROAM JUNIOR - TAREE	3rd
21	JAN	CRONULLA BOARDRIDERS ANNUAL OPEN	2nd
22	FEB	NSW TITLES JUNIOR U19 - NEWPORT	2nd

Above: My junior contest record, meticulously documented by my devoted mum. (*Courtesy Andrew Kidman*)

Left: I was keen for a good psych-up tune from a young age.

Below: One of my first outings as a trialist, at the Straight Talk Tyres contest.

Above: Early trip to Black Rock – this was the first published surf shot for both me and Sarge.

Below left: One of my first G & S boards. That's a Huzza Wuzza model, which was Dick Herbert's shaping name.

Below right: Packing for one of my first trips away, to Margaret River for the Aussie Titles.

Above left: Dog and me driving down the coast in my dad's car. My driving style was set early on – no licence, stolen car and I'm not even looking where I'm going.

Above right: Me, Michael Mackie (*centre*) and Dean Whiteman (*right*) unloading after arriving at Black Rock on a hot summer's day.

Below: Black Rock, early days, in my element – the kind of wave that might inspire you to steal your dad's car!

Above: Learning to turn my Banksy.
Below left: My trusty Rusty.
Below right: The Rusty doing its thing – square tail, hard edge, holding in the pocket.

Above left: Gordon giving me a few pointers on an early Hawaiian trip.

Above right: Practising my Tai Chi, as taught to me by my mate Wayne Murphy.

Left: The magic Rusty after earning me a third place in Japan, even with the nose broken off.

Below: Me and Tom Carroll, finalists at the Tutti Frutti Pro, Lacanau, France, 1984.

Above: Pushing the Rusty hard after getting the nose fixed.

Below left: The first time Dad came down to watch me, at the 1985 Beaurepaires at Cronulla, which I ended up winning.

Below right: Early Billabong ad. (*From left to right*) Banksy, me and Spike.

Bottom left: Posing with a Playboy model.

Bottom right: Prime-time Cronulla. (*From left to right*) me, Sarge, Ratso and Gary Green – ready for trouble.

In full battle cry after winning the Beaurepaires.

you'd have to rug up, and then you knew the swell was coming as those deep winter lows came spinning in. I went up to Durban for the Gunston on a mission. It was a big city, full of people and big buildings, a world away from J-Bay, but I still loved the place and was determined to take care of business. Cheron had introduced me to a shaper called Peter Daniel, and I rode one of his boards that went insane and made it into the final. My opponent was none other than local hero Shaun Tomson – who had won the Gunston about 400 times by then. I still felt like I owed him one for that heat I lost at the Coke contest two years earlier. This was my time and I smoked him. Shaun was always such a gentleman and was really gracious in defeat. I went back to Cheron's place at J-Bay with the trophy, looking like the returning conqueror, and we all went out to dinner to celebrate. My love affair with J-Bay was entrenched forever.

THE OP PRO AND THE GREAT CURREN RIVALRY

I always liked the big-crowd events when I was young. I felt like I surfed better with people watching, as if I fed off the energy of the crowd. But then I got progressively worse as I got older. I'd be like, *no, don't watch me.* Even the commentator could put me off.

But I felt so ready for the '85 Op Pro. I saw an interview I did on the beach during that event recently, and the reporter said, 'Wow, you're really popular,' and I said something like, 'Yeah, I'm doing pretty good for an Aussie. I'm not as popular as Tom Curren, though.' I just seemed so green at the time. But I was right; Curren was like a god to the Huntington crowd, the first top-line pro California had produced for years. We ended up meeting in the final and it was a classic showdown: American versus Australian; natural-foot versus goofy; he was riding Al Merrick's board and I was riding Rusty's, the two top shapers in America. Curren is a Christian, really quiet and conservative, and I was considered pretty outspoken and flamboy-ant, I guess.

It was radical because they were really cheering for Curren, and when I'd get a wave you wouldn't hear a sound. And then he'd just paddle into a wave and you'd hear the crowd slowly build up into a roar. As soon as he kicked out they'd cheer. Every wave sounded like it was going to be a 9.5.

In the final I did this one turn where my foot slipped off the board. Everyone screamed unintentionally in the heat of the moment. I made a weird sort of recovery from half falling with one foot on the board, and everyone started roaring. I thought, *well, at least I got a cheer.* It was intense. I just thought that was the way it always was in finals, but that's probably the biggest crowd I've ever surfed in front of, before or since. It was a real peak for pro surfing.

I'd been quoted in an Australian surf magazine calling the American surfers 'a bunch of wankers', and it didn't win me too many fans in the US. I had to win them back over. I didn't mean it in the way it sounded, and I don't even know why I said it, just jealousy and insecurity probably. I was young and green. It taught me that you really had to watch what you said to journalists. Even in Hawaii, which is technically a part of the US, I copped a bit of flack.

So the final with Curren was especially loaded. Curren was so shy he'd hardly say a word, maybe just a little gesture of hello. But he showed no emotion in the water. We had some heavy paddle battles, and I think I even hit him in the back of the head when we were paddling round the back of the buoy. He was a really good paddler and it was neck and neck, and just with the crowd so on his side, I think I took it out on him. We were all over each other and the buoy was pretty big, so no-one could see what happened behind it, and right when we went round I just kinda went, *whack.* He didn't say anything, though. The funny thing was, Curren was like a hero to me. I was more in awe of him because he came on the scene before me, and his surfing was something to aspire to. I thought he wailed on me surfing-wise, even though I did catch up a little bit. I always thought he was just so super-smooth and way better than me. That final went to three sets and eventually I came out on top. By then I think I'd finally won over at least some of the crowd and got a great reception.

> **Tom Curren:** The Op Pro was bigger than anything else I'd seen before then. It was kind of a circus atmosphere . . . I'd come from a lifeguarding and swimming background, so that kind of physical contact was nothing unusual to me. He did say things at times in the media that he appreciated where I was coming from. I understood that even though it was intense in the heats it wasn't something personal.

All of a sudden everything California had to offer just opened to me. I was staying with Gordon Merchant at Bob Hurley's house. Gordon was over there working with Bob on building up the Billabong brand, so for me to win the biggest surf contest in the US, against their number one guy, was great for the brand. They were so stoked.

Jodie Cooper, who was also sponsored by Billabong at the time, won the women's division, so we all went out to dinner that night on a real high. Having dinner with the owners of Billabong, drinking margaritas, being young Aussies in California, having just won the biggest event in America – it just felt like we'd hit the jackpot. Gordon and Bob were over the moon, Billabong was off and running in the US, it was all happening.

Later that night I went surfing with Gordon. I'd had a few beers and could deadset still hear the crowd. I don't know why we went surfing, I was just that excited, and at Huntington you can go surfing at night because of the lights on the pier. When I took off on a wave I could still hear the roar ringing in my ears, like when you go to a loud rock concert and you still have a ringing in your head when you go to bed.

> **Bob Hurley (former head of Billabong USA):** When we first started Billabong it went pretty well just on the strength of the product. When Mark surfed well at Huntington Beach it just escalated our sales exponentially. It put us on the map. We were on the map in a very small, underground sort of way, but he was controversial, he was setting a new standard. He was the yin to Tom Curren's yang, and they had a huge rivalry, and that really put Billabong on the map in the USA. I'm not a smart businessman, so I was very fortunate. I was just a fan. I love Occy. So I'm like, 'This is too good to be true', and we're selling more stuff and we can pay him more money. It's awesome. I told him at one of the Op Pros, 'If you win this thing, I'll give you ten grand.' He's like, 'Yeah, right.' He won, and I thought, *oh my gosh. I'm so happy to pay him.*

Guaranteed, the parties were pretty big after I won that one, and everyone seemed to want to drag me out somewhere. I have a lot of memories of being locked up with Gary Green in various houses in California, carrying on until sunrise, but always being young enough to shake it off and go surfing the next day. All it would take is driving down Marine Boulevard – the sun is coming out, the marine layer burning off, the chicks are out, the waves are fun, and your hangover seems to disappear with the fog. You're just like, *well, there goes that hangover,* and you're straight into another one.

Huntington felt like home because they did embrace me and I stayed with Bob Hurley and his family, and I hung out with this guy who owned the Infinity surf shop, right on the beach at Huntington. We used to leave our boards there. I hung out with Dougall Walker from back home and his mate Richard Saunders, who were running

Peak wetsuits in the US together. We'd eat at this health food shop called Jan's in Huntington's main street. There were lots of parties but we were eating really good food, and California had so much good health food, so much farther ahead of Australia. I really got into it. It was an eye-opener, don't worry about that, and I wanted to get the best out of everything. I was so psyched. I was listening to David Bowie and Talking Heads, driving on those six-lane freeways. I couldn't believe it all, coming from a place like Kurnell. It was like a fairytale, Disneyland.

Derek Hynd was the Billabong coach at the time and somehow Gordon had agreed to give him the corporate gold card to cover our travel expenses, and we just lived it up. I loved it, and after that I couldn't go back to staying at cheap places. I wouldn't do it any other way. I've always tried to stay at nice places, as nice as possible. It's expensive but it's worth it. Derek would try and keep us all in line but he didn't really stand a chance. Me and Greeny and Ratso were all hanging out together, having a great time. This local guy lent us his car and we were cruising the California coast – it was just surfing, chicks and parties. We were blown away.

One time I picked Richard Marsh up from the airport, and I remember telling him, 'Mate, this place is unbelievable.' We were staying right on the beach, going out every night. You're meant to be twenty-one to get into licensed premises in the US, so we had to drive for miles to this one place that would let us in. I was so keen – one night I went out by myself because I couldn't find any takers. I was just getting amongst it and dancing up a storm when I had a full head rush and nearly passed out. I had to sit down and figured maybe I'd been overdoing things a bit.

> **Jodie Cooper:** It was an exciting era. We both won the Op Pro together in '85. I was with Billabong too, so that was a big thing for both of us. It was really amazing for me. There was the energy of being with a company like Billabong that

was stepping up to be a pretty big player, and winning that event . . . I remember we all went out to dinner and it was a very prestigious moment. The thing that stuck out for me was, as a person, Occ wasn't ready to deal with what was there. He was an eight-year-old trapped in a twenty-year-old's body. He had so much physical ability, at a different level to his mental state of mind. He had a really childish, kid-like manner. But the good thing with Occ, it didn't matter who you were, he had an openness . . . A lot of surfers forget they're human and start to believe the bullshit. With Occ it didn't matter if you were 100th on the women's tour or number two in the world, he always had time for you.

Rabbit Bartholomew: He picked me up at LA airport, and he'd kind of discovered California, and all the trappings of being a superstar. And I know what it's like with people offering you all kinds of gifts, and taking a few of the gifts. It was just like MP [Michael Peterson] at the San Diego world titles in '72, just updated to 1986. It was the same but just a different layer of substances, just the whole adulation thing. It was really the Curren–Carroll era dominating world surfing, but Occy was the superstar.

Kelly Slater: I was about eleven when he hit the scene in US mags. I was blown away by his style, which was so unique-looking, and his brashness where he was just calling out Curren, who I thought was untouchable and too much of a hero to get called out like that by some young kid. He called out American surfing from the top on down. I didn't get to see him surf but heard the news of it from everyone there, and it was exciting and scary that there was this kid from Oz that was that much better than everyone.

Dougall Walker: I lived in the US for two years to set up Peak in the US, and that was in '84 to '86, a very critical period when he became a big star internationally. Setting up a business in the US, that was an enormous boost to our presence . . . He hit it pretty hard, but it's pretty hard not to. There's always something going on around the contest, and there's that many parties and that many girls adoring you and that many surfers hero-worshipping you, it's pretty hard not to have a good time.

Gary Green: Going to California, and Occy winning the Op Pro, it was like the forces of good versus evil, because Curren was the full Christian. Billabong had just gone into America, so it all fitted in perfect. Bob Hurley was the full Christian, too, and Occ would come home at five o'clock in the morning after a bender and pass out in the kids' room, and they'd wake up in the morning horrified. He's got the constitution of a bull . . . Derek Hynd was the Billabong coach at the time and he'd convinced Gordon to give him the gold credit card. Gordon saw the credit card bill at the end of the year and he was spewing. We were styling and all the older guys were spewing at us. Me and Occ used to live it up a bit, and DH was fully anti all that. He was on our case but then he just gave up, because we were still getting results. DH was good – he wouldn't blow smoke up his arse like everyone else. With drugs, the guys who have got it, it's an ego thing for them to say, 'Oh, I was partying with Occy.'

Occy used to lose money – he'd have money falling out of his pockets. He wouldn't give a fuck. He'd wear clothes until they were dirty and then give them away . . . He'd lose everything. He'd lose keys. He actually fucked the ignition on his mum's Celica so he wouldn't need the key, and he'd physically bend the window out and stick his arm in to unlock the door, until it eventually shattered one day. He locked himself out of his apartment – you know how apartments have fireproof doors – he went down to the car and got a wheel brace and hacked a hole through the door. The body corporate freaked, and fixed the door, and two weeks later he did it again. He would have paid for it, but instead of ringing a locksmith like a normal person he just did it again.

Dougall Walker: It was the life of a surfer at that time . . . You go out every weekend and you party hard with your mates and you get up and go surfing and that's that. So you've got this yin and yang: you've got a lifestyle that would kill a normal human being, but because you're surfing during the day your body's expelling everything and you're recovering and you move on. You're detoxing and re-toxing on a daily basis.

We reckon Rabbit used to follow him around and just wait for the money to fall out of his pocket, and pick it up and give it back to him. Then he got sick of doing that and just hung on to it and paid for everything for him. The problem with Occy was he never had a sense for money. He didn't come from a wealthy upbringing, but maybe he got too much money too early in his life. He had a lot of money, but he was fucking hopeless with his finances. He was the kind of kid who could go to an ATM, take out 500 bucks, buy some lunch, and an hour later go, 'Oh, I've got no money left' and go to the ATM again. He'd drop it or whatever.

MARGARET RIVER

My roll continued at Margaret River later that year, and I found myself in a final with the great Mark Richards in huge waves. I was riding a 6'6" in twelve- to fifteen-foot surf, surfing cautiously, avoiding the clean-up sets and ducking in to get the cleaner medium-sized sets. If you got cleaned up, your heat was pretty much over. I was staying with Cheyne Horan and the pro windsurfer Scotty O'Connor in a little caravan, and we had a great vibe going. Scott put on a windsurfing display before the finals, and the biggest sets were more than twice the height of his mast, which was seventeen-feet tall. Most guys were riding much bigger boards and just taking huge drops on the outside, but because I was on such a small board I was doing more turns and snapping on smaller waves but getting good scores.

MR was such a hero to me – I couldn't really believe I was in a final with him, or that I stood much of a chance. Two other really good big-wave guys, Simon Law and Mike Parsons, were also in the final. MR broke his leash halfway through the final and lost his board, which gave me a chance. He was right next to me when he lost his board, and because I was so in awe of him, I turned around to try and retrieve his board. I was about a quarter of the way in, his board bobbing on the inside, and just thought, *what I am doing? I'm in a final!* I turned round and started paddling back out, a bit embarrassed and just kind of grinned sheepishly at MR and went, 'Sorry mate.' I must have looked like a cocky little kid to him, but I ended up winning the final. I didn't know then, but those waves and that strategy would serve me well in Hawaii a month later.

THE 1985 PIPE MASTERS

Rabbit Bartholomew: The Pipe Masters wasn't a sanctioned event those two years in a row, so it was able to go back to a format where they would wait the entire winter and have a one-day event on the most radical day of Pipe. In 1984 it was a good twelve to fifteen foot, but in '85 we got up in the morning and Occy went down to Buddy's place and went, 'Oh fuck, it is so big out there, Bugs, there's no way the contest will be on.' It was one of those days – fifteen to twenty and holding because it was that west. And we looked at it from Buddy's, and we could see it out beyond Kammies just roaring across. And I went, 'It's on. This is the day they wait for. It will be second reef Pipe, it will be all-time.'

By the time I got to Hawaii I was super-confident and ready to go one step better in the contest that meant the most to everyone, in terms of peer respect. I'd won a few events around the world, but until you'd won in Hawaii you hadn't really arrived.

That year it kept on getting bigger through the day. It was already massive, twelve foot plus in the morning, and I spoke to Rab and he said, 'This is serious.' I was like, 'Whoa, then I'm going to be serious too.'

I had good heats all the way through, and all I can remember in the final is everyone else getting cleaned up by this huge set on the third reef. It was massive by then, probably fifteen foot plus. All the other finalists – Michael Ho, Ronnie Burns, Rab, Mickey Neilson and Max Madeiros – they all paddled way out to the third reef. They were having a hassle and they all got out there, and the biggest set came through and cleaned them all up. And I was sitting in the channel, and I went, *yes, they've all been cleaned up.* I ducked in there and got a barrel, and another one, and I ended up getting a few good ones. I didn't think I'd won or anything, but I ended up getting one all the way to the beach as they went, 'Five, four, three, two, one' and I stepped off onto the beach just as the hooter sounded. I went, 'It doesn't get any better than that.' This was before they read out scores, so I was asking everyone, 'How do you think I went?' And people were going, 'You might have won it.' They read out the places in reverse order from six, five, four, and I'm going, *what?* When they announced second, and it wasn't me, I knew I'd won. They put the big lei on me and I just felt like a king. It was all-time.

The whole experience of winning Pipe wasn't so much like a dream – it was more like slow motion. I think when you've got that much adrenalin going through you, you would probably be in a little bit of shock. The day outlays itself in stages and everything is so dramatic, but you're going in slow motion. Your senses are all high and your reflexes are at their peak, and you just do things you normally wouldn't do.

We celebrated at Rosie's Mexican Cantina in Haleiwa that night and Gordon shouted us all dinner. I couldn't legally drink in the US, but I snuck a few sly margaritas that night. I could tell Gordon was really proud of me, and Buddy and a few other friends were there, and we were all just loving life. Gordon used to take surf photos too, and around that time he got a great shot of me at Pipe. I always had trouble getting waves out there in free-surfs, but one afternoon it went a bit onshore and there was hardly anyone out and he talked me into going out. He got this shot of me doing a crouched bottom turn way out on the flats on about an eight-foot wave. Billabong used it as a poster and it's still one of my favourite shots.

Gordon Merchant (from Jack McCoy's *The Occumentary*): I just said to him, 'Treat it like a huge beachbreak. When the sets come, paddle out for your life and when the lulls come scream back in and grab what you can and then shoot back out again. Because the hardest thing to do out here is going to be getting six waves.' It was a serious test of character.

Rabbit Bartholomew: I felt like I was a bit of a warrior at that time, and Occy enjoyed that, being with me and that preparation, and he won that event. We were both in the final and it was a monumental day of survival and go for it, and it was the day he became a world superstar. He probably already was, but he went to another level. It was unbelievable, this kid won the Pipe Masters, the biggest ever . . . Max [Madeiros] and I have got this thing where both those years we were in both those finals. They were these radical days that we kind of prevailed in and loved, and they're the ones that stick with you, I reckon. And obviously a huge day for Occy, the day when he went into a new stratosphere of being a superstar. He had the perfect goofy strategy. That's how you've got to do it as a goofy. Michael Ho and Ronnie Burns kept following me out, and it got to a point of ridiculousness, masochism nearly, where you couldn't go deep enough, you couldn't go far enough out and you were just getting them on the head. We kind of blew each other out. And Michael had to get rescued – I don't think I've ever heard of that before. Michael Ho had to be rescued off Rocky Point. Ronnie and I just got slaughtered. It was just one of those days.

Gerry Lopez: I remember that year. In fact, I remember one wave where he did something I'd never seen anyone else do before. Ronnie Burns was really a strong surfer here, and I thought he would win the contest because he had the most experience. But Occy had a whole different approach that day and I remember one wave, he was paddling out and a huge set was coming in, stacked up to the horizon. And he was paddling out and he was maybe even in danger of getting caught inside by it. But he was too far in to catch the big ones, and what he did was he paddled out and this one came and it capped. There are two reefs out on the second reef, and it capped on the inside one and it had that little foam ball on it. The ones behind were way bigger, and if he had paddled over that he would have been totally toast. And Ronnie was outside waiting for those ones on the second reef, and Occy turned around – I couldn't believe it, I watched him turn around for this wave that was already breaking. It had already broke. There was whitewater on the top of the wave and he caught the whitewater.

I really took note when the kids started doing it later in small waves, the young kids, where they paddled real hard and stood up before they caught the wave, and then they'd be in the standing position when the whitewater hit them from behind. And he did it here at the Pipeline, on a ten- to twelve-foot wave and it was unbelievable. It took my breath away. And I just went, 'Shit, that's it, my time at Pipeline's way over. This kid's something else.' That one moment – oh, there were a lot of moments with Occy – but that one really, really stood out in my mind. He's so incredibly powerful and so beautiful to watch.

THE SUNSET HOUSE

Those years in the mid-80s in Hawaii, staying at Buddy's place at Sunset, were some of the best times of my life. We were surfing so much, having so much fun it was unbelievable. We were doing a lot of yoga – Cheyne Horan was coming around and we had a little program going. We'd eat at Celestial Natural Foods in Haleiwa, which this classic guy, Carter, has run for thirty years. Buddy would take me surfing all over the island, to all these little out-of-the-way places on different winds. The winds would be onshore, and we'd duck away and be getting full barrels. We'd come back at the end of the day, fully surfed out, but we wouldn't tell anyone, and we had that going on for years. You'd walk round Foodland supermarket with the biggest smile, but you couldn't tell anyone. You'd just have this weird suppressed smile on your face.

I've got great memories of those times, surfing with Buddy and another local surfer I became great friends with, Mike Latronic. Tron was all-time. He was always the guy pulling into the biggest Inside Sunset barrels, and we all surfed together a lot. We'd go out to dinner at the end of a day of great waves, smoke a joint and just laugh our heads off, wake up early and do it all again.

I learnt a lot by watching the locals, and I made a point of getting to know them early on. They were great surfers in their home waters, and you could learn a lot by watching them surf and getting to know them. I used to watch Mike and Derek Ho at Pipe, and Mike used to take off switch-foot, and you wouldn't know if it was Derek or Mike. I remember once seeing them at Sunset, on the bowl, both switch-stance. Mike was now goofy-foot and Derek was now regular, foot, and they went through a ten-foot barrel holding hands.

There used to be a really solid crew of big-wave riders out at Sunset all the time, before all those guys riding really huge boards took over. And I loved surfing Sunset in those days. That was probably the best thing about Buddy's place on the point: it was such a good view of the line-up from that angle. There were a lot of days when it was really out of control, and if you'd looked at it front-on from the car park you wouldn't go out. But we used to ride it like that all the time. From our vantage on the point, you could see it was still rideable, and we had some great sessions in huge stormy waves.

And we had some great parties too. We used to play Talking Heads really loud all the time and the whole house would be shaking. One Halloween they dressed me up as a half-man, half-woman, like a Ziggy Stardust thing, because we were all into Bowie. We ended up at a party at Waimea Falls, and there was a guy there who mustn't have liked what I was wearing. He was dressed up in a doctor's mask, and he pulled out this knife. It was so sharp and so big I freaked out and ran for the hills.

Buddy McCray (Billabong's Hawaiian rep, 1979–1985): We got into baking. We baked a lot of cookies. One time we were making the butter and both of us were ringing it out with cheesecloth. We hadn't even eaten one yet and by the afternoon Occy said to me, 'Are you feeling strange? Because I am.' And our fingers were green for, like, three days afterwards. We had some good parties, all-time parties. There'd be an inch of beer on the floor in the morning, in the back house. One morning I got up and looked at all the beer on the floor and went, 'Oh no, what am I going to do?' There was nothing below the house, so I got my drill and started drilling holes in all the deep spots to let the beer drain away. One New Year's I thought the house was going to fall down. There were so many people dancing, the whole house was swaying.

Rabbit Bartholomew: Me and Occy had the Billabong house in Hawaii. It was the first I knew of the company's having a team house. Buddy had the front house and oversaw the whole complex, and Occy and I had the back house, right on the west peak. And we'd go for months at a time and really get it going on. I was at the time heavily into this diet that involved buckwheat pancakes and banana and sweet potato and rice, and me and Occy adhered to that program. But there were some problems because at times the buckwheat pancake mix would end up on the walls and the floor and the ceiling – and it nearly stripped paint. We came back home one day to Rena Merchant tapping her feet and waiting for us, and we spent the rest of the day on our hands and knees scraping buckwheat pancake mix off the walls and the furniture.

Chapter Six

LOVE HURTS

My first experience in love was a pretty torturous affair for all concerned. As fate would have it, I fell in love with one of my best mate's girlfriends. Jenny was going out with Jason Marsh, Richard's brother, and so I lost two friends for a while because of it. No-one planned it, but it just happened that way. It's a really touchy thing when you're young and in love. You fall in love with a girl and she falls in love with you, and her other relationship is pretty much over anyway. You don't want to move in too soon, but it happens. It's hard on everyone. Jenny and I stayed together for years. It wasn't like a fling.

We were all living on the Gold Coast at that point and Kirra was perfect at the time. It always seemed to be a trippy time when Kirra got good, like there was some sort of special energy in the air. Kirra is such a beautiful wave, there always used to be romance or weddings happening whenever it got good. But it was also a heavy time, because Dog really took the affair to heart, and it ended our friendship for a long time. And Jason wanted to kill me. Jenny and I had got together at a nightclub, it was love at first sight, and, sure enough, the next day Kirra was six foot and absolutely perfect. I surfed for hours and hours, thinking about Jenny the whole time, getting barrelled off my nut, in the full bloom of new love, thinking, *this is as good as it gets.*

Then I saw Jason in the water, and he came up and said, 'I don't know why I shouldn't just knock you out right now', and I just put my head down, waiting for the blow. He had me in close range and I was like, *fuck, fair enough.* But he just paddled away. Then I saw him get a big barrel and I thought, *I hope that makes him feel a bit better.* He was a really good surfer and a really good fighter too. A great guy to steal a girlfriend from! So I was shitting myself, but I just felt bad as well. He kind of knew that it was over for him and Jenny, and she was moving on, but it didn't make it any easier. Me and Jason actually made up years before Dog and I.

Jenny and I got pretty serious pretty quickly, as I tend to do. She was doing a bit of modelling at the time, but she decided she wanted to travel on tour with me. So I took her on tour, and all the boys were jealous.

> **Richard Marsh:** The first couple of trips I did with Mark, to Japan and Hawaii, and then we had a falling out so that we didn't travel together anymore. I did my own thing, which was good too . . . I kind of look back at that and wish it didn't happen. But when you're at that age, everything's really serious – especially girlfriends and family – and it's all really your whole world. When you get a bit older you get more perspective on it. That's what's great about getting older – getting past that stage of your life where it's all so dire.

PRO JUNIOR SHOWDOWN

I used to stay in Hawaii for those six weeks of the Triple Crown contests and then stay through Christmas and halfway through January. I'd fly home for the Pro Junior and go straight to Narrabeen.

I was so much fresher than the other guys, because there were no waves at home over Christmas, while I'd been surfing my brains out. I had to jump straight back on a small board, but that was fine with me. I'd feel so strong coming back from Hawaii. You've been surfing big waves and long boards. Rab always said that it's amazing how strong you feel when you get back from Hawaii. You get in Australian waves and they feel so weak and slow.

I remember driving to the north side to compete and having my own stretching routine as I drove the car. I'd be doing stomach exercises and twisting when I was stopped at lights. By the time I got to Narrabeen I was warmed up and ready to go. I beat Dog in '86 round the corner at Warriewood, when it was breaking like a perfect right-hand point break. I was riding a Wayne Roach board and it was going insane. Dog and I weren't on the best of terms, so it was a pretty tense final. It was horrible, because we couldn't park next to each other or acknowledge each other, and we'd been such good friends. But I felt like I had an advantage after being on tour too, because I'd seen some of the best competitors in the world up close and knew how to surf a heat by then.

> **Paul Sargeant:** They were very much at war. Dog had started a thing in Cronulla called SAO, Surfers Against Occy, but he was the only member . . . It was a best-of-three-set final, and I said to Occy, 'Don't take him easy. He's driven by spite and anger.' And Occy went, 'Oh, she'll be right.' And Dog beat him in the first one. Occy came in and went, 'Yeah, you're right.' Then he just went out and decimated him and won the next two sets hands down.

> **Nick Carroll:** By '86 he was a league above it. He was already a highly ranked pro and it was just a walk in the park for him.

> **Mick Mock (Pro Junior contest director):** He was just so far ahead in '86. He was on the tour, he was so powerful, he

was spot-on in his wave selection and totally calm – and he knew it. And he just picked off the opposition very cleanly and then went for it in the final. That's when we had Warriewood, perfect right-handers in the corner. It still hasn't been as good since. It was like a point break.

BELLS 1986 – HEAT OF THE CENTURY

Bells has always been a favourite place of mine, and the '86 Bells contest was a special one for me. I remember that morning I had a heat with Michael Burness, and he turned up halfway through. It was perfect Bells and I got to surf it by myself.

I had a classic preparation. I was going out with Jenny, and we were living really well and eating good food and keeping really healthy. My body was in top nick and I had this bright blue-and-green Peak wetsuit, which was a bit of a favourite. I can still remember running down the car park with my singlet in my hand, feeling as good as I ever have. Curren and I had another great heat, and everyone was stoked and calling it the best heat ever. It was the biggest crowd I'd seen at Bells, and because Tom was with Rip Curl he had a lot of local support. I saw a couple of his waves, heard the roars, and I knew he was on. When I looked back at the footage much later, he was just amazing. He was the smoothest surfer, connecting the dots, always in the right place and never losing speed, just surfing incredibly. We were really pushing each other, throwing everything into every turn, and it was super-close, but in the end he got the decision. At the time it didn't mean anything to me. I was just spewing because I lost. I was just like, *fuck, I'm out of here.* I still really like watching the footage, but it wasn't until years later that I could enjoy it.

Tom Curren: The waves were the right size, the right tide, and it was a good heat. He led the heat for the first half, and then I came back and moved ahead. It was good in that way. There was hardly any sitting there waiting for sets. My boards were working really good. My board was probably a step-up board – one size up from my shortboard – and that might have had a little bit to do with it because there was a bit of bump on the face. There might have been something in that.

There's a really profound confidence when you have a good shaper that you work with for a long time and you have the right boards. It really gives you confidence. You can't really understate that, and it was at a time when boards were improving really dramatically. Boards are always improving, but the rate of improvement is probably a little bit slower now. Al [Merrick] had his way of doing boards. I was actually interested in trying out one of Occy's boards in '86. Rusty's boards had less tail rocker and had kind of that roll going all the way through, flatter over all, different fins. I got Al to make me boards that looked like that, wider and flatter, and they were great. They worked really good across flat sections, quicker off the top. They were a little difficult when there were hollow sections. Occy had more power and that was the main difference, the reason he could do well on boards like that.

Rabbit Bartholomew: That heat set the template for modern surfing, frontside and backside. You could put that heat somewhere in this year's event and it would still be epic. It totally stands the test of time. Two guys at their very best who already had a very famous rivalry. Tom Curren clinched the world title that day, but there was almost more of a cult hero status for Occy.

THE 1986 OP PRO – WHAT A RIOT!

Paul Sargeant: We destroyed places. The tour was like a cyclone or a tornado. We'd turned up, come to town, rape and pillage – not literally – and leave and go to the next one. It was a travelling circus of 220 to 250 people, and every single day at least thirty-two surfers got knocked out, so every night there was a party. He was just so unique. The girls loved not just him or his surfing, but his looks – they just loved him as a *thing* almost. He was like a cuddly koala and he was so naive. He played it up; he played it right up. It was the era of ditzy blonde Californians falling before you, literally. It was like, 'I want you, let's go.' With coke and fast cars and all the boys staying at what were then old run-down hotels across the road, like the Huntington Inn. It was just a running party from room to room . . . It was so hedonistic.

There was a lot of anticipation about the '86 Op Pro when we got to California. The crowd was looking for a showdown like the year before. And word had spread about the heat Curren and I had at Bells.

I've always been really superstitious, especially when it comes to surfing contests. If I was driving to the contest for my heat and I didn't see any of my lucky numbers on any numberplates, I'd be like, *damn, I'm not going to win.* If I was waiting for an elevator and it took too long, I'd be convinced it just wasn't going to happen for me that day. It used play with my mind when I was competing. But sometimes it worked for me. Sometimes you see little signs, like when Mick Fanning saw a dolphin in the water in Brazil when he won his world title, and you become convinced it's a sign just for you. I remember paddling out through the pier during the Op Pro that year, against Tom Curren, and I was so close to the pier as the swell rose and fell, I saw this octopus right there in front of my face, just staring at me. I don't know if they're there all the time, but I was just like, *fuck, I am so going to win.* You see those things in the midst of battle, and it's just what you need to see – it gets you so psyched.

Curren and I met in the semis. It was another great heat, and I won this one. I think I beat him quite convincingly and the crowd wasn't happy, so it was probably all my fault what happened later. I didn't see it, but apparently there was a group of girls sunbathing, and a bunch of guys drinking started telling them to take their tops off. And, much to everyone's surprise, they did! You don't see a lot of topless sunbathing in the US, so the crowd got pretty worked up about this. Then the police came over and tried to get them to put their tops back on, which didn't please the crowd too much. There was a bit of scuffle, and this scuffle turned into a full-blown riot. This is only what I was told later. This was all happening while I was in the water competing against Glen Winton in the final. From the water I could hear the crowd roaring, even when there was no-one catching waves, and I was thinking, *what is going on?* Then I heard a KA-BOOM, like a massive explosion, and I ducked for cover. I saw something on fire, and then there was another explosion – BOOM – and I wanted to paddle in but didn't.

It was another best-of-three final and I'd won the first one. I felt like I'd won the second one, but they delayed announcing the result. We were under the scaffolding and I asked Ian Cairns what was going on, because I was pretty sure I'd sewn up the final. Ian came up to me and said, 'Have you seen what's going on over on the beach? There's a riot. It's out of control. You've won the contest, but you've got to go out and surf this third set because we can't have the people leaving the beach right now or else the riot is going to spill out into the streets.'

I didn't want to go back out there, but he said we had to. I'd been surfing in boardies all day and the water is pretty cold, and I was starting to feel it. I had a steamer, so I chucked that on and paddled out and sat and watched. The crowd was mosh-pitting over each other and things were on fire. I didn't even want to go in. Luckily we got in there and they escorted us up the beach. I'd won, but there wasn't a lot of celebrating that night. We just stayed home because it was too radical in the town that night. Later we went out to a restaurant, and I was really tense because it felt like the town was just going to erupt, and apparently later on that night it did again, in the main street. All kinds of people got beaten up. There was some kind of gang from somewhere just running amok. It really put the contest in jeopardy, because I don't think it was even on the next year.

> **Rabbit Bartholomew:** 'I commentated during the riot. Joey Buran was the co-commentator, and he came up over the back to have a look and came back white as a ghost and just went, 'I'm out of here.' And I went, 'What?' Ian Cairns came up during the final and went, 'There's 50,000 people here. If they go out the back, people are going to die.' We've got the lifeguards going, 'Shut down the PA.' I've got Ian Cairns going, 'Tell them it's a tie and send them back out.' I said, 'But the guys have got to know that it's over. I understand your strategy and I'll go have a chat with them.' And I told Occy, 'Look, mate, you've won but you've got to go back out.' I said, 'Glen, it's two–nil, but there's a riot going on back here. I'm asking you, Occy, to go out there and smoke him, because if you blow it and he smokes you, we've still got to announce that you've won.' They were very professional about it, although Winton did try pretty hard in that one, but Occy still won.

> **Paul Sargeant:** In '86 when we went down to Brazil we flew down together. It was the OP and then Brazil. Anyway, we were late for the plane and we had a rent-a-car, so we just left it at the kerbside in front of the terminal. These days the

plane would not have taken off. That car sat there for days in front of the terminal. I think from memory it was $2500 worth of fines and towing fees. We used to do that sort of shit all the time. Anyway, coming back from Brazil, we got on the plane and everyone was just raging, and all of a sudden, maybe two hours out of Rio, I hear this 'Sarge!' And I knew it was Occ. I'm like, 'What?' He's nine rows back and goes, 'I lost me passport.' I go, 'What?' And he goes, 'I left it on the counter, I think.' And everyone started laughing.

Anyway, we got to LA and I'm at his elbow as they drag him away. They let me come into the room with him, and they go, 'So, you haven't got a passport? You're going to have to go back to Brazil and get it.' Then the guy who went to process him said, 'You're that Occy guy who beat Tom at the pier, aren't you?' And he's like, 'Yeah, yeah, that's me.' And the guy goes, 'I surf, I surf.' We're going, 'That's good, that's good.' He goes, 'I like your surfing. You're good, boy. You know, the President of the United States can't get in this country without a passport, but today you can.' And he came in without a passport. Try and do that in America – you just can't do it.

John Howitt (Peak wetsuits): I'd rented Occy this car and Sarge was driving it because Occ didn't have a licence, and it was on our American Express card. They left it at the airport, and we got this call from the rent-a-car company – 'Where's the car?' And we've gone, 'Oh no, Occy and Sarge have lost the car.' They were going to put the price of the car on our card. We went through all the car parks and couldn't find it. Sarge had driven it up onto the footpath in front of the terminal and got on a plane and left it there.

Dougall Walker: Occy's had some bad influences in his life, but he's always survived them. He lived through that hectic lifestyle, and the lifestyle *was* hectic. I don't know how many times over the years he's come in and gone, 'Oh mate, sorry, I fucked up.' And you go, 'What have you fucking done? Oh fuck . . .' We fix it and move on, and I'm sure he's like that with a lot of people, but there was never anything spiteful or malicious. It was always just fucking Occy.

STEEL CITY

I met this old bloke at the Sands Hotel in Coolangatta the other day, and he told me, 'You know my son. Remember the year you won the contest in Newcastle? You visited him in hospital. He was the guy who got hit by lightning.'

That chance meeting brought back some incredible memories of one of the strangest contest victories of my career. We'd been on Rottnest Island in WA, and this mate of mine, Wayne Murphy, who we called 'Mullman', used to come along as a judge. I got on really well with Mullman and would hang out with him a lot. He used to teach me Tai Chi. He was a very spiritual guy, almost a bit guru-like.

We'd been surfing Strickland Bay, and we stayed on after the contest because the waves were really good. We used to ride our pushies out to Strickland and hide our boards behind the bushes so we wouldn't have to carry them back each time. On our last day there, we rode out to collect our boards and there was this big storm front coming in. It was so trippy because, right where we hid our boards and where we'd been hanging out and doing Tai Chi, this mini-storm erupted right over the top of us, with thunder and lightning going off everywhere. We got caught by the rain and tried to shelter under the bushes while this storm raged all around us. Mullman told me to put my legrope between my teeth in case we got hit by lightning, so I did. It was that serious.

The storm passed and we got out of there okay, and I flew back to the east coast for the Newcastle contest. But on the way I heard on the news about this kid in Newcastle who'd been hit by lightning while watching the trials. It struck me as an odd coincidence considering how close I'd come to being hit myself in WA. By my calculations, it had happened at almost the same time, on opposite sides of the country. I reckon it was the same time, because trippy things like that always seem to happen to me. This kid had been standing on the rocks during the early rounds, right there at Main Beach, Newcastle, just as a South African surfer, Pierre Tostee, was jumping off the rocks. The kid yelled out, 'Good luck' and then he added, 'just as long as you don't beat any Aussies.' As soon as he said that, this bolt of lightning hit him and threw him like twenty feet in the air. Pierre Tostee got flung too by the force of it, but it didn't hit him. They reckon the kid died about seven times, and they managed to bring him back. He was in the hospital right there overlooking the beach, although he wasn't watching the contest because he was still unconscious. When I got to the contest and heard all about it, I just knew I was going to win. I kept asking people, 'How's the kid? How's the kid?' And they said, 'He's going to make it.'

The waves were fun on the final day, three to four foot and clean, and I met Curren again in the final. There was a huge crowd on the beach and the event was televised live on the local TV, because it was such a big event in Newcastle. I got two good waves straightaway in the first five minutes, and then within minutes this howling southerly buster came roaring through the contest and turned the waves to mush. From that point, Curren was never going to catch me.

Afterwards, I told all the media it was a deliberate strategy on my part to get those two quick waves at the start because I sensed the southerly was coming. I think I said something about feeling the southerly salt spray in my eyes, or smelling it or something, but it was all bullshit. The fact was, I'd been warned it was on the way.

The contest director said, 'Do you want to come and visit the kid? Because he's right there in the hospital.' So I visited him after the final and he was lying there in bed; his arms were still going up and down like he had electricity in him and couldn't control them, but he was all right. He was only young, fifteen or sixteen, but apparently he made a full recovery. His old man reckoned he'd been hit by lightning again, and survived, which seems incredible.

Pam Occhilupo: Mark was surfing in the Newcastle event. He knew I was coming up the next day by train, as I had lent him my car. That night I received a strange phone call from one of Mark's mates, telling me he needed to pack a board for Mark and was coming down in a few minutes to do so. I was a little bewildered. I could easily have put the board in a cover, but Richard was insistent. Next day this little old lady carted said board under her arm, weaving through the train crowded with teenagers all going to the competition. After endeavouring to ignore the many strange looks and some outright giggles, I made it to Newcastle and Mark's hotel, only to be told to go off for a walk! Years later Mark confessed to me the reason for all this subterfuge. Poor naive Mum was carrying an illegal substance in the board bag.

I think my disillusionment with the tour began to take hold in late '86. Curren was dominating the tour, and there were a bunch of surfers who seemed to have mastered the contest system and some young guys who were already challenging. I was one of the top seeds, and I wasn't handling losing too well at that stage. A young goofy-footer from Newcastle named Luke Egan took me down in a close heat in Wollongong. I wasn't happy with the decision and just high-tailed it back to Cronulla. I'd heard of Luke through the grapevine, and when I saw him surf I knew how good he was going to be – but it didn't make losing any easier. He seemed to have my measure a lot of the time, and that was the beginning of our battles.

The best thing about the busy contest schedule was there was always another contest the following week where you could redeem yourself. At the same time, a couple of bad results on the trot could really send you into a spin. The Stubbies that year had been moved from March to November, when the waves were usually terrible on the Gold Coast. But the sponsors wanted the pre-summer publicity, and that's the way things went. I drew a young Hawaiian rookie, Sunny Garcia, in my first heat. Sunny's famous quote at the time was 'I just wanna kick some top-sixteen arse', and he wasn't kidding.

I was staying with Jenny at Gemini Court, a high-rise apartment overlooking Burleigh Point, and we were right into our yoga and healthy diet and I was feeling great. But for some reason we decided to go looking for magic mushrooms in the hinterland right before that event, which probably wasn't the ideal way to approach a contest, especially against Sunny. He was so psyched and so confident, and he was giving me a bit of stink-eye and a vibe before our heat that said, *I am definitely going to kick your arse.* I was kind of scared, because he was ripping. I was trying to psych him right back when we were sitting in the water before the heat, stirring the water up around me with my hands, doing my best to look menacing, but I don't think he was very intimidated. He just gave me this look that said, *what are you thinking? I'm just about to smoke you.* And he did.

A DAY AT THE BAY

When we went to Hawaii that year, Billabong was staging one of the biggest events in pro surfing history, a mobile contest that could be held anywhere on the North Shore. But I don't think any of us were ready for what awaited us at Waimea Bay that day. The swell came up huge for the event, and the only rideable place was the bay. Few of the touring pros even surfed the bay regularly or had the right boards for maxing twenty- to twenty-five-foot surf. When we turned up at the beach that morning we were greeted by flawless, sheet-glass conditions – and the biggest waves most of us had ever seen. We were all nervous, scurrying around trying to borrow big boards, and a couple of guys forfeited their heats. I don't blame them a bit. It was terrifying. So many of the guys on tour weren't into it. They went, 'We can't surf that, we haven't got the boards.' Gordon Merchant and Randy Rarick were like, 'You've got to be ready for anything.'

My old Cronulla mate Gary Green was in my heat, and he told me he wasn't going out. I was trying to encourage him: 'Come on, it will be sweet. Just paddle out and have a look.' But then a huge set came through and closed out the entire bay and nearly drowned a couple of competitors. Rob Bain had to be rescued by jet ski, and another guy was washed up on the beach, gasping for his life. Greeny just about turned green watching it all and went, 'Nah, this is so far out of my league.' I said, 'Sweet, don't even worry about it.' You have to make your own call on whether you're ready for a day like that, and no-one else should pressure you into it.

I was shitting myself too, but determined to at least paddle out and catch a couple. After seeing Bainy get cleaned up, I was worried about close-out sets. Sure enough, as we were paddling out for our heat, another one came and I was lucky enough to just scrape over it. I'd left Greeny on the beach umming and aahing about whether he should paddle out, and at that point I hoped he hadn't decided to at the last minute, because he would have copped that set on the head and could very well have drowned.

Mark Richards was in the heat before me and, as I was paddling out, I saw him spin around and take off on one of the largest waves I'd ever seen up close. I paddled so hard from the beach and, sure enough, when I was almost out the back I spotted this big set. I was like, *oh no, here it is*, and I paddled my guts out and just got over it. While I was scratching for my life, I watched in awe as MR coolly turned around and took one of the first waves. I just went, *are you serious?* The wave was over twenty-five feet, and when you're out there you're watching it as if it's in slow motion. Derek Ho took the next one and it closed out the bay. He rode it all the way in and right up the beach. I managed to catch two waves in my heat and I didn't get through; it was best-three back then and I needed another one.

Marvin Foster was in my heat and he was charging, so at ease in the huge waves. It was an epic day, and I was stoked to get over the hurdle and surf it. If I'd got another one I would have gone through, for sure. It was a bummer, because the next day was perfect Sunset, and MR just ruled it. It was great to see the four-time world champ come out of retirement and school all the youngsters, and I think he opened my eyes to how long a surfer can maintain peak performance, especially in bigger waves.

THE SMELLY TURTLE

The World Cup was a specialty event that year, held in big waves at Sunset. After surviving Waimea, I was pumped to do well. It was twelve to fifteen foot, and I made it through the semis. We had about a half-hour break before the final. We'd already surfed three times that day, so I went back to Buddy's house to refuel, but I must have taken too long because I left the other finalists waiting on the podium for me. When I got back, Mike Parsons' dad, in front of everyone, yelled out, 'Did you get enough drugs into you?' Sure, I was no choirboy at the time, but in Hawaii, in public, this was considered decidedly uncool.

One of the big Hawaiian security guys, Elliot, grabbed him and dragged him round the corner. And when I got off the podium I went and confronted him, pretty angry, and had him by the throat. Everyone was going, 'No, Occ, no', so I just pushed him away, but it rattled me. I had to go and surf a final in huge waves, and didn't need something like that playing on my mind. There were fifteen-foot clean-up sets closing out the channel – really radical. A lot of guys were riding the inside bowl. I was on a 7'10" and going way out and trying to tackle the west peak to get a bit of an advantage before moving to the inside. I was way out at sea, all by myself, and I was trying to line up with those big satellite dishes on top of the hill to find the west peaks, but it was really sketchy. Right then a turtle popped up next to me, and the weirdest thing was that it absolutely stunk. It must have just done a poo or a fart or something, but for some reason I took this smelly turtle as a good sign. I really thought I was going to win. That turtle led me, literally by the nose, to the west peak, and I rode some big waves out there. It was so big that one of my rides was from the middle of the channel, going left and then coming back right into the inside bowl. Hans Hedemann ended up winning the event, but I was still stoked with second and felt like I'd made some real inroads in Hawaii that season.

Chapter Seven

Breakdown Dead Ahead

HELLO HOLLYWOOD: NORTH SHORE – THE MOVIE

By 1987 my interest in the tour was already starting to wane. I'd been going so hard and so fast ever since I first went on tour four years prior. I was more than ready for a few extracurricular diversions. When the chance came along to star in a real Hollywood movie, even a corny B-grade surf flick, I jumped at it.

Robbie Page and I heard about this casting in Hawaii for a movie called *North Shore*, and they needed a couple of Aussie surfers, basically to play themselves. So we went along to meet the director early in the Hawaiian season. We headed down to the screen test and had to say a few lines, and I didn't think too much more about it. A few weeks later we found out we got the parts. So then we had to go into Honolulu to get working visas and join the Screen Actors Guild. They didn't start filming until January, and Pagey had to go home to get his visa sorted, so I just stayed in Hawaii.

They were telling us it was going to be a major feature film, but we really didn't know what to expect. When they started shooting on the North Shore they had all these big trucks and trailers and stuff

– Pagey and I even had our own trailer. It was good fun. We met all the actors and they were really cool, and they even cleared the water at Pipe one day for us, which was amazing.

It seemed like a pretty corny script, about this kid who comes from a wave pool in Arizona and wins a trip to Hawaii to compete in the Pipe Masters. We had to shoot this big party scene, which kind of turned into a real party. I thought Pagey was really funny, such a classic Aussie larrikin, which is what they loved about him. A few other surfers made appearances in it, like Laird Hamilton, who played the surf champ that everyone didn't like because he was too obnoxious, and Gerry Lopez, who played this Hawaiian heavy. Gerry's a pretty good actor in his own right. He's done a few things, like *Conan the Barbarian* and *Big Wednesday*, so it was good to hang out with him.

There's this one scene where we're driving along in the cane fields and this guy goes, 'You're Occy, you won the Op Pro twice!' And I roll my eyes exaggeratedly, which was how I was feeling about the whole surf star thing by then. I don't know if they told me to do that, or I just did it. I think maybe that's why Hollywood never called again. I thought I was ripping at the time, but I was just young and kind of cringe at it now.

North Shore became a bit of a cult classic, and there are people who've watched it dozens of times and know all the lines off by heart, like *The Rocky Horror Picture Show* or something. A few younger guys at home still tease me about it every now and again. Like the Harrington twins, Shaun and Dean – every time I see them they want me to say, 'Alex, up ahead!' Just like in the movie. It drives me crazy.

We actually watched some of it the night I retired. Bruce Irons and Kai Garcia had a barbie for me at Gerry's old Pipe house. I get embarrassed every time I see it. I like watching the movie; I just don't like watching my part.

I did like the idea of acting. At the time I thought I was pretty good, in some weird way, I don't know why. But nothing really eventuated out of it, which is probably just as well. I thought Pagey was really good in it, but he never got any calls back either. I don't know why. They didn't even do a sequel. I think they talked about it, but nothing happened, which is really no great shame.

Pam Occhilupo: It was quite possibly the worst movie ever made. Only a mother could love it, and possibly his adoring fans.

Robbie Page: Tim Bonython gave me the tip-off to go down to Gerry Lopez's house because they were doing screen tests for the movie *North Shore*. I got on my bike and went to Mike Latronic's house where he and Occ were playing pool. I got Occy on the handlebars of the bike and rode all the way with him down to Lopez's to do our first screen test. Then we had to wait around for ages, and I ended up overstaying my visa in America waiting to do the film. By the time they sent us down to immigration, me and Occ, they locked me up there. They said, 'You can't leave, you're illegal right now. You've overstayed your visa. You've got to get on a plane home.' And they kept me there. Occ left to go back to the North Shore, and about five minutes later I hear, 'Robbie, Robbie.' I'm walking about out the back in this little office where I'm locked up, and Occ climbs up to this window and goes, 'You got any money?' And I had to give him my last twenty bucks so he could get back to the North Shore.

I finished the year in third place again, which isn't so bad, but it felt like I'd stalled in my efforts to climb the ratings and win a world title. Curren's domination was starting to mess with my head. I lost first round at Bells to Gary Taylor, a good solid surfer from Victoria, but a guy I would normally have expected to beat. I managed a third at the Coke, losing to Tom Carroll in the semis, who went on to beat Pottz in the final. I was travelling over from Cronulla in my mum's Celica, really psyching, and the waves were good. Tom was ripping in our semi, but I had one moment that was pretty special.

Floaters were still a fairly new thing, and Mark Sainsbury was doing those ones where he'd travel over the foam to make sections and float down after the wave had broken. In my semi I pulled a kind of half floater, half re-entry – right on the lip line, riding the falling lip all the way down. I landed it perfectly, and it felt like something new and exciting. That was the best thing I got out of that semi, because that's what interested me: finding new lines and new ways to ride waves. But there was a new breed of surfers on tour who were absolute masters of the competitive system, and they just seemed to have my measure a lot of the time. Guys like Barton Lynch and Damien Hardman and Dave Macaulay were really hard to beat, especially in small waves. They were light and got into a rhythm and just connected the dots all the way to the beach. I could see that my preferred style of surfing was not suiting the contest format.

I remember watching Nick Wood at that event too and feeling a bit worried for him. He was so young and he'd just won Bells at the age of sixteen, the youngest surfer ever to win a major pro contest. He was getting so much attention, and he was shy and couldn't really handle it. I saw him after he lost a heat at the Coke contest, with this little bottle of bourbon in a brown paper bag, taking sly sips. I thought maybe he was just consoling himself after a loss, but he was so young and there was so little guidance for guys like that on tour. There were a lot of casualties, and I could relate because I'd felt that kind of pressure at a young age too, but I'd mostly enjoyed the spotlight. Maybe I saw a bit of myself in Nick, though, because I think I was starting to see the dark side of the whole pro surfing world and the toll it could take on fragile young souls.

MAN OVERBOARD

I was having trouble focusing and was really feeling the effects of all that travel, living out of a suitcase and being away from home. The '87–'88 season opener in Japan seemed to carry a heavy omen for me. I always liked going to Japan, even if the waves weren't always great. We used to stay at the full traditional homestays, with the sliding rice-paper walls and straw mats and the roll-out futon beds and authentic Japanese meals. It was all-time and great to surf there, because the crowds were so into the contest. They really loved it.

To get to Nijima Island we used to get the ferry at night. All the surfers would be hanging around waiting to get on the boat, and you used to be able to buy beer out of vending machines on the street, which always helped pass the time. One year the boys were carrying on, and the Hawaiian boys actually picked up one of the vending machines, put it in the back of their car and took it home. The next year there were no more vending machines. We would just run riot in Nijima. The ferry left at midnight, and if you paid a bit more money you could get a little room with a bed. Other people didn't even sleep and just carried on all the way there.

I slept and woke early to see the sunrise and was doing my yoga on the deck, psyching for the contest. It was a three-storey ferry and I was on the top deck, just taking in the sights over the ocean at dawn. I looked down and there was this old guy climbing over the railing. I thought, *what is this guy doing?* Before I knew it he just fell in the water. He was looking up at me, not asking for help or anything, lying flat on his back. I was in shock. There was no-one else around and I didn't know what to do. If I jumped in after him then we'd both be in the water watching the ship disappear into the distance. We might never be found. I ran to the captain, screaming, 'Man overboard! Man overboard!' But I don't speak Japanese and they didn't speak English. I was trying to explain what happened and they didn't understand.

So I grabbed this guy and went to throw him overboard, just to show them what I meant, and then I thought, *hang on, they're going to think I've just pushed some guy overboard.* I was freaking and they eventually worked out what I was on about and turned the boat around. They did a couple of circles but couldn't find him. Someone explained to me that it happened a bit – old people who can't deal with the pressure of their jobs or supporting a family and stuff and just jump off the boat in the middle of the ocean.

In Nijima the police came and interviewed me. They had to ask me what had happened and try to work out who the old man was. It was heavy, just in the middle of the sea, no-one around. It rattled me, that's for sure. Winning a surfing contest didn't seem like such a matter of life or death after that, and I lost early to Dave Macaulay. That started a run of mediocre results for me through '87, and my frustration and disillusionment with the tour grew. I missed the South African leg, sick of the constant travel and the contest scene. When I did compete, I'd make a final one event, then lose first round in the next event to guys I should have beaten. It was an unhealthy cycle of peaks and troughs that was never going to end well, but I just didn't have the maturity at the time to see it.

FRENCH CONNECTION

The redeeming feature of the tour that year for me was getting to know Maurice Cole and his family in France. Maurice is a great character and an excellent surfer and shaper from Victoria, who had relocated to France and was more than happy to show me all the attractions of the French lifestyle. He'd been telling us about the waves in Hossegor for a while, but that year I got to experience it for myself.

Surfing was really new and fresh in France: the industry was in its infancy, there were no crowds, and miles of quality beachbreaks were dotted with nude sunbathers. Maurice would take us to surf a high-tide bank all morning in unbelievable waves. And just when you think you're going to come in and get something to eat, Maurice goes, 'Nuh, there's a low-tide bank that is going crazy right now.' So we'd go there, miss out on lunch, then we'd surf La Gravier on the high tide in the afternoon. By the end of the day we'd be almost delirious with exhaustion. Maurice is such a surf nazi when the surf's good, and we were surfing the best waves ever. There were nude girls on the beach and we'd often surf without legropes. You'd get barrelled, lose your board, swim in and have some naked beauty hand you your board. It was pretty crazy.

They were epic times. Maurice had a little house at Capbreton and a dog called Doc, a big horse of a dog. His beautiful wife, Anne, used to treat me like a son. I would babysit their two young kids, Damo and Marine. I had a real family environment with them in Hossegor and I fell in love with it. Maurice would cook pasta with cream sauce and then this spicy tomato Basque sauce. He'd make us surf all day, so he had to fill us up with carbs. After surfing for hours we'd go home for one quick bowl of pasta and get back out there. It was unbelievable. Then Maurice built this beautiful house just a short walk from the beach, and that was a *real* nude beach. The French would get nude anywhere, but at the designated nude beach *everyone* was nude. There always seemed to be lots of old nude French guys with moustaches flying kites, which was a bit disturbing. But, that aside, it was pretty close to a surfer's heaven.

But while the free-surfing experience was bliss, the contest scene was providing me with little joy, and I was losing too many heats that I knew I should have been winning. Tahitian surfer Vetea 'Poto' David knocked me out early in Biarritz that year. Poto was such a funny guy and great to travel with. He came up to me once and, in his thick Tahitian accent, said, 'Occy, Occy, I can't handle it because every time the commentator says, "He's going to do a turn", I can't do it. It really puts me off. Do you think I should wear earplugs or something?' And after that it started putting me off too . . . So maybe it was Poto's fault I quit the tour.

Gary Taylor from Victoria was another guy who seemed to have my measure that year, so maybe we should blame *him* for my quitting the tour. Then there was Brad Gerlach, a loud, flamboyant American who used to inevitably break out his Occy impersonation at parties. I hated it. He did it once at the presentation for the Beaurepaires in this really high-pitched Aussie accent. I didn't even think it was that good. I'd just leave the room, and everyone would be laughing. That might have had a bit to do with me retiring, so we'll blame it on Gerr. It didn't help that he kept knocking me out in heats either.

Of course, the truth is it wasn't anyone's fault but my own that I was growing disillusioned. I couldn't have imagined then where that disillusionment would take me.

EASY RIDER

Hawaii was where I would normally expect to redeem an ordinary year with a few results, but I struggled even there. One incident that Hawaiian season seemed to sum up my life at the time – the way I seemed to flirt with disaster yet somehow land on my feet.

I was bitten by a centipede, and someone told me you had to drink a lot of alcohol to get the sting out. So I drank a bottle of tequila. I was so drunk, and the poison from the centipede and the alcohol had a really bad reaction. I was just off my head . . . I don't know what I was thinking, but the next day I decided it would be a good idea to borrow this guy's Harley-Davidson. I wasn't drunk anymore, but I was still feeling weird.

I was riding into Haleiwa and I thought I was ripping, so I started looking around to see if anyone was looking at me. All of a sudden I saw Cheyne Horan and Tom Carroll, so I revved it really loud and they looked over. I started waving furiously. Then the car in front of me came to a dead stop. I was doing about forty Ks when I hit it and went straight over the handlebars, like it was in slow motion – headfirst into the air, did a complete somersault and landed perfectly, on my feet, in front of the car. Tom and Cheyne couldn't believe it. They were just standing there in shock. The guy in the car was a tourist and he wanted to call the cops and fill out an accident report, and I just picked up the bike and drove off. I couldn't get it started at first, and I'm going, 'Yeah, no worries', and those guys were laughing at me. I finally got it started and was gone. When I saw those guys a couple of days later they said they were in hysterics, nearly wet themselves. People hear the story and they don't believe it, but I've got witnesses.

> **Tom Carroll:** Cheyne and I were going to the local market there at Haleiwa, and we saw Occy riding this motorbike, no helmet or anything – I don't think he had a shirt on – cruising along. He kind of started waving to us and this guy stopped in front of him and he didn't know and just kept waving . . . I clearly remember him getting launched over the car, did a complete flip and landed on his feet. And I'll never forget it because it looked so natural. There was just utter disbelief. He got up and ran straight to the bike and just took off back towards Sunset. Somehow he just pulled it off. Me and Cheyne were in hysterics – 'How did he pull that?' The bike was okay. He got away. The guy in the car was just left there shaking his head, going, 'What was that?'

I don't know whether it was an accumulation of everything I'd been through in a few short years on tour, but that Hawaiian season I went on a bit of a bender. I'm not sure how else to put it. It's not easy to look back on or talk about, because I hurt a lot of people I cared about. But in the midst of something like that you have no perspective on things. You're just swept along by events.

I fell in with the wrong crowd at some point over there. I was always so keen to get on well with the locals, and the more successful I became the keener people seemed to be to get to know me. It was great, for a while. At some point you realise you're hanging out with people who like the *idea* of who you are, the pro surfer, without really knowing you as a person.

I'd experimented with drugs on tour, it was hard not to at that time. Everywhere we went, there seemed to be parties thrown especially for us, full of people eager to show us a good time in their part of the world. It was all too easy to succumb, especially when results aren't going your way in the contests. It's like the chicken and the egg. Which comes first – the dodgy results or the partying? One leads to the other in a downward spiral, and pretty soon you've lost your way.

By the time Jenny came over to join me in Hawaii, I was almost a different person and the relationship was never going to survive. I was partying too much and out of control. For me, that Hawaiian season turned into a trip to the wild side, one that I almost didn't make it back from.

Pam Occhilupo: We had been hearing reports of various misadventures in Hawaii, but on New Year's Eve,1987, Fleur arrived with a very long face and said she had something to tell Luciano and I. Jenny had been ringing her from Hawaii over the last few days with disturbing news about Mark's weird behaviour, and she felt it was too much of a burden to carry alone . . . According to Jenny, Mark had been involved in an accident, riding a motorbike into a car, was being chased by the police, being thrown out of restaurants and generally behaving in an erratic and obnoxious fashion. It was horrifying news, although not completely unexpected . . . Luciano, who was always marvellous in a crisis, told me to book a seat on the first plane over there. I begged him to go instead, but he said he had no patience with the drug scene, which we were pretty sure Mark was involved in. Not that I relished the thought of it either, but he told me that I had more understanding from my training in counselling, whereas he knew he would just become angry, which would not solve anything.

Jodie Cooper: For me, I saw a side of Occ that was the fine line between genius and an absolute fruit loop, a vulnerability. . . . I saw that at a real young age. He had all this talent. When someone surfs like he does, his style is so mature, people think his brain is like that too. But too much stimulus could really rock his world. It sent him a little bit loopy. He was like an artist – one day he'd paint a masterpiece and the next he'd cut his ear off. Some days you would walk up to him and he'd be talking in a munchkin voice, like a four-year-old, like he's in some other world.

It is hard to imagine a time when a high-profile, professional athlete could quietly slip off the radar, in the grip of a terrifying, narcotic bender, and not become front-page news. We are so accustomed to the blood sport of celebrity scandal, it is difficult to fathom an earlier age when a protective circle of friends and family and a compassionate media could allow a sports star their personal struggles and healing in private. But that's how it was when the wheels began to come off Occ's spectacular career.

I was a surf magazine editor at the time, and even I had no idea of the depths he fell to during his Lost Hawaiian Winter. There were no paparazzi lying in wait when he sheepishly skulked through Sydney Airport upon his return from his extended Hawaiian season, or camped on his lawn when he slipped into seclusion and stacked on the beef out at Kurnell. I'd like to think we kept a respectful distance, hoping to see that magical talent rekindled when he was ready. Occ had already earnt that kind of goodwill, in the surf community and beyond. He'd bob up now and again; surf well enough to allay our fears and quell the rumours of his untimely demise; appear in Jack McCoy's surf movies, apparently fit, well and still capable of destroying a wave like no-one else; then vanish for extended periods while we wondered as to

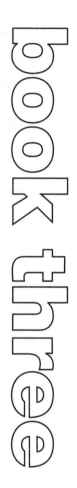

book three

The Fall

his fate. A serious comeback wasn't even contemplated; we just hoped he'd survive, not become another sad casualty in a long line of self-destructive surf heroes.

– T. B.

Chapter Eight

The Lost Hawaiian Winter

Looking back, I realise I was so in awe of Hawaii that I really wanted to *become* Hawaiian and fit in with the local scene. I was over the tour, and I liked all the Hawaiian crew and the lifestyle. I wanted to live there and get a regular job and just be one of the boys. I was hanging out with local surfer Mickey Neilson, getting into all kinds of trouble, going out to the Pink Cadillac every night and surfing all day, and going out again. At one stage I started labouring, just to try and be a regular guy, not a surf star – but the romance of manual labour didn't last too long. It was hard work. And it ate into your surf time.

Mum flew over to try and help me, but I wasn't interested in help, and she flew home distraught. Then Mum and Dad came together to try and bring me home, because they were so scared for me, but I rejected their help. I was just too wild and out of control. I was having a ball, but everyone else was really worried about me. Jenny and I had broken up because she couldn't deal with all the craziness, but I was oblivious to how I was hurting the people around me.

I met a Brazilian girl, Patricia, and suddenly decided that we should get married. I've done this a few times, maybe latching onto someone for security in the middle of my confusion, but it was never going to last. She couldn't stand my erratic behaviour and lifestyle either and flew home, and just as quickly I took up with a young Hawaiian girl named Robyn. She was a real good-time girl, who didn't seem to mind the wild times in the slightest, and in that way at least we were a good match.

I know everyone was really worried about me, but I thought I knew what I was doing and that I was old enough to make my own calls. The way I saw it, I was just really getting into Hawaii, like I'd always wanted to do, and rebelling a bit, I guess. Prior to that I was staying with Buddy or Gordon and really concentrating on the contests. I was still really young when I started coming to Hawaii, and I guess I wanted to break out of that whole surf-star mould and really live the Hawaiian experience. I went flitting around the outer islands, being put up in fancy beach houses by my new-found friends. I got to know all the heavy local crew on the North Shore. I felt a bit like Maxwell Smart, from that old TV show *Get Smart*. People said I was in danger, that I was hanging out with the wrong crowd or self-destructing, and my response was: 'And . . . loving it.' I really wanted to see that side of the North Shore. I'd been going there for four or five years and I wasn't a kid anymore.

I got to know Eddie Rothman really well, and a guy who had a place under Eddie's house, Dan Nakasoni. Dan was a really good guy, and he shaped really nice boards. He made me a board and I painted it with this wild paint job, which seemed to reflect my state of mind at the time.

I definitely was on the party program, no doubt about that, and there was a point at which I even scared myself. Robyn and I had been up for a few days. I was driving around the island to her mum's house, and I suddenly got a massive nosebleed. It felt like there was a big cloud over me, like the world was caving in on me. I pulled over and went, 'Faaarrk, I've had enough.' And I asked Robyn to marry me. She was a real fun girl, but I don't think I was in love with her. I brought her back to Australia, but as soon as I straightened up we broke up.

They were some wild times. You learn from your mistakes. And when I finally came home, I just wanted to stay home. It was full-on for everyone.

Pam Occhilupo: I woke around midnight one night in Hawaii to hear Mark banging around in his bedroom. When I poked my head around the door, I could tell he was really irrational – he was opening and shutting doors while Patricia lay quietly sleeping. When I asked him what he was doing, he turned on me and shouted that he was looking after his sick wife! He was writing too; there were screeds of notepaper beside him. I made myself a cup of strong tea and sat in the lounge, and soon he came out and apologised for yelling and showed me what he had been writing. I still have it – a crazy jumble of things about passports and bringing cocaine into the country. He said 'they' were after him, investigating everything. He also started talking about Luciano, saying he was head of the Mafia in Italy and could get anyone to do anything. Delusions of grandeur! Typical drug-induced schizophrenia . . . I was torn between feeling very, very sorry for his poor confused brain and quite petrified about what he would do next.

Buddy McCray: I was majorly concerned about him. I tried to steer the trouble away from him, and steer him away from the trouble, but it was out of my hands. Any time he'd go out I'd tell his friends, 'Keep an eye on him. Don't let him run off with these morons who keep him out all night.' But there wasn't much I could do. I remember going to have dinner with his mum and dad at the Turtle Bay, and his mum was going, 'What can we do?' I said, 'The good thing to do would be to send him off to the desert somewhere, make him do all the camp work, and keep him away from all the shit for a couple of months. Let him get his head clear.' And I said, 'Don't give him any spare change. Don't give him any money. If he blows through his money, then that's the end of it. If you give him money, he just runs out and buys himself some candy.' Literally, he walked in while we were having this conversation and asked his mum for twenty bucks, and she gave him twenty bucks, and he went straight out and bought himself a bag of whiz.

He was a super-popular, gregarious guy, so everybody wanted to be around him. He was such good energy. It's like any kind of celebrity – you get your entourage and people who want to hang on and be a part of the scene. And he wanted to be a part of the local scene too. It got really ugly. I was worried that he might not make it back, but I knew he was so strong-willed and he always had that part of him that he developed through surfing. To surf so well at such a young age – any-body that can get to that level of ability has so much energy and focus for what they're doing. That's an inner strength that can carry over into other things. That was the main thing that got him through, at least as far as I can see.

Mike Latronic: There was stuff going on with Occy that wasn't kosher. We like to have fun, but he was dealing with elements that were beyond our control. As a really close friend, I look back and it hurts. I always wonder if I was a good enough friend. We'd just tell him, 'You've got to know, these people aren't your friends. We're your friends and we fucking won't tolerate it.' He had to go find somewhere else to stay.

I always wanted to help him. He was spending all his money and I remember when he was sort of disillusioned or uncomfortable with his success. He wanted to go home and get a job pouring concrete. It was kind of delusional. I was like, 'Dude, you have no idea how good you've got it. There's nothing wrong with an honest day's work, but when you've got a talent to surf and you're being paid to do it, let it flourish.' It was hard to see that get thrown away week after week, day after day.

We'd talked about strapping him down to a chair for hours at a time so he couldn't leave the house. We didn't know what his consumption levels were or what he was consuming, but I knew he was in trouble . . . Everyone wanted a piece of him, and if you were some hot shot with some good weed – 'Come do this with me, Occy.' Everybody wanted to hang with Occy and impress Occy, one of the best surfers in the world and a charismatic guy. He probably followed his nose too many times.

Tom Carroll: It was absolutely unsustainable. I saw him one time and I was shocked. He's a really sensitive character, and for his sensitive nature the tour's unforgiving. When you're moving at that pace, there's no feeling of being yourself. You're really out there, and he was really young. There was so much at our fingertips when we were travelling the world. He was very well-known in the '80s. It was a gnarly time, the '80s. It was pretty hard-core – more dangerous than the '70s in some ways – and Occy was kind of living through it in a very sensitive state. On the North Shore I saw him a few times and I know the crew that were there with him, and he was vulnerable to that stuff that was going on. People like Occy, it's part of human nature to play out your desires until you reach rock bottom, until you experience enough suffering to move beyond it. It was a bummer. Some part of me as a competitive animal was going, *maybe I've got an opportunity here*, but another part was going, *it's his life, it's really sad*. I was really torn.

At that time I thought that was the end of Occy forever. I tried to look and learn from it at the time – *this is what could happen.* We all had all these paths open to us and, for Occy, he never knew when to pull up. A lot of that heavy element on the North Shore, it had this alluring thing for me too. I liked that heaviness and risk-taking . . . I think that sensitive nature, people actually took advantage of it, people who were pretty sick people in themselves and wanted to drag someone else down.

Brian Surratt: There was some radical shit going on . . . He showed up and the guys took advantage of him – took his credit card, took his rental car, charged up thirty grand. And he would show up at my house, and I'd be like, 'Whoa, whoa, whoa . . .' He was coming unglued, going, 'Where's my board? I want to go surf, Uncle Brian.' We got him in the house and talked a bit, and he was going through some hard moments again with drinking and drugs. I said, 'Where you been?' And he said, 'At these people's house.' So I got a couple of guys, went over to the people's house and said, 'Ay, you been taking advantage. What the fuck's going on?' I got him away from those people and took him in like family.

I had a big fishing boat and would wake him every day at four or five o'clock to go fishing. We did that for a while. He loves to fish. We'd go out for the whole day – marlin, big yellow-fin tunas, mahi mahi. He was great on a boat. We got along really well . . . Let's put it in Hawaiian terms – we call it 'ohana. That means we always accept our real good friends, like adopting them into the family. Occy was very, very special.

Grandma Surratt (Brian's mother): He was good, then he was bad, then he was good again. He was a rascal. He got involved in the wrong crowd. He was very young when he first came out. He was like one of our kids. He was a good kid who just got into trouble when the drugs came into it, but he got over it fast. My husband, George, was very worried about him.

Pam Occhilupo: I was like a tigress fighting for her cub, and I went to see everyone I could possibly think of to try to help. Casting around for ways to extricate Mark from his predicament, I rang John Laws, a brilliant radio announcer who I respected greatly. Of course, I rang anonymously, but unfortunately the situation was not common and many people picked up on it. John Laws is such an intelligent man and we have quite a rapport. I had rung him on a few occasions in the past, and he has always been polite and helpful, a perfect gentleman. This time I said my son was in Hawaii, self-destructing on drugs. John managed to elicit from me that Mark was a professional sportsman, and I suppose people had only to put two-and-two together to realise what sport it was – and who the sportsman was. Off the air, John spoke to me, letting me know that he knew who I was and assuring me that he would do anything in his power to help.

The first thing that happened when I got off the phone was a ring from *The Daily Telegraph*, saying that they knew I had rung John Laws that morning and did I want to talk about it? I denied it, of course, but was starting to feel qualms about what I had done and what effect it would have if it ever got back to Mark. Then Graham Cassidy, the editor of *The Sun-Herald* where I worked, and president of the ASP – also a good friend to Mark – rang and said, 'What have you done, Pam? Everyone is talking about Mark and trying to find out what is happening.' I told him that I felt compelled to try every avenue. I knew he was just trying to shut me up because of the bad publicity for the surfing association.

Graham Cassidy: I've spent my life trying to keep a lid on things . . . Having been a journalist, you make a judgement when people have been in the shit, when they deserve to go down and when they don't. In my case, I was prepared to go in to bat for him, wanting to uphold the good name of surfing. It was the obvious position for me to take . . . In a way, I put my reputation on the line in terms of wanting to convince people that what they were hearing was overblown, it was an aberration. Why crucify him on the strength of an aberration? No-one knew the depth it was going to go to. We actually sincerely believed that he could come out of this, and what we should be doing is trying to protect him from massive bad press, which could inflict more wounds emotionally and make the situation worse.

John Howitt: I gave him a progress payment and three days later it was all gone. He came in and he was out of money. Even though he wasn't due for it, we gave it to him anyway because he was the star. That's when he got stuck in Hawaii and they were trying to get him home. At that stage he was like a superstar, and everything had fallen in his lap and he'd gone off the rails. All his desires fell from the sky. I gave him that money and he went to Hawaii and he put it all up his nose. When his mother rang John Laws, I had this reporter in the factory blaming me for supporting his drug habit.

Paul Sargeant: That year in Hawaii, we went to all sorts of lengths to get him back here. And I forget who the lifeguards were, but they were friends of Robbie Wood's, and Robbie was really helpful. He rang me and he said, 'I hear Occy's in all sorts of trouble.' I said, 'Yeah, we're trying to get him back from Hawaii, but he's just going mad on his credit cards and won't return phone calls. Half the time we can't find him.' And he goes, 'Well, I know a couple of lifeguards over there. We'll set up a thing where we fake a bust.' I said, 'What do you mean, "fake a bust"?' He said, 'We'll get two local lifeguards in police uniforms, go over there and tell him that we've been watching him. We know he's doing drugs and stuff and he's got a choice. Either we'll take him to the airport and he can get out of here, or we take him to the station and book him.' So that's what we set up and, the day before, he got tipped off. He went over to Maui, and it fell through. That's when Pam went over the first time.

His American Express card got to forty-four grand, and we cut it off. He'd just bought his first property before he'd gone off on that tangent. It was a great two-bedroom apartment, the best of everything: stereo, leather lounges, that sort of thing. It cost seventy-six grand, I think, eleventh floor, views all the way round. Anyway, he got back and he was forty-four grand in debt on his credit card.

We cut off his cash so he couldn't draw cash, and he went to his credit card. He was buying the boys trips to Maui or Molokai or wherever in return for coke. So then we cut the credit card off as well. When he came back to Australia we just said, 'You've blown it. You're going to have to sell your unit.' So we went through that process . . . I found out one day Occy had given someone his $3000 leather lounge for, like, 200 bucks. It was like, *these people are supposed to be his* friends. *What are they doing*? He sold someone else the stereo dirt cheap . . . It was just the full fire sale.

Nick Carroll: I did quite a bit of reporting on it. It really was fucking heavy. I went over to Cronulla looking for him, and I ran into Richard Maurer and Pottz at the North Cronulla pub. They were both going, 'What the fuck happened to him?' Richard said he'd never seen him drinking or eating junk food before, and he'd just seen him down the beach drinking a sixpack and eating McDonald's. Pottz said, 'It's the tour. If someone told you not to do something, you would immediately go off and do it.'

The ASP was pretty tough about it. They said they weren't going to let the standing of the other top surfers be affected by one surfer going off on a binge. There were a lot of people working to try and shut everything up, and stop it from blowing up. I did an interview with him and he'd been such a bright light, and it was like the light had totally gone out in him. None of the light that had shone in him was there. It was kind of baffling for the entire sport. People say it was about the waves – it was a soul move. It wasn't that at all; he just spun out. After that it was only a matter of time before he would eventually bail altogether. He found it very hard to talk about.

From *The Sydney Morning Herald*, 11 June 1988: 'Most Sydneysiders didn't take too much notice when ten weeks ago an anguished mother spoke on talk-back radio about her son's cocaine habit, but the Honolulu Narcotics Vice Squad certainly did. The woman is the mother of a highly rated Australian surfer and she has since been to Hawaii, where she was interviewed by police . . . When he left Hawaii earlier this year, the surfer returned home with 'quite a few debts', his mother says. He had also received a warning from his sponsors which, in effect, said that they were not prepared to watch their money go up his nose. 'I was horrified when I found out he was using cocaine,' she told the *Herald*. 'At the time he said, "I'm taking cocaine and I like it." I was really scared that he was killing himself or that he was going to end up in jail.' . . . As well as speaking anonymously on radio, the woman contacted Federal Police, who searched

Occy

her son when he arrived at Sydney Airport. When the *Herald* contacted the surfer, his father threatened legal action if his son was identified. 'I can tell you one thing,' he said, 'every kid is experimenting with drugs these days.'

I eventually came home sore and sorry and with one hell of a credit card bill, but it had taught me a tough lesson and I knew things had to change. My surfing didn't seem to have suffered too much – I stumbled into the season-ending Australian leg and managed a semifinal finish at Bells. But that was my only result. In another telling heat, I lost in the second round of the Coke Classic at Manly to Luke Egan. I already knew he surfed good and embodied all the energy and enthusiasm I was lacking, and he smoked me. Maybe I passed on a bit of a torch that day, because I felt like Louie was really flying the flag in the years ahead as I discovered the joys of the couch. I finished the year in ninth place, which was a disappointment. I knew I could do better, but I also knew that I couldn't keep going the way I was going. Something had to give. In hindsight it was kind of weird, because if I was ninth in the world right now I *so* wouldn't be quitting, but back then I guess ninth was like a failure. I'd had so much success so quickly, and then I started going through the motions at an early age, going backwards instead of forwards. Tom Curren had dominated the sport for a couple of years, and there were new and hungry challengers coming up all the time.

I embarked on the new season in a daze, somehow managing a third in Japan, after losing to Curren in the semis, and another third at the Gunston in South Africa. But I was on autopilot. I missed events, went through the motions when I did show up, lost heats I should have won, and grew increasingly weary and disillusioned with the tour. At the heart of it, too, I just wanted to go surf some good waves, and the tour at the time was stuck in chasing big beach crowds at mediocre city beachbreaks in holiday season. Even though it had been my dream since I was a kid, I knew I had to quit the tour to heal myself and get my life sorted. The tour was going back to a calendar year ending in Hawaii in December, which should have suited me, but December seemed a long way away and I didn't think I'd last on tour that long.

What I really needed to do was stop, completely. Just stop. Whatever else was going on in all the swirling craziness around me and within me, some part of me knew I needed simply to rest. That's what Mum would say, bless her, excusing all my excesses: 'He just needed a rest.' And it's true. I just needed to be still for a while. And despite my ragged state, I had the good sense to obey. I just stopped.

> **Cheyne Horan:** Occ came to me around '88 in Japan and we were out there looking at the moon. We were staying near each other; we spent a lot of time together in Japan, did a lot of yoga. We were looking up at the full moon, and he said, 'I'm going to quit the tour. They're never going to let me win. They can only see Curren as world champion.' I can remember Larry Blair saying the same thing to me in Japan ten years earlier.

PULLING THE PIN

By the time I got to California for the Op Pro, I knew I couldn't keep going. Partly it was the whole party scene catching up with me, and partly it was the living out of a suitcase and never being home. Sometimes I would literally wake up in hotel rooms and wonder what country I was in. It all started to take a toll and I really felt like I'd missed out on my youth. I'd been on tour for four or five years, and I just started getting really depressed and homesick. I didn't tell anyone about any of this at the time, which probably only made it worse. I was travelling with Derek Hynd and Greeny, and I was surfing in the Op Pro at Huntington, the scene of some of my biggest wins and wildest times on tour, but it all seemed a bit hollow now.

Occy

I didn't tell anyone, but I said to myself, *when I lose, when they all go on to Europe, I'm going to hop on a flight home.* But the worst thing was I couldn't lose. My first heat, my opponent just didn't catch a wave, and all the little dribbly waves came to me and I got through the heat. It was the first time I was disappointed I won. The next heat I was up against a guy called Jeff Novak, and I thought, *I can't let this guy beat me.* I made it all the way to the quarterfinals. We were due to leave for Europe the next day, but I'd made up my mind that I was going to fly home. I thought, *if I don't lose today, I'm not going to be able to pull it off.* Their flights were at the same time, and they'd want to know why I wasn't checking-in as well.

I was against Gary Elkerton in the quarters and I deadset made myself get a paddling interference. All the good waves came to me and I was beating him by a mile. So when he had priority and paddled for a wave, I just paddled for the wave with him. Everyone went, 'Why did you do that?' And I just went, 'Oh, I didn't realise.' I did it so slyly that no-one even noticed it was deliberate. And then I just packed up and went home.

> **Paul Sargeant:** He went off the tour, and if he hadn't he probably would have self-destructed. Both him and Pottz at the same time – seventeen, eighteen, on tour with all this money, all this fame, got whatever they wanted, whenever they wanted it – they never got to know the value of money, even friends. As far as I know, apart from Hawaii when he did that little bit of labouring, the only time I'm aware of when he ever worked, he went and did one day's work experience at Cronulla leagues club, peeling prawns, and he ate so many of them that he went home sick at lunchtime.

> **Rabbit Bartholomew:** It came as a bit of a shock to me to hear that Occy had bailed out. I knew that he'd had some problems. There had been some signs that year in Hawaii, the

year he did the flip over the motorbike. There was no way he should have survived that. And he was definitely doing certain substances to excess, and he just got caught up in that whole thing. But I didn't realise that he was totally burning out.

I spent the rest of 1988 at home, not doing much at all, just resting and trying to get myself together. I actually made it to Hawaii that year, but I was already a bit overweight and my heart wasn't in it. Billabong was sponsoring the biggest event of the year at the end of the season in Hawaii; they wanted me to compete and hopefully get my mind back on the job. I got knocked out early in the Pipe Masters but I did better in the Billabong Pro, which was a mobile event again and just happened to be held at perfect Pipe early in the New Year. I had a pretty good heat against Damien Hardman in the third round and beat him. He just had to beat me to secure the title. He was coming out of this barrel and put his arm up to claim it, and the lip just caught him by the arm and threw him off. It was big perfect Pipe, and I was riding a 7'10" and starting to feel really good, getting through heats, getting the old feeling back.

Then I ran into some trouble in my quarterfinal with Luke Egan, and I think I even started throwing a few punches in a paddling hassle. He got me on an interference and I wasn't happy. Luke was a mate, but I wasn't myself and was starting to lose my grip. I was probably a bit jealous, too, because he was the new young goofy-footer making his mark at Pipeline, like I had just a few years earlier, but already my star seemed to be on the wane.

Luke was sitting wide at one point, and I felt like charging so I paddled deep and took off on one and Luke just dropped in. I went, 'What are you doing?' And he goes, 'I've got priority.' I hadn't even realised. I just went, 'Oh no, you do too.' I hadn't surfed a heat in six months and had forgotten all about the small matter of rules. And that was the end of my run. Luke ended up making the final against Barton Lynch, who won the contest and the world title that day in a fairytale finish, but my head was a million miles away. I finished the season in forty-fifth place and a lot of people quite understandably figured my pro surfing career was coming to an inglorious end, another casualty of the tour lifestyle.

Rabbit Bartholomew: It was really bad, it was primitive. There were several casualties . . . I was on the ASP board of directors, and that was something I was very aware of. You couldn't have sixteen-year-olds on the world tour, just throwing them bucket-loads of money. You couldn't do it – it was going to fuck them up. No mentorship, some sporadic coaching, no financial management, no-one working out the itineraries and your life. No-one. Young guys seventeen years old were just given a wheelbarrow full of money, and they can tell everyone to get fucked and they're encouraged to. It's a recipe for disaster. There's a long list – so many.

Jodie Cooper: You either saw him absolutely trim, so physically fit – the full athlete – or he looked the other way, he really let himself go. There was no in-between: so buff and lean or he had that tendency to put on the pork. And you could see that in his mental state. He was quite overweight – hair in his face, long and greasy, food on his face – and you could just see where his head was, because he was at that stage where he didn't care about anything.

Someone like Occy, with such legend status, there's people who want to latch on to that and bleed him dry to boost their own credibility, taking him down the wrong path. I witnessed a lot of that. Occy definitely had that really vulnerable side. He's a really extreme guy, there's no middle ground – he's a gladiator or a sloth.

Chapter Nine

The Elvis Years

I tried to get my act together and jump back on tour in '89, but the old feeling and focus just wasn't there. It was never going to work. I had a couple of results – a third and a fifth in France most notably – but my head was elsewhere. I was beginning to discover the joys of travelling to great waves for film and photo shoots; the sort of exotic travel to quality waves that I'd been missing on tour. It was like therapy for me. We had a great trip to G-Land for a classic Billabong movie called *Filthy Habits*, with Ronnie Burns, and that wave on the edge of the Javanese jungle just blew my mind. Ronnie was super-impressive there and really opened my eyes to the joys of drawing long lines, and making big turns and long barrels the hallmarks of your surfing. It just all felt a lot more real than the pro tour theatrics in shitty waves, trying to fit three little snaps into a two-foot shorey.

There was another epic trip to Reunion Island, featured in the movie *Pump*, again with Ronnie. That place really suited my surfing – this big wrapping left that kept bending back at you, just asking to be belted. There was no-one there and the place was just amazing: beautiful girls, warm water, great food and no crowds. We were staying just across the bay from this wave, St Leu, and one afternoon it was pretty small and I was the only one out. A few sets ended up coming through and I had an amazing session. The cameraman noticed I was getting a few waves and decided to shoot it right from the house we were staying in. It turned into one of my favourite video segments.

Andy Irons: The first time I heard of Occ was from my cousin Jason. He was the guy that got me into surfing, and his favourite surfer was Occy, so he showed me a bunch of shots of him in the surf magazines and this one surf movie, Billabong's *Pump*. It was the best movie I'd ever seen, especially that section in Reunion when he was all by himself. I just thought it was amazing, just his style and how fast he went and how cool he looked – he looked like such the cool person. He had the long hair and epitomised everything I wanted to be like. Perfect style and everything.

Pam Occhilupo: Mark's behaviour continued to be erratic. He was living with a friend on the Gold Coast, having had to sell his lovely unit to pay off his debts. He surfed only occasionally, competing in some events and bypassing others. I didn't see much of him that year as one or both of us were travelling a lot. In 1990 I took six months off work to go on my own world tour – halted when I met Luciano in Cairns, and now, four children and thirty years later, continuing. Strangely enough, as I set off, I met Mark completely by accident at Sydney Airport. He was just returning from spending Christmas in Hawaii, and we sat down and had a very special hour together. Times like these were precious. Mark would open up and talk freely about his hopes and his feelings, as he wouldn't do on other occasions. He told me about his new girlfriend, Anna, a top model who he was very much in love with. This was the first serious–sounding relationship since he had broken up with Jenny a year ago – a long time for Mark – and I was thrilled for him.

LOSING LUCIANO

I have always been able to put on weight quickly and lose it quickly, and my weight fluctuated wildly during my time off tour, as I'd try and muster the energy for some sort of comeback. But it was just too soon. By mid-1990 I was doing all right, competing regularly and ranked thirty-sixth, but then I got the news that my dad was critically ill. I just came straight home.

Dad hadn't gone to work one day, which was really out of character, so my sister Fleur took him to the doctor and they found a brain tumour. He was given six weeks to live. I was living on the Gold Coast by then, and I came down to see him in hospital a couple of times, but as he deteriorated I just found it too hard. And when he passed away I couldn't deal with it. It was a really sad time.

That generation of men seemed like such strong figures. They never said much about how they were feeling. You knew you were going to get in trouble if you mucked up, but you didn't get a lot of accolades when you were good – which just made you try harder to win their approval. I know there were times when my dad was really bummed at me, when I was getting into trouble. He'd always say to me, 'Whatever you do, don't you ever go anywhere near drugs.' And I'd say, 'I promise, Dad.' And he'd say, 'I'd never talk to you again', trying to scare me, and it *did* scare me. But then he'd find out that I'd been messing up and he'd be so angry – scary angry. When he was gone I felt terrible that I'd ignored his advice and we had never had a chance to talk about it. I wasn't that bad at a young age, but I wished I'd had the chance to confess how out of control my life had become at times, and maybe that would have helped.

I also really regretted not wanting to know his culture. It was hard in Australia at the time I was growing up because we'd be called 'wogs', and so I distanced myself from my background. But I was always fascinated by it, despite myself. I can still remember hanging in the pool on a Sunday afternoon, listening to them talk Italian and play Italian music while they drank KB Lager. I'd take a couple of sly sips when no-one was looking. I always wondered about Dad. 'Luciano Occhilupo' sounds like a Mafia name, and my dad always promised me that he wasn't in the Mafia. But if I'd had a few too many beers, it was always a good story for the boys.

It's like the old saying, you don't know what you've got till it's gone, and I was sorry I'd never become closer to my father. But he was such a good dad to me, and I missed him terribly.

Pam Occhilupo: It was in Urbino, coincidentally the birth-place of my ancestor, the great painter Raphael – my maiden name – that I heard the terrible news that Luciano was dying. We had been speaking frequently on the phone while I was travelling. He had sounded really happy and carefree, mak-ing jokes. Funnily enough, he sounded better than he had for some time . . . My life fell apart at that moment because, in spite of our volatile marriage, I still loved Luciano very much and I knew he always loved me. I must admit that I was too shocked and steeped in my own grief to think of how the chil-dren were coping. It must have been much worse for them being alone and witnessing Luciano's deterioration.

Mark had been contacted, of course, and had come down to Sydney. He had always had a fear of death, even as a toddler, and would continually ask me deep questions about what happened when we died. He had already experienced the deaths of three of his close mates through accidents, drugs and alcohol, so I felt it was going to be especially tough for him. When I finally got back to Sydney after many long hours on the plane, Alex picked me up and we went straight to the hospital. I was prepared to see a very sick man, but I couldn't believe my eyes. This wonderful handsome man was now a mere skeleton, his head exposing an enormous scar where he had been opened up and closed again because of the inoperable tumour.

Fleur Occhilupo: Alex rang me and said, 'Dad's at home.' He never missed a day of work. He was a hard worker. I said, 'What's wrong?' She said, 'I don't know.' I'd only been studying medicine for six months [in Newcastle], so I got in the car and drove all the way to Sydney. I got home and Dad was standing in front of the computer, where he always was, in his study, and something had gone wrong with the computer. All the numbers were swimming on the screen. And I said, 'Dad, why aren't you at work?' And he said, 'I don't know, I forgot.' I asked, 'Dad, have you got a headache?' And he replied, 'Only when I think about it.' So I thought, *oh, here we go.* So I got the local GP to come over. This was the hardest day of my life.

The doctor said it was due to isolation, because Dad was living there on his own, and he sent him to a psychiatrist. So we were sitting there in front of a psychiatrist, and it only took her two minutes before she said, 'Send him for a CAT scan.' Dad started playing around like a little kid. He was rapidly going downhill, because when you have a tumour in your frontal lobe it can be there for years, but then there's a cut-off point where it just becomes too big. And so he went and had the scan, and then I took him straight to my GP, my mentor and one of the reasons I studied medicine. She looked down and said, 'Fleur, six weeks.' Dad was playing with her stethoscope and I said, 'Dad, stop playing with that – that's expensive equipment.' She said, 'Don't worry, let him play with what he wants.' He looked at me and asked, 'Why are you crying,

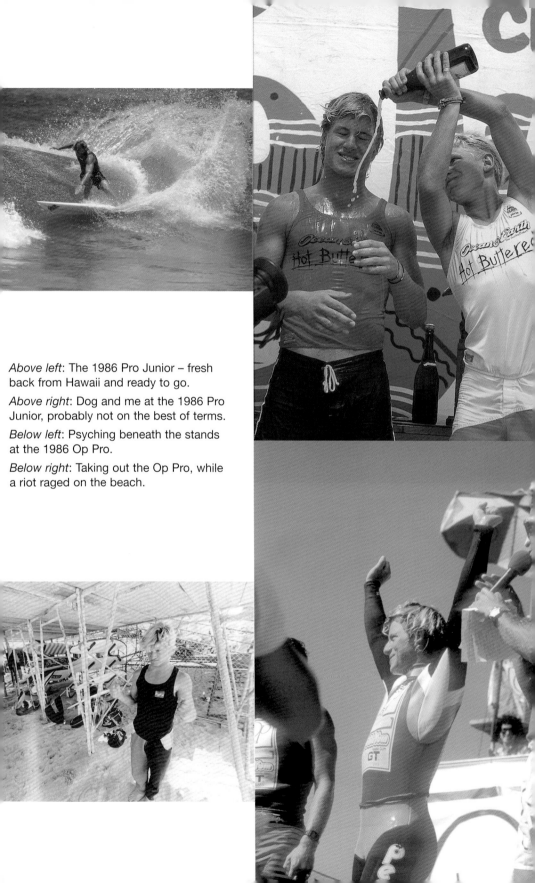

Above left: The 1986 Pro Junior – fresh back from Hawaii and ready to go.

Above right: Dog and me at the 1986 Pro Junior, probably not on the best of terms.

Below left: Psyching beneath the stands at the 1986 Op Pro.

Below right: Taking out the Op Pro, while a riot raged on the beach.

Above: Finding my line on a glassy Bells wall, 1987.

Right: A rare shot of me declining a beer from Gary Green at the Fosters comp in Newquay.

Below: Me and Geoff Booth in an early Peak wetsuit ad.

Above: A classic Peak ad, shot on an almost flat day at Steamers Beach in a one-foot shorebreak after a fruitless drive to Black Rock. One of my favourite shots. Thanks, Sarge.

Below: Thinking about home and ready to jump ship at the 1988 Op Pro at Huntington Beach vs. Gary Elkerton.

Above left: The colourful board design I came up with during my wild Hawaiian winter.

Above right: Luke wondering what the hell I'm doing, dropping in at the 1988 Coke contest.

Below left: Carrying a few extra pounds at the 1988 Billabong Pro in Hawaii.

Below right: Greeny and me, synchronised surfing at the Coke contest.

Above: Shooting for the sky as I take on the role of free-surfer.

Below: Big stormy day at Sunset.

Above left: Anna and me on the beach, before I started packing on the pounds.

Above right: Getting into my junk-food period – looks like a Mars Bar in one hand and a sausage roll in the other.

Below: Surfing down at the farm, my little south coast retreat during my reclusive days.

Above: The result of my failed comeback attempt in 1992 – my boards that got trashed by the beach tractor in France.

Below: Getting into my free-surfing in my time off tour, early 1990s.

Above: Soaking up the morning sun at J-Bay at Cheron's house, one of my favourite places in the world.

Below: Enjoying cutting loose in my time off tour.

Fleur?' And I said, 'Do you want to know, Dad?' He said, 'No, not really.' He forgot to go to work one day and my GP was right: it was six weeks to the day.

Pam: The first few days he could speak in English, but then he only spoke in Italian. I spent most of my time in the hospital, and he was speaking in odd words. The nurse said, 'Oh, he can't take his eyes off you. How long were you married? When did you marry?' I couldn't think and he piped up with the date . . . Luciano was different from anyone I'd ever met. I had lots of boyfriends, and a husband before him, but even after thirty years together he just always made me feel all weak. I never got over it. He was gorgeous. No other man ever interested me.

Mark and I made a long chain out of flowers from the funeral and, in true surfing tradition, went down to the beach, where Mark donned his wetsuit and surfed out to lay the flowers on the ocean. That was a moment which stays vividly in my mind – just Mark and I casting flowers on the ocean in memory of our beloved husband and father. I felt Luciano could see it too, and to this day I have felt his presence beside me. I still ask him what I should do and receive the answers too.

Fleur: Dad was an amazing man, a tower of strength, and when he died we all fell apart . . . Mark was born on the sixteenth of June and Dad died on the fifteenth of June. I think Mark felt that he disappointed Dad, and I think he found that hard to deal with while Dad was dying. But I just said to him over the years, 'Dad was so proud of you. You're exactly like Dad, even bigger and better and stronger.'

Pam: Later, at a family conference, Luciano's specialist told us that the tumour had probably been growing for twenty years. So this was why my husband had gradually changed from the charming, witty person I fell in love with to someone who never appeared to get any joy out of life. He had never complained of headaches, but after he died I found packets of pain tablets hidden all over the house.

With Mum on her own at Kurnell, and me still undecided about my future, I decided to move back to Sydney and live with her in the old family home. There was another reason for wanting to go home. My girlfriend at the time, Anna, was a successful model. She was from Mudgeeraba on the Gold Coast, and I'd met her up there, but she wanted to move to Sydney for her modelling career, because she was working with Chadwick Models and there was more work in Sydney. I wanted to be with her, but she couldn't do the tour with me because she had a career of her own. So we got to hang out at home, and I really liked it. I put on a lot of weight but she didn't care. She's like a country girl, so she loved Kurnell.

It was such a different lifestyle for me. I'd take her to modelling jobs sometimes, or we'd go down the coast – all the way down to Geroa, Seven Mile Beach. I had this little beach hidden away in between there and Kiama, a good little surf spot where no-one used to go. There was an electric fence there to keep people out and the cows in, and I buzzed myself a few times clambering over it. The bigger I got the more I got buzzed! I was pretty big by then and I didn't want anyone to see me in the surf, so I'd sneak down there once a week by myself.

At first, I loved being at home and I loved Kurnell. I'd been on tour from age sixteen to twenty-two. I still really felt like a teenager, or felt like I missed my teens, and I just wanted to go home and see my mates. But then I got stuck at home and didn't want to leave, or couldn't.

Soon after, as if to compound my grief, the great Hawaiian surfer and dear friend Ronnie Burns was killed in a trail-bike accident.

We'd travelled a lot together for Billabong and were really close. I was devastated and flew to Hawaii for the funeral. Ronnie was good friends with Buddy McCray and used to hang around the house at Sunset. We often surfed Rocky Point together, and the inside bowl at Rocky Lefts is still know as RB's because he always used to surf it. He would hang in that rip and surf those little left suck-ups, and that was my favourite place too. And you can only imagine how good he was out at Pipe. They called him Big Red, and he had the longest arms. Every time a fifteen-footer that no one wanted came through, he'd be on it, because he had the arms to paddle into it. Losing him so suddenly in the prime of life was a huge blow for all of us who knew and loved him.

All of this contributed to me losing the will to surf and slowly sinking into a depression where I just didn't want to get off the couch or see anyone. I started watching TV all day long and getting chicken and chips from the take-away place next door for lunch and dinner. I might have been okay if it had still been a fruit shop. I might have just got into my yoga and really veged out, literally. But while I'd been away on tour it had changed to a take-away food joint. The chicken and chips were too good, and the bacon-and-egg rolls were too good in the morning. That place became my nemesis. The owners, Steve and Effi, are still there – they're really nice Greek people, just like family to me. But there went my waistline. It was no fault of theirs, I just couldn't keep away from the joint. This diet, combined with a daily sixpack while spending the days reclined on the couch watching TV, led to what I politely refer to as my 'Elvis period'.

Pam Occhilupo: Mark decided to come down to live with me and brought Anna with him. We were a strange three-some: Mark and I still trying to cope with our grief and not much help to each other, while Anna was full of joy, living with her lover and immersing herself in the heart of the modelling world. Mark had gone onto his 'chicken-and-chips diet' and watched TV all day. His weight blew up and he avoided all phone calls. I was becoming an accomplished liar, manufacturing excuses as to why he couldn't (read *wouldn't*) answer the phone. He very rarely surfed, and avoided his friends. In fact, he was sinking deeper into depression every day.

Anna went home for Christmas, and Mark and I could wallow in our own misery. The first Christmas without Luciano was pretty tough. Alex invited us to her place, and poor Mark had nothing respectable to wear because he had put on so much weight. He had been living in an old stretched tracksuit for months, and now I found myself searching cheap clothing stores for a pair of shorts large enough to fit him. The very largest size only just encompassed his thickening girth. He was so reluctant to leave the house and would have preferred, I'm sure, to eat chicken and chips for Christmas dinner in his own home.

I always worked at the *Herald* on Christmas Day, and Mark had to get a taxi in to meet me. I remember coming out of the building to see this grim figure sitting on the kerb outside the *Herald* building in Broadway, with head bent and eyes glued on the ground so no-one would recognise him. The sight almost broke my heart.

Paul Sargeant: He was out there for seven months, wouldn't answer phone calls or whatever, and after seven months I just went out one day and parked in the driveway and went, 'Occ, I know you're in there. I'm not moving until you come out.' And I think Anna was there and she said, 'He won't come out', so I started beeping the horn. I said, 'Come out or I'm just going to lay on the horn.' And, anyway, this huge, fat, white, greasy whale came to the door. He was massive, like the old Marlon Brando: puffed cheeks, double chin, hair was black and greasy and down to his shoulders. He was *white* – he just looked like a greasy fat wog. I couldn't believe it. He went, 'Don't tell anyone, will ya.' That was the period when all he'd leave the house for was to go to the fried chicken shop next door. That was pretty rad. That was a reaction to his father's death. He didn't accept it at all. He never really acknowledged the grief.

Richard Maurer: When he had his first fat stint down at Kurnell, me and him used to go for quick little quiet surfs by ourselves down at Garie and that, once a week on Sundays. And we'd still go down and have a little hit of tennis at the rec club, just to try and get him fit. I really didn't like seeing him how he was, but I knew he needed time because he'd been on the circuit since he was sixteen and never had time to take a step back. The pro circuit is really no holiday; it was a party scene every weekend. During the '80s the tour was fast. He told me, 'On the tour you race to see who can eat fastest.' That's fucking ridiculous.

After the first time he gave up, he wasn't even wearing Billabong wetsuits. I was living up on the beachfront, and he came up to my window and goes, 'Hey, Rich, do you want to go for a surf?' I've just gone, 'What the fuck are you wearing?' He goes, 'Oh, I gave all my wetsuits away.' I go, 'What do you mean you gave all your wetsuits away? You're sponsored by Billabong and you're wearing Rip Curl.' He's like, 'What's the matter?' I went, 'What's the matter? You're hanging up at these guys' place smoking heaps of bongs.' I thought that was really uninspiring for him, and it sort of got worse. At that time he was probably doing a lot of drugs. It just got him down. He missed out on a lot. He was in a full depressive state then. I probably didn't help getting up him, but I thought, *I'm not going to not say anything* . . . He'd put on heaps of beef but, the thing is, at Kurnell nobody saw him. He'd go down the Kurnell rec club and play the pokies and have a few beers, go home and buy half a chicken and chips and a Pepsi.

Nick Carroll: He was no longer a force in the sport, and the sport was changing so fast with Kelly Slater and company coming into the picture. It was completely inconceivable that he'd make a comeback. Gordon at the time was totally against Occy trying to make a comeback. People further down the track have said Gordon should have believed in him more. It wasn't a matter of believing in him. It wasn't a matter of him making a comeback. He had psychological problems. It wasn't a good idea for him to be going back on the tour. You could only see it totally destroying him. There have been a lot of casualties, and you just don't make it back. But when you're talking about a surfer of his ability, anything's possible. It's lucky that he was actually still young enough to make it back. When he exploded he was still pretty young.

Vince Lawder (former Billabong team manager): When it's evolving, you don't realise it's evolving that badly until the wheels totally fall off. He just came home and turned into a recluse and stayed in Cronulla for ages and ages and ages. I remember ringing him up for this and that, and it wasn't going to happen. I remember trying to get him motivated to do something, and I eventually talked him into coming down to Bells: 'You don't have to do much, mate. Just go out and do the expression session and get a couple of photos and hang out; and if the waves are going off somewhere, just grab some of the grommets and get in the car and go surfing.' And he did it, and I remember the expression session that year was perfect six-foot Bells. He was carrying the extra weight, and a lot of people were wondering how he was going to surf – we all kind of were a little bit. He'd just come off the bottom and do these big turns and take chunks out of the wave. That beautiful Occy flow and style and power, and with the extra weight he was actually throwing a couple more gallons of spray . . . It was pretty impressive. The juniors were watching, just going, 'Wow, that's Occy.'

ROTTNEST ISLAND AND THE KILLER WHALES

Eventually, I lost the weight quickly. I had a dream one night that I lost the weight and started surfing again, and when I woke up the next day that's exactly what I set about doing. I was still big but I slowly got my surfing back into some kind of form. Billabong encouraged me to get out and stop being a recluse. I was wary of jumping back on tour and Gordon was dead against it, but they sent me on a few trips interstate and it helped to get out and see a few people again.

Rottnest Island has always been a really special place to me. It has some kind of trippy energy. I've heard old stories of Aborigines being massacred, and there are definitely spirits lurking out there. I've had some wild experiences over the years. Around this time, I'd go along to the Billabong junior events, surf with the kids and put on expression sessions. It was a good way for me to keep in touch with the surfing world while I wasn't on tour, and we always had a good time. There are heaps of waves on Rottnest, and this one day we were surfing a place called Cathedral Rock. It was only small but it gets really good, kind of a deep-water wave breaking close to the cliffs.

I was out there with a few of the grommets and my old mate Wayne Murphy, and Vince Lawder was on the cliff videoing. I was the furthest out and remember being in a really relaxed zone. I can even remember the song that was going through my head at the time. It was Queen's 'Bohemian Rhapsody', that bit at the end where it goes, 'Nothing really matters, anyone can see.' It's a weird song and I've no idea why it was in my head, but I was right at the end where it goes, 'Any way the wind blows . . .' And just as I got to the end, only ten feet away, this dorsal fin appeared. I swear it was six-foot high out of the water, like a scene from *Jaws*, and its eye looked straight at me. I turned white as a ghost. I figured I was staring at the biggest shark on Earth. It turned out to be a killer whale, but I had no idea. I couldn't even move for a second or two. It was swimming in a wave, and I just shat myself and tried to catch the same wave, but it wouldn't break. It should have broken because it was a set wave, but the whale was so big it stopped the wave from breaking and I missed it.

I turned around and another killer whale jumped clean out of the water, just behind me. All the kids saw it jump, and there was absolute pandemonium in the water. It was radical. No-one else had seen the first one but they'd all seen the second one jump. The next thing we knew there were fish everywhere, salmon jumping out of the water and throwing themselves up onto the rocks, trying to escape. The whole ocean was suddenly so alive. We did a pretty fair impersonation of the salmon and just about ran across the water up onto the rocks as fast as we could.

It was almost sunset, and we could see about twelve killer whales swimming around. We sat on the rocks and watched them swimming in formation in two groups of six, crossing over and herding the salmon and then chowing into them. The water just went green. It's a really rare occurrence, but our friend George Simpson, who's a professional fisherman, reckons he'd seen it once or twice before. Vince rang the TV station and the Channel 7 helicopter flew over to film it and interviewed us for the news that night. We were all pretty shaken up. We were staying at this brand-new resort on the island, and Mullman kept coming to my room that night going,

'Fuck, I can't believe what happened.' He'd had about twenty beers just trying to come down.

> **Vince Lawder:** It went so quiet, all the marine life disappeared. Murphy said the only other time he'd seen it like that was at Cactus [South Australia] just before a shark attack. We were up on the hill and could see what was going on, the orcas just coming up out of the water. No-one had ever seen them there before, but they were following the salmon. There's a little harbour there, and we saw one of the killer whales come in behind the boys and herd all the salmon back to the rest of the pack – there was just a feeding frenzy. One of the big ones came out of the water with so much power.

EASTERN TENGGARA AND OCCY'S LEFT

I started getting myself together, working on my surfing and fitness. I felt like a bear that had been hibernating and was slowly coming back to life. The trips away with film-maker Jack McCoy to make the Billabong movies were always a great way for me to get back in tune with my surfing, free of distractions, to clear my head and get fit.

Jack was always on the lookout for new locations and he had a good friend, Claude, who was building a resort in a really remote part of Indonesia. We flew from Bali on the milk run to Eastern Tenggara on this dodgy little domestic plane. We were picked up at a tiny airport in the middle of nowhere and drove for at least four hours on the bumpiest dirt road you can imagine. I think we were all starting to have our doubts, but it turned out to be one of the most amazing trips of my life.

Sunny Garcia was with us, and he likes his mod cons and wasn't too sure about the whole deal. The place was so primitive.

When we got there the huts weren't finished, and we had to make these little makeshift mattresses on the floor. The restaurant wasn't finished either, but they managed to feed us each day.

The surf was only around three feet, but you could tell it was a quality wave. Jack was filming from the water and his offsider, Gordo the Great, was shooting from the land. We were surfing by ourselves all day, but Sunny was pretty over it. He didn't like roughing it and didn't want to stay. He lasted about two weeks and he was ripping, and we were having a ball, but the surf was small. Jack was begging him: 'Please stay, there's a swell coming.' But he said, 'Nuh, I'm out of here.'

I stayed because there was no way Jack was going to let me go, but I was also having fun. And I wanted to see the wave with a bit of size. Sure enough, a few days after Sunny split, it was six to eight feet and I was the only one out. Jack and Gordo filmed, and I surfed all by myself like that for two days. It was unbelievable, some of the best sessions of my life. Jack would never let you come in when it was like that. 'Get back out there, get back out there,' he'd growl whenever I wanted to come in and eat or just relax for a little while.

One time I was out there paddling for a wave and this shark, a brown shark, came swimming along beside me. I could almost touch it. I shat myself and paddled straight into the impact zone, duck-dived a wave and let it take me over the falls. I came up with a snapped board, just freaking. Jack just looked at me and went, 'What the fuck are you doing?' I could barely speak. 'There's a massive shark,' I babbled. Jack was cool as a cucumber. 'They're out there all the time. Don't worry, they're nothing. They don't even bite. Get back out there.' So I had to get another board and get back out there.

One night all these villagers came down with spears and made a bit of a scene. They weren't after us, but they weren't happy about the workers who had been brought in from another island to build the resort. I don't know what had gone down, but it looked like trouble. The local tribes in the area still settled their differences in bloody battles, and we were freaking out. So we ran to get Claude, and he had to come down and talk to them in their native language and managed to calm things down.

Gordo the Great is always fun to have on a trip – there's never a dull moment when he's around. One day we went into a village to do some filming and check it all out. The people were really cool and seemed happy to have us. They're right into their betel nut, and they were all chewing away with that classic red-mouthed, toothless smile. We all tried a bit – it makes you a little high, like kava, all relaxed and floaty. I was actually shitting red poo for ages afterwards. I thought I had piles. You're not supposed to swallow it, but it's hard not to when you're not used to it. I was chewing it and chewing it, trying to get a buzz, and Gordo the Great was filming us. I had red stuff running down my cheeks – it looked just like *Amityville Horror*. We were all laughing with the locals. The men chew it so much they lose all their teeth, and they get their wives to chew it for them first to soften it up. And I noticed this old granny chewing some betel nut; she must have been about ninety years old. She chewed it all into this slobbery ball and then offered it to me. I just went, 'Ah, no thanks' and nearly threw up.

Then Gordo walked around the corner from filming something else. I said, 'Hey, Gordo, this lady's got some betel nut for you.' And Gordo, being Gordo, just grabbed it and shoved it in his mouth. I went, 'Aaaah, that just came out of her mouth!' Gordo turned green and bolted – I'm sure he threw up. I was on the ground laughing so hard I think I actually wet my pants. Gordo's such a comedian, and he's usually the one playing practical jokes, but I got him that time.

The trip out was even worse than the trip in. They couldn't get a car for us, and in the end we eventually rode out in the back of a milk truck. It had no windows in the back, so we had to leave the doors open to get some air and then just about choked on exhaust fumes. We got our flight back to Bali on the sketchy plane, but we knew we'd been blessed with a unique experience.

John 'Gordo' Gordon: The chief took a bit of a shine to me and Occ and Jack, and we were the only three taken into his house. We've gone in and they've 'fessed up and told us how the Japanese did some really horrid things when they came through in the war. That's why the village is on this peak up high, so they can see anyone coming. Their most cherished possessions from this conflict are the actual scalps – these Japanese soldiers; they killed a few, and they had kept the scalps. Like the American Indians, they'd scalp them. The government got wind of them and confiscated six scalps, but they stashed another six. They were like trophies, like, *they gave us hell, but look what we've got.* So, the chief's there and we're on the betel nut, swaying around, and then we've been given the scalp show. I've been a cameraman for twenty years, I've seen a fair bit, but that was like, *wow, this was some Japanese kid who was probably twenty-two years old and a solider. Heavy, heavy . . .*

I come out and I'm still in shock from the scalp show. I was in a daze and looked the other way, and right at that moment this old lady – ninety years old with wrinkles on her wrinkles – has pulled a globule out of her mouth and offered it to Occ. I'm looking the other way, and he goes, 'Nah, I'm fine, but my mate Gordo, he'd love it.' And I've turned around and Occ goes, 'It's for you, put it in your mouth.' There's 300 villagers standing round in a semicircle out the front of the chief's house so I thought, *crikey, don't want to offend.* It'd be like spitting the kava out in Fiji. I've thrown it in my mouth and I'm sucking away on this globule, and Occy goes, 'She just had it in her mouth!' And I've thought, *oh well, I'm infected already, I don't want to lose the respect we've earnt.* I've sort of tied my neck in a knot, and nearly gagged, but tried to make out like I was savouring it. As I put it in my mouth the whole village has just erupted, so I saw the respect that was given straight back to us – so I've taken my lumps. But that night I did gargle a bit of Listerine.

Rod Dahlberg (shaper): When Occ was big, Sarge got me to make him a board, a 6'6". He rode that board in *Green Iguana*. By the end of the footage his pants were falling off. He would have been wearing a size 36 at the start, and the weight was just falling off him because Jack had him over there training. That board went unreal, and the surfing was really, really good. As I started shaping Occy's boards, and he started losing weight, we brought the volume down until we got to the magic dimensions: 6'3" by 18¾ by 2⅜. It was a lot easier to refine things once we established those dimensions.

Rusty Preisendorfer: After I launched my own brand in late '85, I did T-shirts for a couple of years. None of the big clothing companies seemed to mind too much. I wasn't really taken as a threat at the time. Then we segued into apparel in about 1988 or '89. As the R-dot gained momentum at the retail apparel level, more and more of the established surf apparel companies took a stand. At the time I was very bummed. I felt I had a lot to offer Occy – a natural chemistry and an intuitive understanding of what he needed in his equipment. On the flip side, after being in the clothing business for a few years, I understood and was somewhat flattered that I was taken as a commercial threat.

As the years ticked by, I always made a few boards for Occy, usually when he was passing through on his way to Europe. At one point an edict came down from the top at

Billabong: he, or any other Billabong team rider, was forbidden to ride my boards, logo or no logo. Even so, I would always build a couple for him on his way through to Europe . . . small logos and a can of white spray-paint included.

Gordon Merchant (from *Surfing Life*, 1991): When his father died, that was a very difficult period for him. He found it very difficult to cope. I was concerned about him and my future with him, where we were going. Just the fact that I've known him for such a long time, I knew what to do in the situation. I had a lot of faith in him, that he'd come through it. I just picked up the phone one day and he said, 'I'm back . . .' Now he wants to go to Hawaii and surf in the contests. I don't think he's got anything left to prove there. I think he should concentrate on getting footage for videos . . . You can get a surfer of less ability but more consistent who can get up the ratings. If there were ten or twelve contests with long waiting periods, I'd be more enthusiastic about it. It drains people. Occy's surfing better now than when he was on the circuit, particularly towards the end when he'd lost interest. They lose a lot of their free-surfing ability.

Chapter Ten

Manic in France

In 1992 I was on the comeback trail. I'd lost all the excess weight and felt like I was surfing well enough to make a serious run at the tour. There was a new two-tiered system, which meant instead of the old trials system there were two separate tours – the World Qualifying Series and the World Championship Tour. Because my ratings had fallen, I'd first have to slog it out on the WQS and do well enough to re-qualify before I could hope to make it on the WCT the following year. I did about ten WQS events that year, but the results weren't coming. I got a fifth at the Drug Offensive/Cleanwater Classic at Manly, but that was about it by mid-year.

The best thing I'd done for myself was buy a block of land up at Bilambil with the money I'd inherited from my father. It was about seventy grand, and I was really worried about blowing it, because money has always had a way of just slipping through my fingers. My old mate Rabbit was living up at Bilambil, I'd been to visit him there once or twice, and he was always raving about how nice it was. His place backed onto a golf course, and it was like the country up there – sweeping views of the coast and still close enough to town and the beach. Terranora Lakes Country Club was right there and Rab didn't mind the odd hit of a pokie, and neither did I back then. I bought this block of land just up the road, and it was probably the smartest thing I've ever done with my money. I was so proud of that block. I had it for years before I eventually built on it. I'd get a couple of mates, China O'Connor and Reg Riley, to come up and help me slash it every so often, pay them a bit of money or just buy a case of beer. We'd spend a few hours slashing the whole block by hand with machetes. The grass would grow about eight-feet tall in six months, and I used to love getting the boys up there and going at it.

Rabbit Bartholomew: He came to me and said, 'In about a week's time I'm going to get a cheque for $70,000,' which at that time was a pretty decent-sized cheque. And he said, 'I'm really, really worried about it', and I asked, 'Why?' He said, 'Well, I'm really worried about what I'm going to do with it.' And I said, 'Got ya, totally got ya. Mate, we're going to get you a piece of dirt. Meet me here, I'll pick you up, we'll go up to my house at Bilambil, we'll get on the blower, talk to all the real estate people.'

We drive up to Bilambil, McAlister Road, and we come round the corner and Occy goes, 'There, Rab, there's a block for sale.' I said, 'Okay, get the number, we'll put that on the list. It's going to be a long morning, let's start with that one.' And he gets on the phone and I start busying myself doing something else. When I tune into the conversation, he's going, 'Okay, um, so seventy-two grand? Okay. Can I buy it tomorrow?' And I raced towards him and go, 'No, you've got to haggle – no, don't do this.' And he goes, 'Can I buy it tomorrow at eleven o'clock?' So I got on the phone and said, 'Look, Mark doesn't have a lot of experience with this.' But, I swear, that moment he decided he was buying that block of land and nothing was going to stop him, and that's how it transpired.

This was around the time of the big tour meltdown in Europe, the massive one . . . I get a phone call while Occ's having the meltdown in Europe, from the real estate agent going, 'This contract – it's lapsed. He's lost his ten grand.' The moment you go over the thirty days with a contract like that, you have done your deposit. The guy can put it on the market again and pocket the money. Luckily, he was saved and we managed to settle the purchase. Occy was like Mr Magoo in a way. He was lucky he always had Gordon there, and Rab was there trying to do my little bit. Lots of people – Richard Maurer . . . there's a big list of people.

Somehow I managed to win a minor event in England in July '92, the Hot Tuna Surfmasters in Newquay. I was staying at a little bed-and-breakfast and had a nice walk across the golf course to the beach. I was staying by myself – over the years I've always won more contests when I've been staying by myself. Being so superstitious, it's just easier to get into your own rhythm and eat the same food, walk the same way to the event, all the little things that seem to be working for you. I hung out with this local guy, Grishka Roberts, a good surfer and a cool guy, and I was starting to feel the old flow coming back.

That win gave me the incentive to carry on and have a real crack at a comeback, but it was probably the worst thing that could have happened to me. When the tour was in Portugal we received the news that a much-loved Australian pro surfer, Mark Sainsbury, had died surfing his local break, at Avoca on the NSW Central Coast. None of us could believe it. He was a fit, popular, hugely talented surfer cut down in his prime, apparently by a brain aneurysm. The whole tour was in shock and, in our grief, a whole bunch of us went off the rails.

Paul Sargeant: In '92 when we were in Portugal, Sanga died back home and everybody lost it . . . Found drowned at Avoca. How could he *drown*, you know? Later we found out it was an aneurysm . . . Ross [Clarke-Jones] had minded a couple of Sanga's boards so he didn't have to take them all the way home, and we took one down to the beach. It was just super-grey, cold, freezing. We lit a fire, there was like twenty-five of us, on the sand flats on these little dunes before the beach, and we went round the circle and everybody said something. It got to Doug Silva and he started crying, and everyone was like, 'It's all right, man.' And we found out then that his father had died that week . . . And then we all started crying, every-body, it was incredible, just sitting there, freezing cold, really grey, foggy. And Ross went, 'Okay, let's burn this board.' He was only in board shorts – we were all wrapped up. We lit the board and, the second Ross put it in the water, the clouds parted on the horizon. There was this huge orange ball. We just all went, 'Wow.'

What started as a wake turned into a prolonged bender throughout the European leg, and by the time I got to France I was in full-on meltdown. Then we got the news that my old mate Rabbit had been diagnosed with a malignant melanoma and was having an operation to remove it. When you're a young pro surfer travelling the world you sometimes feel a bit invincible, but suddenly it just all felt so precarious. I was so upset by Sanga's death and Rabbit's news, it was just like another body blow after my father's death. I felt that familiar sensation creeping back of losing my grip, and people were really worried about me. And I did feel like I was losing my grip on reality. On the surface, I was having a wild old time, going out every night and going extra hard, but everyone could see I was out of control.

I was staying with Nicky Wood, and it was really heavy because ordinarily Sanga probably would have been staying with us. I just didn't cope. My girlfriend, Anna, heard the stories back in Austra-lia and flew over to France to try and help, but I wasn't ready to be helped and just shunned her, and she flew home heartbroken. I can only vaguely remember even seeing her, but I just didn't want to be tamed. I wanted to keep going mad. It was pretty scary for everyone, except me, because in my own mind I felt like I knew what I was doing. But it was becoming increasingly obvious to everyone else that something was seriously wrong. It was hard to ignore when I decided to bury my surfboards on the beach in Hossegor one day. It took me a long time to dig that hole, and I thought it was a great idea, stashing my boards at the beach instead of having to lug them back to where I was staying. It seemed to be some kind of sign the next morning when a tractor was criss-crossing the beach collecting rubbish and virtually destroyed them.

I had a heat with Barton Lynch that morning and I was surfing without a leash, even though it was four to six feet. I was so sick of signing autographs by then but, when my board washed ashore and someone picked it up for me, I decided to sign an autograph for them. Then I figured I may as well do a few more while I was at it. I spent about ten minutes on the beach signing autographs while Barton surfed the heat on his own. Needless to say, I was knocked out, and set about wreaking more havoc on land.

I was drinking all the time and eventually got kicked out of the contest area. I was hassling people, ripping people's T-shirts, wanting to fight, being a complete idiot. I honestly don't remember a whole lot about it, but I heard all the stories later, almost as if they were about someone else. I got in a fight on the beach with this French guy flying a kite, because his kite took a dive and almost hit me. It turned out he was an off-duty cop, so then the cops were after me.

Barton Lynch: He tried to spear me in the head with his board. I had him that morning and wasn't really aware of where he was at. I rocked up and the waves are three to five feet, perfect right-handers. I'm trying to prepare myself for what I figure is a real battle: Occy in perfect rights. He's looking a bit second-hand and going, 'The waves are fucked, let's shut it down' and he started trying to push the contest scaffolding over. And then he sits down and starts eating sand. I gave him some water and went, 'Here, rinse your mouth.' I was starting to feel a little uneasy about it. I had a pretty good heat, I think I had him combo-ed, and he got priority and said, 'You're not going to get another wave.' I said, 'I think you need a wave, not me.' I sucked him into one, he got one, and I got the one behind it. As I ride by he throws his board at me, tries to hit me in the head with it. Then he's walking along the beach signing autographs.

Paul Sargeant: The following week we went to Hossegor, and the party just continued. We just got completely drunk, we destroyed that hotel in Portugal, we were driving around in the hills going crazy. In Hossegor, it just continued. We got completely and absolutely smashed every day – Herring, Powell, myself, Occy – we'd be there first thing in the morning. Herro had started to spin out. He always followed what Occy did. The two of them have an incredible parallel in their development, both freaks. And I think Sanga dying really brought on the gush and the realisation of his father's death . . . Occy would turn up at the Rock Food about eleven o'clock wearing blue board shorts and carrying a blanket like Linus and a piece of bamboo. He was staying at Maurice [Coles'] place. He said, 'You've got to book me a ticket to China, Sarge.' I went, 'Why, Occ?' 'Well, look, it's bamboo. I found it on the way down here. It's a sign – I nearly tripped over it.' 'Really?' And he started going weirder and weirder . . . We were all starting to get worried about him and talking about it with Maurice. 'What are we going to do? What are we going to do?' It started getting to the point where we were having to threaten him: 'Mate, you're going to have to slow down or we're going to put you on a plane.'

Kelly Slater: I actually surfed against him in a heat in '92 at Hossegor, which ended up ironically being my first win on tour and, I think, his last event for a long time. It was when he buried his boards in the sand and forgot about them, and they got run over by the beach-cleaning machine. He tried to fight me the week before on a dark sidewalk. He was out of control. The competitor in the back of my head was thinking, *fuck him*, but a bigger piece of me was watching a hero of mine, and future friend, fall – and it was sad and frightening. There was nothing I could do but hope he didn't get himself killed.

Maurice Cole: He knocked on my door and I saw him arrive at the house. He was running up after coming from Portugal. As I opened the door, he burst into tears and just sort of went, 'Mate, can I please stay?' And I said, 'Mate, you're always welcome.' I didn't really understand at that stage . . . He started really getting weird, and by 'weird' I mean he wasn't that interested in surfing and he was starting to drink and smoke a lot. Then he couldn't sleep, so he'd go out at night to Rock Food or wherever. But what he was doing was coming home on light, in the morning, and then trying to go surfing. Then I realised he wasn't sleeping. He hadn't slept for a couple of days.

I was in the shaping bay really early in the morning, I remember it was still dark, and he came home and had this stick in his hand, and this stick in his hand was going to help him get home. And I said, 'Oh, you're going home?' And he said, 'Yeah, I'm gonna swim home.' I went, 'You're going to swim home. Okay, okay, you're going to swim home.' He said, 'I'm going to stop in Tiananmen Square and do some Tai Chi, and this is my Tai Chi stick.' And I looked at him and I was going, *huh? What the fuck's this*? Then he said, 'I'm going to have a shark cage.' And then I realised he was sort of semi-serious. His girlfriend, Anna, was on her way over, and I said, 'Anna's going to be here soon. It will all be good.' And he went, 'No, no, no, I don't know Anna anymore.' Then he just sort of wandered off again . . . It was getting a lot worse.

He was going out at night, and there was a kid going by on a little moped and he coat-hangered the kid. The kid had about five or six brothers, fishermen in Capbreton, so they were hunting him and wanting to kill him. We knew Occ was in the middle of having some kind of breakdown. I spoke to a psychiatrist and he said, 'You've got to get him to sleep.' And because he was staying with us, he'd come in a few times and scare the living fuck out of the kids, which really started to concern me. Because they loved him that much, they started getting scared of him dribbling around. He wasn't noticing the kids, where he was usually really attentive to them. So they picked up on the madness.

I remember Anne said, 'Right, you're eating now.' We made this big baguette sandwich for him and put two of the heaviest French sleeping pills you've ever come across in it. We all sat there and watched him, the fucker. The bull came out, and he fought those two sleeping pills for about an hour. He was nodding off on the couch, but he fought them and came to and walked around. I said, 'Just sit down, mate . . . cruise', and the next minute he was up out of the house. I had people everywhere trying to make sure he couldn't get into any trouble. This was part of his comeback tour, this was him relaunching himself, so to speak.

The ASP were so concerned that they wanted to get him arrested and locked up, and they'd come to me and gone, 'What can you do about it?' They laid it on me. 'If you can't control him and get him out of the public eye, if he's going to keep going like this, on behalf of the ASP we're going to call

Occy

the police and get him arrested and get him committed.' I was nearly in tears, I didn't know what to do. I've got Occ sitting in front of me, and I'm going, 'Occ, are you there? Can you hear me? Are you going to get this? You've got to fucking behave yourself. We've got to get you away from here. You're not allowed to come to the beach anymore, because they're going to put you in a fucking mental hospital. They're going to lock you up, mate. They're going to put you in a padded cell. Am I getting through, mate?' I can still see it now. The tears welled up in his eyes and he just went, 'Don't let them do that to me, Maurice. Don't let them do that.' I was fucking in tears, going, 'Look, I'm not going to let them do it to you, but I've got to get you off the beach.' None of us knew what to do.

Every now and then, when I'd thrown that scenario at him, there were a couple of moments of real clarity and sense, where he was actually getting it, and I thought maybe he's going to pull this off and he's going to come right himself. But we didn't even know how to get him home. If he blew up on a plane, he might bring the plane down, because he had that – I had a couple of wrestles with him – insane strength. For the first time in my life I had to deal with something where I had no idea what I was doing. I didn't know if I was doing good, bad or otherwise. I'm just running on gut feel. Luckily, he had people around. He had a nucleus of people who really cared about him and looked after him.

I decided I needed to lie low for a while and bolted down to Spain. I had some friends at a surfboard company called Pukas and hung with them and managed to mellow out a bit. They were cool guys and I felt like I could relate to them. I was virtually penniless by this point, and they took me in and looked after me. The guys on tour were freaking out, going, 'Occy's gone to Spain and he's never coming back.' And I thought I might never come back. I'd been staying with

Maurice Cole in France, and he was really worried about me and was ringing Inigo, the owner of Pukas, to see what was going on. And Inigo was telling him, 'It's okay, he's cruising, he's mellowed out.'

Spain was perfect for me because they didn't speak English and I didn't speak Spanish, so they didn't think I was crazy. I was having a great old time, going out to all the bars in this little town called Zarautz. I had left everything behind in France and had no clothes apart from what I was wearing, and this one old pair of gym boots with the soles falling off. I'd wrap the laces around them to hold them together. I must have been quite a sight. Inigo's wife, Marian, would just laugh at me and took me to San Sebastian, where all the best shopping was, and bought me this beautiful new pair of boots. They were called Panama Jacks and they were so nice.

After spending a couple of weeks in Spain, I was starting to feel okay again and, with my new boots and some new boards from Pukas, I thought I was killing it. I started surfing again and went back to France to say sorry to Maurice for going crazy and freaking everyone out. Then I headed home with my new boots and boards, thinking I was ready to get back to business and rekindle my surfing career. But I was about to learn it wasn't going to be as simple as all that. I had a long way to go before I was going to be ready to even think about competing. I flew home straight into a friend's bucks party, and the partying just continued, which did me no good at all.

Chapter Eleven

Elvis, Revisited

I eventually retreated back to the Gold Coast to lick my wounds. Somehow I pulled myself together enough to conjure up a fourth at the City Beach Pro at Surfers Paradise, but that proved to be my last hurrah for quite a while as my second Elvis period kicked in. That's when I met my future wife, Beatrice, and began what would prove to be a long hibernation. Rabbit dragged me out one night to Surfers Paradise, because he was worried I was turning into a bit of a hermit. I think Beatrice was supposed to be set up with Rabbit, but she and I just clicked. We started talking and I thought, *wow, this chick's pretty cool.* She said she was studying psychology and I said, 'Perfect, because I'm crazy. I can be your case study.' I guess I was still kind of out there, but I was home amongst friends so I felt safe. She started laughing and went, 'You're funny.' And I went, 'No, I'm serious!' And she said, 'No, no, you're way too young.'

But I was really taken with her. I thought she was gorgeous and I kept ringing up a mutual friend, Mandy McKinnon, going, 'You've got to set us up' and she'd go, 'No way!'

Then one night I ran into her at the Hill Street nightclub in Coolangatta. We just picked up right where we left off, talked all night and were virtually inseparable from that moment on. Beatrice was older than me and had a young son, Rainer, and I think I welcomed that whole family environment at that point.

Beatrice Occhilupo: We actually met through Mandy McKinnon. We were going out for dinner – Mandy and her husband, Andy, and Rabbit, and we were going to watch the *Green Iguana* movie when it was first released. At the time I didn't know about pro surfing – that it even existed or that they got paid for what they did. The McKinnons were trying to match-make me to Rabbit the whole night. Both he and Mark were sitting opposite me at dinner, and Mark just kept staring at me. The next morning I was hanging out with Mandy again; we were at Cabarita Beach, maybe for an indigenous contest. Mark was there and saw me. At some point I started walking up the beach to go for a swim. He followed and came up alongside me, trying to make conversation. I pretty much ignored him. I didn't want to talk to him and just kept walking – and I guess that maybe that made him 'keener' or something.

Two weeks later I saw him at the Hill Street nightclub. He came home with me and we talked all night long. He wouldn't leave. I kept saying, 'Haven't you got somewhere to go?' And he just kept saying, 'No!' The first thing he'd done when he walked in the door was open a beer and started saying some weird things. He was making some crazy statements, and all I could think was that I just wanted him out of my life. Anyway, I ended up driving him down to Coolangatta, where he picked up his board, and then he directed me up to Bilambil to show me his block of land. We ended up back at my place and had a barbecue. He was like a lost little boy, and my heart just went out to him. He was just so lost, and I guess I was in rescue mode. I guess I felt I had to take care of him.

We started living together, but the drugs and alcohol indulgence became too much, and I had to say to him that I had an eight-year-old kid; I didn't want that sort of stuff going on around him, and that if he didn't stop, he'd have to go . . . And he stopped doing it! I remember sitting there at home one day, his head in my lap, just stroking his hair. He was clinging to me, wanting someone to rescue him. He wanted an anchor. He was like a bit of wood drifting in the ocean. He needed someone to grab him and save him, and that's sort of what I did. It took a while, but he straightened his act up.

Pam Occhilupo: When he met Bea, that was terrific, that was great for him. I thought, *she's an angel, here's the angel that's been sent to help him* . . . The week before the wedding, Bea had been driving home with her sister when she turned her head to look at the wedding dress that they had just picked up. The car collided with another vehicle, and Bea attended the ceremony in a neck brace. To complete the picture, Mark held his bucks party the night before and after several drinks was running down the street when he fell and broke his ankle, so he ended up on crutches. They were a funny-looking pair, I'm afraid.

Billabong were really good during this down time, and Gordon was always so understanding. I would talk to him every now and again, and he'd want to know what was going on. It was great of him to give me that time off, because I did it twice. Whenever I met a lady and fell in love, I'd seem to get all homey and put on lots of weight and not surf. I did it when I married Bea too. And that's when Gordon really gave me a lot of time, and I put on a lot of weight.

We were living in Palm Beach, on 15th Avenue, and I really didn't want to see anyone. If the phone rang I wouldn't answer it, because I'm one of those people who can't say no. So I figured it was better not to answer it. It was a really tough time. I was missing all my friends and was thinking, *no-one likes me anymore.* I would suffer anxiety attacks whenever I left the house. All I wanted to do was stay home. Home was safe. And out there you might run into someone. It was a kind of paranoia. I just didn't want any confrontations and wanted to stay home and stay safe.

At one point I tipped the scales at seventeen stone. I'm usually about twelve or thirteen, so I was really big. I didn't even want to go to Billabong and get those sized board shorts. So I'd either go and buy Billabongs at a shop, or just buy a no-name brand – those really stretchy ones – and just slob around the house.

I was pretty depressed, so I'd sleep in till eight or nine, have a big bowl of Coco Pops and go back to bed for a nap. I'd wake up hungry and have my chicken and chips for lunch and watch *The Bold and the Beautiful*, if the midday movie wasn't any good, and often have a nap during that. I wasn't drinking during the day, but I was in a real routine. I've always been a real routine kind of guy, though I probably appear far from it, even if it's a bit of a weird routine. I was stacking on the pounds and it was happening really fast. I was a total recluse, and every day at five o'clock I'd watch *The Price is Right* and have my sixpack of beer and cheese-and-bacon balls as my little treat. Then Bea would cook me a beautiful dinner, and I'd go straight to bed after dinner. I was sleeping like a bear.

Nothing against Palm Beach or the people who live there, but it was a depressing time for me. The surf was pretty average out the front most of the time. I was only one unit back from the beach, but I didn't go out much. Shaper Nev Hyman lived across from us, and he often had a lot of good surfers out the front of his house. That stopped me surfing, because I didn't want to paddle out if there were any good surfers around. There were a few times I got some great waves out there, but usually I'd sneak out when no-one else was interested or around.

Beatrice Occhilupo: I started noticing that he was sleeping in a lot. Normally he would jump out of bed at five o'clock in the morning and go surfing – that was his morning regime – but then he started not getting up, and sleeping longer. It started gradually, but was definitely noticeable over time. I thought he was just burnt out, like he'd been doing so much, so full-on, and I thought he needed to rest to come back. I didn't think he was manic depressive or anything like that. I didn't think it was anything serious at first, but it just got worse and worse and worse.

We moved into the apartment at Palm Beach and he was sleeping more, drinking like a carton of beer a night and obviously putting on weight. He would have Coco Pops for breakfast, a whole barbecued chicken and a massive serve of hot chips for lunch. I'd cook him a healthy meal for dinner, but it was obviously the beer and the chips that put the weight on. He got so big I had to go to 'big men's' shops to get clothes to fit him. He was like a size 38 or 40, and he wouldn't go outside, except to ride his bike up to get his chicken and chips for lunch every day, and there was a little shop across the road where he'd get his Coco Pops . . . I'm not sure where he was getting his beer from. He was gambling really heavily too.

Paul Sargeant: He used to think nothing during that reclusive period of going down to Seagulls and putting in the coins, just loading the machine up and have maximum bet. Every push of the button was like forty bucks, and he'd just sit there – *brrrr, brrrr, brrrr.* It was crazy. Full-on gambling addict . . . I'd hate to think how much money he has wasted, but that's just him. He never learnt the value of money, never learnt what work was. Money was just something that he had to have to get what he wanted, and he just had no understanding of it.

Rabbit Bartholomew: I was shocked when I went up to his house and he was lying on the couch – it was just like seeing Marlon Brando in *Apocalypse Now*. He was this big cow on the couch, eating chips and drinking beer. He had the TV all lined up and he just wasn't getting off the couch. And that went on for a very long time.

STIRRINGS

It turned out to be very fortunate for me that Beatrice was a psychologist, because she recognised that I was suffering from depression. She couldn't really treat me because she was my wife, but she did get me to go see someone. The first counsellor I went to was this really wealthy lady who lived in this big house, and the session was super-expensive. I dreaded it. The days I had to go see her were the worst ever, like having four root canals done at the same time. Beatrice had been talking to Gordon, and he thought it was a really good idea – he might have even been funding it. But it just didn't feel right, so I didn't go back.

Then Beatrice rang up this place in Burleigh, and it wasn't at all expensive; they only asked you to pay whatever you could afford, and the guy was really cool. His name was Warren and he was a former priest or something. He just made me feel really comfortable. He was able to sum up everything that had happened to me and make sense of it, how I started on tour so early and all the partying I used to indulge in. I was drinking a fair bit at that stage. I don't know if you'd call it alcoholism, but I just felt like I needed a few beers every night to relax.

He listened to my story and said maybe I did suffer from a bit of depression, but it was natural given what I'd been through. He said, 'Don't worry about it too much but just keep an eye on it and start looking after yourself a bit better.' He helped me feel strong again and proud of myself, and that was the start of my comeback. I hope if he ever does read this book that he gets some satisfaction from that, because going to see him was one of the best things I ever did for myself.

A lot of people are shy or embarrassed about going to get counselling, but it's such a good thing to get another point of view on your situation. There are plenty of surfers I know who have struggled with depression and haven't known how to get help. Surfing gives you such huge highs – and they're natural highs – but lows are always going to happen in life. You've just got to be able to accept it and recognise it, I reckon.

I used to smoke a bit, but I wasn't smoking at all at the time because it would just weird me out. One day someone came over with a joint and I had some, and because I hadn't been smoking, it really hit me. I looked in the mirror and, for the first time in a long time, I really saw myself. And I didn't like what I saw. I was fat and pale with greasy hair hanging down over my face. On a whim, I decided to try on my wedding suit, and it *so* didn't fit. The button on the pants was about three inches from the buttonhole, and I could barely get into my suit jacket. If I'd moved my arms, the whole back would have ripped, like the Incredible Hulk, except I wasn't cut like the Hulk.

Gordon used to come around, and he was sweet. He always knew I'd lose the weight – I'd done it before. But when I got to seventeen stone, he must have been having his doubts. We were renting in Palm Beach and it was a tough time for us. I had the block of land in Bilambil and we really wanted to stop paying rent and build a house on our land. So I asked Gordon if he would help us out, and he was nice enough to say yes. He just went, 'Yeah, sweet. I think it's a good idea to have a house back there in the country.' So he funded the house. But he also said, 'I need you to lose weight. That's the deal, because I need to use you in ads and videos.' So that was the start of it.

Rabbit Bartholomew: I always give a lot of credit to Beatrice, because she met him when he was still on the descent. And she realised he had to bottom out at home. But then the moment he turned the corner she really was there, and she fussed over him and she managed him and kept him motivated. I think without Beatrice and Rainer he may have not come back. There would have been some self-pity in there and, plus, I think the badder elements would have got to him. She was his guardian angel.

Pam Occhilupo: Bea got to work and designed a house suitable for the site which would make the best of the 180-degree view up and down the coast, from Surfers Paradise to Fingal Beach and beyond. While Bea supervised the building, Mark lay on the couch, not even enjoying the surf at his door and refusing to even view the construction process. Why, I don't know. Maybe he still needed time out . . . Bea had created a beautiful home for him, decorating it like a showpiece. Finally, when it was ready, she took Mark up there, virtually moving him from one couch to the other.

Beatrice Occhilupo: The house backed onto a golf course, and he only had to go up the backyard and across the course to the clubhouse. That's when the gambling problem went through the roof – and he was still drinking a carton of beer every night! At the end of that year, we went to get the bulk of his contract money from Billabong after we'd been taking out our basic living expenses, and there was nothing there. That year I reckon he'd gambled something like $50,000. That was when I went to Gordon. At that time my sister Naomi was going out with Gordon, and I went to him and said that I couldn't handle it anymore and needed help. I said, 'Why can't we send him somewhere to lose weight and get him out of this sleeping thing?' I still really loved him, but it was a horrible time. There was also a lot of pressure getting the house built up at Bilambil Heights too, and he just didn't want to know about it.

Rabbit Bartholomew: He always maintained a sense of humour. There was one very, very funny time – and it was also a cringe. We'd talked him into coming down to Bells, between Vince Lawder and I. We said, 'We've got to get him down there. We know he's fat and people are going to be in shock, but we've got to try and bring him out.' We didn't want him to do the whole MP thing, and we were just worried about him being a hermit and going deeper inside and really having big problems and never coming back. We'd really massaged him into the place and coaxed him along and shielded him. We were at a Billabong Pro Junior and there was this moment. The late Professor Brian Lowdon, who was a friend of mine, was saying hello, and he's looked around at Occy and goes, 'Oh my God, what happened to you?' And I went, *right, it's all over – meltdown.* Just the way he said it was such a shock. It did take us a few more days to get Occy back out of the house on that one.

He was very self-conscious, and we had this expression session and I said, 'Come on, let's get out there.' It was just hilarious because him getting into a wetsuit was like one of those big ladies trying to get into a corset. I was going, 'Hold your breath and we'll get the zip up.' His face was blowing up and we got out there, and it was deadset two-foot Rincon – fun little surf but not too strong. Occy was out there paddling, and at that point you could see his arms were a bit short because of his girth and he wasn't getting anywhere. And his head was blowing up, even his feet, toes and fingers were fat. He really blew up. I was thinking, *this is kind of gnarly but at least he's out here.'* And this wave came – it was quite a good wave – and it looked like it was going to be fun. I was going, 'Go Occy, go mate', and he paddled and huffed and puffed and he was right there on this wave . . . and couldn't catch it. I went, 'Oh shit.' And then I looked over at him and he looked over at me, and for the rest of that expression session we laughed hysterically. We were falling off our boards laughing. I was laughing at him and he was laughing at himself, and we were both laughing at the ridiculous situation. And I think it was a therapeutic thing. He knew he had to do heaps of work.

Vince Lawder: I remember when he was going through that 'big' stage, I was trying to get him out to go to events or surf trips. I said to Jack McCoy, 'Let's try and get him to Bells, because if there's one event he'd like to go to it's Bells.' We talked him into going down, and that was the turnaround. Jack came down, and Peter Wilson got a lot of great shots. Gee, he was big, and people were wondering if he could still surf, but when the swell came up the weight actually sort of worked for him – he was just going up and taking chunks of wave out. He was ripping. When he did that he got that confidence back, and he realised it's not that bad out there and people still loved him. He was just out there cruising in these waves, doing those nice, big, flowing carves of his. He did a few turns and the whole beach was like, *whoa, that was pretty awesome.* No-one cared how big he was then. Quite a number of times I put Occy on trips, and you just hope he's going to be there, but he did the old disappearing act quite a bit. Just getting him to Bells was a big turnaround, just everyone talking to him, because he'd been in this little cave.

Taj Burrow: I always remember him tearing apart the bowl at Bells. That's my favourite memory of him for sure. When I was young, him and Margo and a couple of others used to go out there for an expression session. I was just blown away by their power. I was this little kid out there doing tail-slides and stuff, and Occy would come along with the most amazing backhand style in the world and hack it to pieces. That was one of my favourite things, the way he attacked it out there. Everyone loves the way he surfs backhand, and especially out there. I just love those grab-rail bottom turns straight into the biggest hook and then straight into another grab-rail bottom turn. That will never die.

Vince Lawder: It got to a point where Gordon went, 'Where do we go from here?' Everybody gets to that point. That includes everybody on the team. There's a decision to be made by the company about who will be supported. You don't want to be throwing money away, because there could be some young kid who needs some support. And a lot of the time, the surfers don't get that second chance. Money goes into the young kids coming through all the time because we had a pretty extensive junior team. Occy looked at Gordon as a father figure. They were really close.

Occy was a freak, one of a kind, and I know Gordon did want him to get fit again. That's when we stuck him on that trip to Bells and he got through it okay. Jack [McCoy] went good, and we threw him straight into a little trip with Jack. I think he might have flown from Bells straight to WA and hung out with Jack for two months – then Jack started filming the comeback. And Jack would ring up and give us a little report every now and again. He was stoked at Occy's progression. I think Occy had had his holiday and his time off, and he had this new lease on life. I think that played a huge role in his comeback.

Beatrice Occhilupo: My sister Naomi suggested that we send him over to Jack McCoy in Western Australia . . . and so we did! Mark didn't want to go. He was crying. We decided to send someone with him that he knew and liked, so Fergie [Andrew Ferguson] went. He's died since. It was really hard for me too, because I knew I wouldn't see Mark for a while. I think it was eventually for about two-and-a-half months. They went over there and Jack trained him, put him on a good diet . . . I think Jack had more control over him than I did. He flew back two or three months later. He walked off the plane still looking heavy, but he had lost heaps of weight, and he was really confident and it was obvious that he felt good about himself.

Once the house was built, I knew I had to make good on my deal with Gordon to lose the weight and get back into surfing. So I went off to WA, to stay with Jack McCoy and his family, and their friends George and Tracy Simpson, in Yallingup, near Margaret River. They had a great house out in the country, and beautiful kids. They became like a second family to me. I stayed for a couple of months, and I kept popping back and forth after that to see them. That's where I lost my weight. They had me on the best program – I was running and surfing every day, and they were cooking me the nicest food. They're really good eaters and super health conscious, especially Tracy. George is a fisherman, so we'd either eat fish or vegetarian, a really clean diet.

I was surfing heaps and Jack was filming me sometimes, but I was pretty overweight for quite a while. There're some waves in the *Occumentary* video that, if you look closely, I'm still really big. But the weight just started falling off. I'd go for big runs through the country, and it felt amazing to be fit and healthy and surfing well again.

My whole comeback was like a Rocky movie, and I was really living it. I was running in a tracksuit because Dad loved running in a tracksuit, and I got that from him. My mates at Kurnell used to laugh at my dad because he was a fanatical runner and he had this really funny running style, and he'd always run in a red tracksuit all year round. In Sydney, on forty-degree days, he'd be running in his red tracksuit. I used to run with him when I was young. They were really good memories, running round the streets of Kurnell with him, and I felt like I took that spirit with me when I started my comeback. I'd have my big Billabong trackies on and I'd run down the street or in the middle of the West Australian bush, listening to that theme song from *Rocky*. This wasn't like my other attempted comebacks; I was giving it 190 per cent, because I kind of knew it was now or never for my surfing career, and I was running out of time.

Jack McCoy (from *The Occumentary*): Every morning he'd go for a run about six o'clock. We'd give him a nice big healthy breakfast, and then off we'd go to the beach. Occy was a little shy during his Elvis period, didn't want to go to many of the main breaks. I wanted to bring my gear with me to do some filming, just to show him, to give him some more confidence in believing that he was still worth taking pictures of. He went back to the Goldie a lot less heavy and a lot more stoked. I just tried to encourage him to believe in himself and that he could do whatever he thought he wanted in surfing. He returned and Beatrice really kept up the same positive program we'd encouraged him with and, Occ being Occ, he took the bull by the horns so to speak – and the rest is history.

Taj Burrow: When I was a grom I used to be really close to Jack McCoy, and Jack brought Occ over for one of his movies. I was so excited he was coming to town. I remember he was huge when he came. He was ripping and I was so stoked I got to go for a surf with him. And I clearly remember I used to ride, like, 5'6"s, tiny little boards, when I was young. I thought

I was ripping at the time, doing little tail-slides and reverses. And I was so excited for him to come and to try and throw a little reverse in front of him or something. And it would have been six-foot Bears, which is kind of a big left, and it just didn't suit me at all. I was on my backhand and it was big and I couldn't do anything that I wanted to do, and he was just ripping. I was bouncing around on these chops and couldn't do a thing. I remember being so bummed that I couldn't do anything cool in front of him, but it was awesome to surf with him.

Rabbit Bartholomew: Very soon after that I saw him at 5 am on the top of Duranbah, and from that moment on the weight started coming off and he got his motivation back. I remember very clearly – I reckon I was there at the exact moment he turned it round. It was dawn at the top of Point Danger. I went up there at 5 am and looked over, and there was Occy checking the surf, at dawn. And he said, 'I'm going to do it.' And that was the morning he started stripping the weight off unbelievably. No-one surfs earlier than Occy, and that 5 am surf has served him well. It brought him back.

I sometimes get asked how I managed to come back from such a low point, and there were a lot of contributing factors. I think, eventually, I just felt like I was wasting my life by *not* surfing. I'd enjoyed the role of being a free-surfer, and working on the movies with Jack helped me keep my surfing at a high level. Getting away from the world tour and the craziness and everything else I got caught up in and meeting Jack and doing the movies with him was a big part of my comeback. The guys I was surfing with, like Margo, Luke Egan, Andrew Ferguson and Munga, good friends who were all ripping, helped me lift my surfing. I had to be ripping too, or I was just going to look stupid in the movies, so I had to lift my performance, but without the pressure of competition. Just being out in the desert and some of the remote locations Jack took us to really helped enlighten me about another side of the surfing lifestyle, made me appreciate life and calmed me down.

Jack and I really hit it off right from the start. I liked his philosophy and approach to life. He's always happy, really grateful, has really good morals. He told me one time in WA, 'All you need to be happy is someone to love, something to do and something to look forward to.' And it just struck a chord with me. I was like, *that is so right. I want to find them all.* And I ended up finding them all. It's a surfer's life: you've got something to do and something to look forward to every morning you wake up and wonder what the waves are doing. Surfers are uniquely blessed in that way. All you need then is someone to love. Going on trips and going in events in the long run gave me something to look forward to as well. Jack was the perfect guy I needed at the time, so I was lucky to get hooked up with him for all those years.

Jack would always get us to do all these whacky time-lapse sequences, running around in circles and doing weird stuff. A lot of the guys didn't like doing it, but I didn't mind too much. It just looked like I was still a bit crazy, so no-one paid too much notice.

Sunny Garcia: I remember one time Jack was trying to get me to do a time-lapse sequence for one of the movies, and I just plain refused and sat in the car. Occy was already in the car, and there was a stand-off as Jack started yelling at me to get out. When he realised I wasn't going to budge, Jack started telling Occy to get out of the car and do it. There was a long pause, then Occy called out in this squeaky voice, 'Sunny says if I get out of the car he's going to bash me.'

Vince Lawder: We used to do trips and take Joel [Parkinson] and Dean [Morrison] and Rasta [Dave Rastovich] – they were still grommets back then and would get out of hand. Occ was real good in that all the kids really respected him, and I couldn't be everywhere at the one time – kids would be playing up here, there and everywhere. If Occ thought something wasn't right, he'd grab the kid and the kid would be like, *shit, Occy just had a go at me. He just tuned me about what I should be doing.* I think a lot of the kids learnt a lot from that, and saw another side to him.

You think he's not on top of what he's doing, but he's totally on top of what he's doing. He'd just do it in his own way. He wouldn't get fazed by what was going on around him, but if he didn't want to do something he didn't do it. It was hard sometimes, just hoping that he'd turn up at the airport, and sometimes he didn't. You'd track him down and he'd get on the plane the next day.

Dougall Walker: I give a lot of credit to Gordon Merchant there, and Gordon copped a lot of criticism from certain people for the way Occy's money was managed for him. But if Occy had got his full pay cheques, it would have all gone. But Gordon set him up to buy his house and the money went into his mortgage. There was living money – *healthy* living money – more than the average wage. Occy was so trusting, and often he'd trust the wrong people and some people took advantage of him along the way. He's also had a lot of people around him who were looking out for him. There were times at conferences, when Occy had gone completely off the rails, and virtually everyone was like, 'Right, yeah, it's time to cut him loose.' I remember one in particular, and even Gordon was unsure. And I remember Bob Hurley getting up and going, 'You guys are kidding . . . No matter what he's doing, we've got to stand by him,' and it was a real defining moment. It was one of those moments that was a wake-up call, and you go, *shit, that's right.* There were a number of those. And you've got to remember, most athletes, sponsored sportspeople, fade quickly. Occy had the ability to plateau and then move again and move again and move again. From a company's perspective, you can't sacrifice the livelihood of thousands of people if someone's going down. If you hang on, you're going down with them. It might sound very mercenary, but the fact of the matter is it's a business to create income for the people who own the company, obviously, but there's a lot of people who make their livelihood out of that. And lots of times it was looked upon as: 'Okay, is Occy going to sink the ship here?' But it never happened. It's very interesting.

I honestly believe it was emotion, and Occy's personality and ability to be new to a new generation, because that's what the surf companies – and all the youth companies – are all about. They need to be new to a new generation every time. And you can go too far with someone and they lose their appeal – all of a sudden it's, 'That's the old guys' company. That's the old generation, and we're the new generation.' And if you hang on too long, you get pushed to the side with them. Occy was so valuable to Billabong as an athlete because he continued. It was always a good association. It didn't become a negative association. At times it got close, damn close, but I also give credit to Gordon Merchant and Bob Hurley for their loyalty – not only to Occy, but their understanding that he had this ability. No-one thought he'd go on to surf on the tour until he was forty . . . No-one's even gone close. Once upon a time at thirty you were over the hill.

Rusty Preisendorfer: Occy always had a positive outlook on things. I think it paid back in dividends. Especially when he went through a period of personal challenge. His golden karma and a few good people helped him pull through and realise his true potential: one of the greatest surfers to ever grace the waves with his gift. We stayed in touch. At times it was through Paul Sargeant. Sarge was always a staunch advocate for Occy. At one point I had a sponsorship agreement worked out for him. I was headed to Fiji for my annual vacation there; I usually mixed holiday with work, bringing team guys along to shoot photos and work on videos. Occy was looking for support, not just in the financial sense, but just trying to regain his footing, and I was ready to help if I could. I had a sponsorship agreement that he was good with and a plane ticket waiting. At the last minute Gordon stepped up. I'm happy for Occy that it worked out. I've never, ever, wanted anything from him other than that he would be appreciated and looked after. He was such a gifted surfer and such a nice person. I just wanted to see him back on track.

It's dawn at Snapper rocks, at the southern end of the Gold Coast, where an exquisite build-up of sand has coincided with the first cyclone swell of the year. The sun is barely over the horizon when I pull up into the carpark, just as a familiar figure races along the base of a towering wave. Occy compresses through a low-centred bottom turn, drives vertically up the face of the wave and tears a devastating gouge through the cresting peak. He flies out of the top of the wave – for one impossible instant, I swear, completely upside down, clawing the wave face and raking his board through the lip – then drives back down the face and into the next bottom turn.

Surfers love Occy because the lines he draws look like pure, unbridled, animal instinct – no hint of the calculated repertoire of safe manoeuvres that made pro surfing a sham in the '80s, nor the jelly-legged tricks the kids are pulling these days (to the ongoing horror of the purists). He simply looks like he was put on this Earth to surf.

Occhilupo won the first WQS event of the new season, the XXXX Classic on the Sunshine Coast in January. It was his first win in five years. 'I just got that special feeling I've missed and I haven't had for so long. A real complete kind of feeling. After the wave that I clinched it on, I got a real good feeling of euphoria – a real strong feeling. A kind of feeling that you want again.'

book four

Rise Again

The feeling. Occhilupo has always been driven by it. Opponents, spectators and judges could see it written all over him when he possessed that air of invincibility and the result was a mere formality. It's that feeling, the most potent drug of them all, that Occy seems to crave – more than the glory and the spoils of victory. 'I want to blow my own mind and blow everyone else's, and I know I can do that in the water,' he declares. 'I know the waves we're going to have, and I just can't wait. I want to surf like I never have, and I know I've got that in me.'

The feeling's back? 'I've been getting it lately,' he almost whispers.

– from 'Re-birthing a Legend', *Inside Sport*,
March 1997

Chapter Twelve

The Challenge

In 1995 I took my first tentative steps back into the pro surfing world. I spent some time down at Bells that year, prior to the Easter contest, and scored really good waves. It was probably the best Bells I ever surfed – six foot, dead offshore and straight as a ruler. The footage from those sessions ended up in a classic surf movie called *Litmus*. We'd been down at Johanna and spent the night at Lorne on the way back to Bells, and when we got there it was absolutely pumping. I remember driving back along the Great Ocean Road and drooling at these perfect conditions out the window, knowing that Bells would be all-time. I couldn't get back there fast enough and, when I did, I just wanted to unleash my surfing on these perfect waves. I felt like my surfing really came together during those sessions at Bells.

Andrew Kidman (*Litmus* film-maker): That was the best surfing I ever saw, at Bells the year before he qualified. I remember seeing the footage and thinking, *that's the best surfing in the world.* Peter Kirkhouse had been filming him, and he brought it back to the house and said, 'You should see this footage of Occy I just shot.' I remember saying to him that I'd never seen anything like it, and he knew we were making a movie. He said, 'You can have it for the movie if you like.'

I was like, 'Fucking hell.' It was pretty unbelievable. He was turning up under the barrel.

I talked to him about it later and he had such a vivid memory of it. He said he finally felt like he'd come back to surfing after that session, so I guess it must have meant something to him. It's still the best surfing I've ever seen.

THE CHALLENGE

Occy (from the film *The Mystery Left*, the first Billabong Challenge): I'm not disappointed not having the world title. Most of the time I let my surfing do the talking, and just to be known as a great surfer to me is pretty good. I'm happy.

Rabbit Bartholomew: At the ebb, things had unravelled to the point where, between the winter in Hawaii and the meltdown in Europe – and things in between – and the California stunts and incidents, Occy had obviously fucked up, to the max. Billabong was going global, and Billabong USA had made a decision that this guy was bad for the company, that this guy's image could not be associated with them. He couldn't be the poster boy and they actually wanted him gone, and understandably so. I could understand their point of view, so I could see this coming down. And it went to and fro and it was quite a big debate. All points led to him going, but I knew that Gordon always had that last parachute . . . There were a lot of little things that helped spark Occy, but I always thought that him knowing Gordon came in and protected him at his lowest point, like the cavalry, was something that he thought was worth fighting for. Part of the whole strategy with the Challenge was to give Occy a stage. It was unbelievable. Everyone loved him being there, and he just loved being back. He was in among his own.

I'd lost the extra weight and was getting my surfing back to a level I was happy with, but it still looked like a big leap to try and make it back on tour. And that's when Billabong came up with the idea of the Challenge, a specialty event designed to put the best surfers in the world in the best waves. The concept also had the added benefit of reintroducing me to top-line competition in a good environment and good waves. It was really the perfect vehicle for my comeback.

The first Billabong Challenge was up north at this desert left, which shall remain nameless. George Simpson was running the show, so I felt really comfortable with him, and I had a really supportive crew around me. The Challenge was the joint brainchild of my old mate Rabbit, who was a special projects director for Billabong, film-maker Jack McCoy and Gordon Merchant. Everyone shared the vision of taking a select bunch of top surfers away to a really special environment and setting us loose in great waves. I'd been up to the desert before with Jack and George and loved the place. I was so stoked. And to have this amazing group of surfers come along just made it better.

Kelly Slater, Shane Powell, Rob Machado, Johnny Boy Gomes, Sunny Garcia, Kalani Robb – it was a great cast, and everyone loved camping out under the stars and getting some sick waves. It was so far removed from the average surf contest. The camp set-up was amazing, with really good food and table tennis in one of the tents. Beatrice came away and helped with the catering – lots of the crew brought their partners and it had a real family vibe. I felt like I was back among my people. I took a little bit from each of the surfers at that event to help improve my surfing.

These local Aboriginal people came out and cooked kangaroo tail for us one night and had a little corroboree. We'd had a few beers and they were teaching us how to cook it. Apparently you're supposed to eat the bottom part of the tail, and I must have taken a big bite out of the top part. I just got a mouthful of fur. Everyone was laughing at me, and I was coughing up fur balls for about two weeks after that.

It felt great to be back in competition in such a supportive environment, and I ended up making the final and gaining a lot of confidence. Rob Machado won the event in perfect barrels, and everyone went away feeling like they'd been part of something special.

Two weeks later we went to Jeffreys Bay for the second Billabong Challenge, this time going right, on one of the world's great point breaks. We had to sit and wait a while for a swell, but no-one minded too much. We had Johnny Boy Gomes with us and, even though he had a couple of run-ins in the surf and punched out a kneeboarder's fins one day, he was generally really mellow and good to hang with. He had his girlfriend at the time with him, and it was good to see him relaxed and enjoying life. We waited for about a week, checking the point every morning at dawn, only to be greeted by an almost flat ocean, when finally the swell started to show. It was about four foot at first light – corduroy lines to the horizon. Rabbit took one look at it and went, 'This is the day.' The swell just got bigger and bigger until it got up to about eight to ten feet, just unloading on itself. Kelly seemed to have it on a string all day, and I'll never forget one crazy barrel he rode down at Impossibles, while we all screamed from the beach. Local surfer Warren Dean surfed really well too, getting three barrels on one wave and really showing his knowledge of the line-up.

It was super-windy and really heavy going all day, and I made the final again. I jumped from my 6'5" Dahlberg, which had been going really well but was starting to skitter on the bigger sets, to a 6'10" Tokoro. It was built for Hawaii and felt way too big on the waves, but it was just good for the paddling power – I needed all the help I could get at that point. You don't really want the big waves at J-Bay on a day like that, because they don't hug the point like the smaller ones. I ended up getting second to Kelly, who was almost unbeatable at that point, and the party that night at Cheron's place was unreal. We'd worked so hard all day, our arms were just about falling off, and beer has never tasted so good. Kelly was in a great mood, enjoying the relaxed atmosphere and novel format away from the tour. There were only eight surfers, and the whole thing had a really soulful feeling. All the locals came to the party and seemed happy to have us there. It was epic. Someone asked me recently, if I could go anywhere in the world, not to compete but just for a holiday, where would it be? I didn't have to think too hard. I'd go back to J-Bay and hang out at Cheron's place in a heartbeat.

You couldn't come up with a better way to prepare me for a comeback. The Challenge was Gordon's baby, but I don't think my return to the tour was his master plan. He would have preferred I just travelled and surfed in the movies. But surfing great waves with some of the best surfers in the world was an ideal stepping stone towards the tour, which was starting to hold contests in the world's best waves in prime surf season.

I really felt like a lot of those surfers were supporting me in my comeback by coming all the way to the Challenge events. It was such a long way to go, to the WA desert or South Africa, but everyone was stoked to be a part of it. The format, the prize money and the locations must have had a bit to do with it too, but all those guys at the Challenge events played a part in my comeback, whether they realised it or not. Those things were almost better than the tour, and contributed to the evolution of the so-called 'Dream Tour'.

I can recall one afternoon watching the young Hawaiian guys Ross Williams and Shane Dorian surf this bombie by themselves. It had probably never been surfed before. It was late in the arvo, and we were all sitting in the car watching them take on these huge rights, drinking beers and screaming our guts out when they got a good one. They were such good times.

Kelly Slater: Billabong did really well by creating that event and putting Occ in. It must've been a huge help to his expression and confidence. That was the time I really got to know him, and we became pretty good friends at that point . . . dinners at home and golfing together, arm wrestling. It was really nice to see him supported by Beatrice and gaining steam and confidence in himself. Brought a smile to many faces to see the life back in him . . . That was definitely a part of the mystique for me. Occy's always been a huge inspiration for me. To have some real time together back then was so memorable. He's got a keen wit at times, but he's such a kid at heart. I was stoked to see him coming back and getting himself together. I know it was a true-blue Billabong event and marketing idea from the get go, but I think the energy of it was just the spirit of surfing. I have great memories of that time, and finally getting to know Occy well from those events was a huge bonus.

Jack McCoy (taken in part from *The Occumentary*): Once Gordon felt that Occy wanted to seriously make a comeback, we came up with the idea of the Challenge. It had two objectives: it was to help Occy get a chance to surf with the world's best and get their measure. Also, Gordon was tired of putting his money into pro contests where the final was held at a city beach on a Sunday arvo at 2 pm, regardless of surf conditions; we knew we wanted to do something different and created our vision of how we saw pro surfing. Occy was the seed and the Challenge grew from there.

He was really stoked to hang with Kelly, Rob and the rest of the guys. They were on top at the time. Once again, the Challenge was a family affair, with everyone involved in making the day-to-day life run smoothly and fun. The surf was very funky for most of the time, but there were a few days when the boys went head-to-head and Occ held his own. He was sick for the final day. He was weak and not that confident. He ended up getting fourth, which was great. I think if he was feeling better, he might have done better, but it was a start and he was really stoked to be competing with that level of surfers again. He was also stoked to be part of what would become the template for what today has become the Dream Tour.

The Challenge films were also the first of that type of coverage of surfing events. There were a lot of imitators, both film and contests, after they came out. Occ was always the cornerstone for me in all of the Challenge programs. I always had him as the thread of each in some form or another. Occy was always stoked at the events and keen to make sure all of the other surfers felt like the Challenge was sort of a family thing. He was also always guaranteed to come out with something classic. One of my favourites is when, after surfing his first heat of the J-Bay Challenge, he announced during his post-heat interview that, 'Even my big toe was getting cold out there.' Pure Occ.

Kelly Slater (from *The Occumentary*): He was telling me how he's always stubbing his toes, and we're walking out over these lava rocks and all of a sudden I feel the ground shake, and he just goes, 'Oh mate, I've done it again.' And I look down and his whole toe is flayed open, just bleeding profusely, and we're just about to jump in the water. It's really sharky there. I just remember looking at his toenail, his skin was like over his toenail – just exploded. I think it was me and Rob Machado. We're looking at him, almost crying because we felt bad for him, but also because it was really funny. He was talking about it and just, bang, hit his toe. It's just Occy, he does funny stuff like that all the time.

Vince Lawder: People thought we were mad, but that was our vision – to get the best surfers in the best waves – and that's what people wanted to watch. And we believe that that was the start of the Dream Tour, where you get the waves and the conditions. Occy would not have survived going back on tour in two-foot slop. To have Teahupoo, Pipe, Mundaka, Jeffreys Bay – it's no coincidence that these are the contests that Billabong sponsored.

Richard Maurer: Once he went over to WA I knew something was happening, and he didn't want to be a pork chop in front of the rest of the Billabong Challenge crew. He really wanted to do well in that. He got in the final and sort of went, 'Okay, I've still got it here, I can still have a go.' I knew after that he was going to get more inspiration.

Dougall Walker: Gordon did a lot of good things for Occy. Gordon's no angel – trust me. There's a lot of people in the world who feel like Gordon screwed them over at some time, but one guy who he looked after unbelievably well was Occy. It was a father–son relationship. Gordon really took a special interest in him. He was one of the few guys who had a direct line to Gordon at all times. Gordon would always slap him into line a bit, not physically . . . Gordon was smart enough to take the pressure off when he could and pull him into line when he could.

I DON'T KNOW BOATS

I headed back to Hawaii that year with no expectations, just wanting to work on my surfing and show Beatrice all my old haunts. It felt great to be back in Hawaii – fit and healthy and surfing well. My friend Kaui Hill had been living on Molokai and invited us to come and visit him. Kaui was the owner of Straight Up Surfboards, who I'd been riding for, and he said we'd love the unspoilt beauty of Molokai.

Kaui was also a well-known comedian who created this character called Bu La'ia. Bu was this classic Hawaiian pidgin-speaking 'moke', which is a slang term for Hawaiians, but Kaui could get away with it because he was Hawaiian. He even ran for governor of Hawaii as Bu La'ia, and attracted about 8000 votes.

There's a big beautiful bay at Halawa Valley, and as soon as you go past that bay it's sheer cliff for ten to fifteen kilometres, before you get to a little beach called Wailau. That's their North Shore. People camp at Wailau, and there's a good little wave there too. Kaui took me there on a jet ski once. To get there hiking takes a few days but to get there by boat takes about half an hour. His jet ski started konking out about halfway, and I was like, 'What would happen if it conked out?' I shouldn't have asked that question, because the next time I went there I found out.

The north coast of Molokai is amazing. They filmed *Jurassic Park* there. The entire coast is sheer ocean cliffs, with waterfalls tumbling down here and there. It is so inaccessible that they used to take people suffering from leprosy here in the old days so they couldn't escape. There is one small peninsula of land at the base of the cliffs where the Kalaupapa leper colony still is. Of course, leprosy is treatable now and the residents are free to leave, but a lot of them choose to stay there because it is the only home they have ever known.

Kaui wanted me to go and pick up a friend of his from Halawa Bay in this rubber duckie, or Zodiac. I tried to tell him, 'Mate, I'm not really that good with boats', but he didn't want to hear it. He had two rubber duckies. One motor didn't work and the other duckie was flat, so he had to switch motors and then it was sweet. This little local kid called Jaya said, 'I'm going to come too.' Which was fine by me – I figured I needed all the help I could get. Bea was one of those women who always got a feeling about certain things, and I remember telling her I was taking the Zodiac to Halawa Bay. She said, 'I don't know, I've got a bad feeling about it. You don't really know boats.' I should have listened, but I was always up for an adventure.

We had a surfboard in a cover to deliver to someone. And then Kaui said, 'By the way, catch a fish too while you're out there,' so we had to throw a rod in as well. It was two o'clock in the afternoon, and I had to get there and back before nightfall. I figured I'd be doing well pulling *that* off, let alone catching fish.

As soon as you come around the corner to the north shore, you're in open ocean. The swell was coming up and I was driving. I don't know why Jaya wasn't driving, except that he was just this young kid. The swell was from the north, so it was going our way, and we were cruising down these little swells, catching little runners. But we were about two kilometres out to sea – I was keeping a wide berth from the cliffs because I was freaking.

We were riding down this one little runner when, all of a sudden, a hole opened up as the swell drew water off a reef in front of us, and we just nose-dived into the reef. The duckie folded in half and we both got flung out – and the duckie kept going. We had the fishing line out, and somehow Jaya grabbed the line and started wrapping it around his arm to try and stop the duckie. And before I could even say, 'What are you doing?', the lure came up and went straight into his arm. And then he was getting pulled under by the boat. So I grabbed the line to give him some slack and screamed, 'Pull that fucking thing out now!' He pulled it out and the line just went *whirrr*, and the boat was gone. We were two kilometres out to sea, in some of the most shark-infested water in the world, and the duckie was vanishing into the distance.

Luckily, the surfboard had got thrown out of the boat too, so we took it out of its cover. Jaya was starting to panic, and then I started panicking because he was bleeding. We grabbed the board, about a 7'0", and I put him on the front. I got on the back and we started paddling together.

We were both freaking, because we were a long way from the coast and it seemed like we were getting sucked out to sea, but we managed to get into a bit of rhythm and started making some progress. By the time we got in, the swell was about five or six foot, crashing on the rocks, and we managed to clamber up on the cliffs and suss out where we were. It was about four in the afternoon by then, and I was going, 'We're fucked' and started panicking. And then Jaya came into his own, and I started losing it. 'We're fucked, we're fucked . . .' My eyes were all blurry and bloodshot. I couldn't see properly and I didn't want to go anywhere. I said, 'We've got to stay right here.' He said, 'No, we've got to decide which way we're going to go, because there's no-one coming to look for us.' And then I started crying like a baby – 'No, no, we're staying here.' He was like, 'There's no-one looking for us, we *cannot* stay here. We've got to choose one way.' And whichever way we go, it's all cliff and boulders as far as the eye can see.

We had to go high, then come down low, and then a wave would come and we'd go high again. Then we got to this sheer cliff and we had to swim – and by then the swell was ten foot. I carried the board the whole time because I knew this was coming, so I jumped on the board and Jaya swum for it. And then there was another two-hour hike after that. We climbed along the base of the cliffs for hours, and pretty soon it was dark and we were just groping along by feel. We finally got back about eleven at night. My feet were completely red-raw, and Kaui was like, 'Where the fuck have you guys been?' They found the duckie two days later off Oahu, and it had run out of petrol.

I came back to Oahu after that and thought, *if I can get through that, then I can win Pipe no matter how big it is – because that was way more scary than any wave at Pipe.*

THE '95 PIPE MASTERS – THE RETURN

Beatrice Occhilupo: We went to Hawaii together quite early in the season. Joel Fitzgerald came over and stayed with us. Mark and he trained together incredibly. They were doing like a thousand sit-ups a day, running the beach, doing that under-water thing carrying boulders. He got a wild card to Pipe that year. Sunny was up for a world title, and he and Mark were drawn against each other. Everyone was threatening to send Mark home in a coffin if he beat Sunny. We got threats from everybody. Even his best Hawaiian friend [and board sponsor], Kaui Hill, said he had to lose the heat. Gordon said, 'Just don't do it – you do what you do and don't listen to them.' Mark started getting depressed again, no doubt because of the pressure of it all, and started sleeping again – in Hawaii! I was thinking, *oh God, not again!*

That year in Hawaii I was staying with Gordon and training with Joel Fitzgerald, and we'd run and swim and surf every day, no matter what the waves were like. Joel is a great surfer, especially in Hawaii, and he was really good energy to be around. I'd done a fair bit of training before I got there, and I was ready to make a serious run in Hawaii. But at the same time, I didn't even know if I'd get a start in the events. Looking back on it, there's no denying I was on a mission. Joel and I got on this program where we'd do 1000 sit-ups a day, and we'd get up super early and just start busting them out. It can get kind of monotonous and we'd have little breaks, but I don't think there's anything better for surfing than core strength.

I wasn't even really thinking about the tour, or world titles, I just wanted to re-establish myself as a surfer. But that Hawaiian winter gave me the inspiration to make a serious comeback to competition.

The Pipe Masters is one of the most prestigious contests in the world, and Pipe is a really challenging wave. No-one surfs it better than the local crew, and there was always intense competition for the few spots in the local trials to get into the main event. Because I was unseeded after my time off, I had to compete from the first round of the trials, and there was a bit of resentment about me even getting a start at all.

In the first round of the trials I had Braden Dias and Liam MacNamara in my heat, two really strong Pipe specialists. I remember Liam was so desperate to get through that he grabbed my legrope and I kicked his hand away. It was an intense welcome-back to competition. Liam's a good friend of mine, but he's just so devoted to the local Pipeline guys getting a shot in the Pipe Masters. He was going, 'You shouldn't even be out here. This is for the Pipe guys.' I was like, 'Far out, whatever – just get off my leash.'

It was pretty solid Pipe. I started to get my old rhythm back and was going through one heat after another, building momentum the whole time, and made it through to the main event.

Early in the main event, I came up against local favourite Sunny Garcia, who was going for the world title, and I had a real dilemma. There wasn't really anything at stake for me in terms of ratings points and world rankings, while Sunny was chasing a world title, with all the local support behind him. It was a difficult situation, and I made a decision that I didn't want to interfere with the world-title race and actually tried to let Sunny win our heat. But it was another one of those weird things: no matter what I did, I couldn't seem to lose. All the waves kept coming to me, and then Sunny broke his leash and I ended up winning.

Sunny Garcia: Occy did everything he could to let me win the heat. He sat wide and let me take any wave I wanted, and when I lost my board he tried to give me his. But it just wasn't meant to be. When I got to the beach, some of my guys were saying, 'We should get him for beating Sunny.' And

I told them, 'He tried to let me win, it wasn't his fault.' It's not often in surf contests that you have your competitor trying to give you their board.

Kelly Slater: Sunny broke his leash and got a back-up board paddled out to him. I grabbed his board on the way out to bring it back to him and help him out, but by that time he got his other one. Occy was trying to give him waves, and also possibly get an interference, so that Sunny would win. He was probably stressed he would be banned from Hawaii if he beat Sunny, so he tried to help him. But there were bigger forces at work that day, for whatever reason, and it wasn't to be. In the long run, it made Sunny work harder and probably appreciate winning the title more. And it gave Occy the confidence to go on and win one as well. You never know why something happens until later sometimes.

Rabbit Bartholomew: I was very close to that incident, because early on in the event Occ came to me for some advice. He'd drawn Sunny, and the thing is, I may have ill-advised him that it might not be a good idea to get through that heat, because we were looking at the whole perspective – his comeback for the following year. He'd done enough, but it was going to be next year that counted. We were thinking down the line a bit. There was nothing at stake for him. That's what I said to him: 'You're on track, but this is not your track, this is not the one you have to win.' And I may have ill-advised him in that way, and then he won. I was always into making it count when you had to make it count, and not interfering with other people's world-title races.

Paul Sargeant: That was a really, really gnarly thing. Sunny was going for the world title and Occy was expected to throw the heat. And me and Beatrice were like, 'No way, don't you dare throw that heat. You just get out there and surf your best.' The contest was on standby for two or three days leading up to that showdown, and we were checking the surf at Rocky Point one day. Liam MacNamara came up and went, 'So, Occy, you're going to beat Sunny? I guess you got a choice: you can beat him and go to the airport or you can lose and stay around.' And all these people were coming around giving him advice. And he went out and won it, fair dinkum. And I think at that point, that really threw the Hawaiian weight behind him, because as much as there was local aggro before it, it turned into respect. He always had respect there and he was always everyone's favourite, but he just went to a new level I think. He didn't back down. It was like it was meant to be. You can't say he laid down, because he surfed good on the waves he got. He gave concessions as far as wave selection went and all that. When he won, everyone went 'Oh shit', but nothing ever came of it.

Gerry Lopez: A lot of people really think highly of him here. That whole thing with Sunny, I think that showed a lot of the Hawaiian people, a lot of Sunny's friends, this guy's trying to help Sunny out here. It didn't happen that way, but they all saw that he made a real effort to do that for Sunny.

Beatrice Occhilupo: It was a horrible time. It was really, really horrible. Mark felt so bad. One thing about Mark, he really feels for people. He doesn't like to upset anyone. He doesn't like confrontations. He was friends with Sunny and he was thinking, *maybe I should just throw the heat and let him have it*. But I kept saying, 'No – just go out there and do your best. What would Sunny do? Do you think he'd do that for you? That's the way it is! It's dog eat dog in this surfing thing – you're competing against your best mates, but you just don't give them the waves because you feel sorry for them.' I went and told Gordon what was going down. He went to Kaui and told him to fuck off, and then he pulled Mark aside and said, 'You just get out there and do your best. Don't you listen to anyone!' Mark was still very vulnerable at that stage. The whole thing really hurt Mark. Anyway, the day came and Mark just went, 'Nah, fuck it.' He later said he didn't actually 'mean' to beat Sunny – 'But the waves came to me and I caught them.'

Once I'd beaten Sunny, I really wanted to go all the way – and I just kept progressing. In that one event, I surfed through eleven sudden-death heats, through the trials, into the main event, and all the way to the final against reigning world champ Kelly Slater. It was like a fairytale. I'd come to Hawaii with no expectations. I didn't even know if I'd get a start at Pipe. And now here I was in the middle of the closest world-title race in years, in the final at Pipe against the world champ.

I was doing pretty well in the final until I broke my board and Joel Fitzgerald paddled out with my spare board without a leash on it. I went, 'Where's my leash?' And he went, 'You don't need it.'

I knew then I was right behind the eight ball. I'd already lost time by breaking my board and getting the replacement. I think Kelly had me 'combo-ed', meaning I needed two solid scores to get back in front. It was about eight- to ten-foot Pipe and, if I fell without a leash, I faced a lengthy swim in and more lost time. But I'd got that far and wasn't about to give up. I got another really good barrel, but I came out of it a bit high on the wave and nearly lost it, clinging on in this weird layback position, trying to hang on to my board. I knew if I lost it, my chances were over. I scored a 9 and put myself back within striking distance. With seconds to go, right at the end of the final, I got a really wide one, and I was in the barrel for a long time – real sandbar stuff. If I came out of that, I reckon I could have won it.

But I didn't, and Kelly claimed the Pipe Masters and the world title. Still, second was a nice welcome-back to competition.

Kelly Slater: I was fully surprised to see him back fit and focused and in the game in '95. Pipe was huge for him and a fairytale for the both of us, if you know the story. The wild-card comeback takes down Sunny and meets me in the final, where I have to win to pass Rob Machado, who passed Sunny, in order to take the title. We're all friends and it's a heavy battle. I knew that final was as important to win for him as it was for me in that moment – if nothing else for him to look Sunny in the face and feel like he finished the task at hand. I could see the stress on his face before our final. When we hit the water I told him, 'I know this heat is as important for you as it is for me, so just go for it and don't worry.' I could visibly see the stress leave his face, 'cause he was still an active role in the title, but that's ultimately where he wanted to be, so it was good. There was a genuine part of me that wanted to see him win. If he did, Rob would take the title and that would've been heartbreaking, but fine with me in the end.

Gerry Lopez: I had heard that he was on Maui briefly a few years earlier, and somebody said that they'd seen him. I said, 'Where is he? Bring him around!' And they said, 'He's laying low, he doesn't want to see anybody.' And I respected that because all of us have gone through some difficult times. Not so many people from his generation, but a lot from my generation didn't make it. I sort of knew if he made it out of that dip in his life that he was going to be better than ever, and it sure turned out that way. But he even surprised me. He was resurrected, a whole rebirth, and came back much stronger than he was even the first time around. That was pretty damn impressive. It was like the Cinderella story, to come from the very bottom, because the trials were vicious, and it hardly ever happened that someone from the trials would make it very far. But to have Occy come right to the very edge of that, it was like Pipeline let him down in the final heat. It wasn't anything he did. The waves just went to sleep a little bit, just didn't come through for him. That would have been a really great thing. It was a really great thing as it was, but to come from the bottom and win the event . . .

Maurice Cole: Ross had a house directly in front of Backdoor Pipe, little grey house, and Ross and I were walking out of there one day and I've heard, 'Maurice! Ross!' from thirty metres away. And here is Occ, looking pretty fit and healthy, just running towards us, with the grin, the flick of the hair. He grabbed us in a bear hug, and I had no idea what to do or say, from where we left off. And here was this incredibly vibrant Occ – he looked like a young kid in an older body, just beaming with light, glowing. 'Oh mate, it's so good to see you. I wanted to catch up with ya.' And he actually did, he apologised: 'I'm so sorry about what happened last time.' And when he did that I went, *wow, he does have some sort of accountability and responsibility for his actions. That's pretty good*. And he goes, 'You're not going to believe it – I got married' and all this, because we'd heard all those stories. *Oh no, what's he done . . . Who's he married?*

It was 31 December, and we decided we were going to have a quiet one. And Occ's gone, 'Can I come round tonight with Bea? I can introduce you.' He came round, we had dinner, we all sat out there on the balcony until the sun came up. We had fireworks, we were on our own on the beach at midnight, nearly blew ourselves up, just laughing, having the best time of our lives . . . We met Bea and realised, *wow, Bea's really got her head together. Bea's really sorted him out.* In the conversation there was still talk of requalifying and world titles, and Ross and I were like, 'Fuck yeah, bring it on.' We knew he had the ability. When that window of opportunity's there, fucking take it. We were party to this whole new push for Occy to win a world title. And if it happened or not it didn't matter – it was part of the healing for Occ. Bea seemed wonderful and fantastic, and we got to know her. We were believers, and he always knew that, that we were going to support him. If he wanted to give it a shot, we were going to back him all the way.

I was talking to Steve Perry [at Oakley sunglasses], and Pezza was going, 'Is there anyone else out there that's worth sponsoring. If you see anyone, just let me know, will ya?' And I took the biggest, deepest breath and went, 'Okay, I've got a wild one for you. I've got a wild punt for you, but I'm backing it all the way.' And he said, 'What?' And I said, 'Occ. Occy is on the way back, Pezza. Back him.' And he went, 'What? Occy?' And I told him the little story, and he's gone, 'Okay, I'll just take that back to the marketing people.' And he got back to me and he's gone, 'Mate, they all just laughed at me. They said, "What's fucking Maurice on?"'

I said, 'Pezz, mate, it's a wild call, it's a punt, but I don't reckon you'll ever get a better punt than this. And he just went, 'Maurice, just tell Occy and his new wife, we'll put in ten grand US.' And I remember going back to Bea and Occ with that and, other than just people's support, that someone would come in and do that, that was such a big building block for his self-esteem. And it showed other people, *shit, Oakley are giving him sunglasses, giving him money. What's going on here*? He had a stigma attached to him. Pezza gave him a chance, his friends were backing him to the max, but the whole rest of the institution of surfing weren't backing him at all, because of all the stories from France of the breakdown, whether he got to the 150-kilo mark . . . There was such a negative spin on him, until people actually lived it with him and experienced it with him, they had no idea. The energy was back, the glow was back, the aura was back, know what I mean? And it took people nearly a year or so to get on board.

Steve Perry: Jack McCoy said, 'You've got to get on Occy. Occy's making a comeback.' Maurice Cole said, 'Get on Occy, he's gong to win a world title; no-one can beat him, he's surfing that good.' So we did a new contract, gave him some money and the rest is history. Just the fact that Occy was back – where he'd come from and where he'd been – we always knew how popular he was and his personality. For ten grand to get him to wear your product, that's a good bet, because he's Occ . . . It was just because he's the Occ. Maurice was really impressed, and I took his opinion on board. It was more about the fact that he was back. He's a great personality to be endorsing your brand. You get Occ to wear your product, you don't even have to think about it – it's a walk-up start.

Occy went on to sell more Oakley sunglasses for us than any other three men standing in the surfing world. Shane Warne was huge for us, and I'd probably say Occ and Shane Warne were two of the most iconic sportsmen I've dealt with. There's a lot of similarities between them in a lot of ways, very similar. Warney's got the same sort of generosity as Occy's got. People write Warney off, but he's an absolutely sensational person. No-one hears of all the stuff he does for charity. Him and Warney are two icons of Australian sport. Occy's beyond surfing. He's an iconic person in any pursuit.

Above: A rare moment when I had the better of Kelly, pulling in while he's caught inside, 1995 Pipe Masters. (Although he probably paddled out and scored a 10 after this!)

Right: Bea, me and Rainer – a winning team.

Above left: Bea congratulating me after another win at the Skins.

Above right: Tonka, my much-loved prize for winning the Skins.

Below left: The Warrnambool crew, providing my own cheer squad at Bells, 1997. Thanks, boys.

Below right: Ringing the Bell for my dad at the 1998 Rip Curl Pro.

A hook in the pocket at Bells – a move that has served me well over the years.

Dropping into big, perfect G-Land at the 1997 Quiksilver Pro.

Above: Right in my comfort zone at good, mid-range Teahupoo.

Right: Gordon giving me a guiding hand, again, studying a heat sheet in Hawaii.

Above and below: Two views of what I like doing to a big, wide-open shoulder at Cloudbreak, Fiji.

Above: The boys from Bure One. Hoyo, Luke and me loving life.

Right: Super-caddy Hoyo and me celebrating another heat win.

Left: Holding down the bar with Luke at Namotu.

Below: Right at home at Namotu, manning the barbecue. Stand back, girls.

Above: What I hope to be doing a lot more of in retirement, right at home at D-bah.

Left: Mae and me on our wedding day. (*Occhilupo family collection*)

Below: My wonderful family. (*Clockwise*) Mae, me, Jay and Jonah. (*Occhilupo family collection*)

Chapter Thirteen

The Second Coming

After Pipe, I told Gordon I really wanted to requalify for the WCT. He was against the idea. He just wanted me to cruise and free-surf and do film and photo shoots. He didn't want to see me slogging it out on the WQS in really bad waves in four-man heats and fail, and maybe damage my reputation. But I was determined to do it, and Beatrice was really into and ready to travel the world with me. In the end Gordon said, 'Do what you want to do.' He wasn't completely calling the shots, but he had kind of been calling my shots for a while. He's always been like a mentor, guiding me and advising me on what I should or shouldn't do, and he's always made good calls. But this was one time I went against his advice. I know it caused him a bit of anxiety, which gave me extra motivation to succeed.

It was going to be hard work, though, qualifying through the WQS, which was a whole different deal to the trials system I came through the first time way back in '83. There were way more surfers for a start, hundreds of them from all over the world: Brazil, South Africa, the US mainland, Hawaii, Europe, as well as Australia. They were all young, fit, pumped up and full of dreams. The WCT had moved to the world's great surf spots in season, with waiting periods and the ability to go mobile, and this was a big part of my motivation to make it back. But the WQS still went to mainly mediocre metropolitan beachbreaks, fifty or more events, zig-zagging all over the planet. This was the kind of schedule that had brought me undone the first time round, but I just knuckled down to do it. I also had Bea by my side, cooking me great food, helping organise my travels and keep me on the straight and narrow. And her son, Rainer, was a great surfing buddy and often caddied for me during competition.

Rainer and I had become good friends, and he'd grown up fast. He was just a kid when I first started going out with his mum. I remember him jumping up and down in the back seat of the car whenever I put music on, and thinking to myself, *this kid's a bit radical.* I'd be like, 'Settle down there, boy!' But he became a really well-mannered young man, and I'd like to think I had a bit to do with that. By the time he was fifteen or sixteen, he could really hold his own in the surf. He got big fast, and not too many people dropped in on Rainer. He became good friends with all my friends, especially Joel Parkinson – they loved surfing together. I was proud of him. Everyone loved Rainer and we became a really good team on tour, getting through airports, grabbing luggage and hire cars.

> **Rainer:** Oh yeah! He was a great father to me. He taught me everything I know! Well, I've got a head on my shoulders. I'm not too bad. My real dad left when I was two, and I never had any blokes around, just Mum and her sisters and stuff. And then I met Dad and he taught me everything to know about being a man, having respect and being tough . . . and whatever else. Respect was the biggest thing, and that's one thing I do have for him, and a lot of other people. I know about respect.

It was nice to travel as a family unit and we decided to do it in style, staying at the best hotels. It was a far cry from my early days on the tour, and it worked. I'd be in bed by 7.30 and up at the crack of dawn, amping to surf.

The main thing I knew I had to do if I was going to requalify was speed up my surfing. Barton Lynch gave me that bit of advice, and it was so true. He said, 'You're surfing really well, but you've just got to speed it up.' It was a hard thing to do, but it was probably good for me. It changed my surfing. The main difference in the time I'd been off tour was that surfing had got a fair bit quicker. I always believed pure, powerful surfing was the way to go, but there's nothing wrong with being quick too. If you blend the two together . . . well, that combination probably helped me get back on tour. You have to adapt to the new thing, the latest. I saw other surfers trying to come back; they were still surfing beautifully, but they didn't have the speed. They just looked a bit slow and a little cruisy – and there's nothing wrong with that if that's what you're into. That's good soul surfing – I like it. But it just doesn't blend in when you're in competition, being judged alongside other guys surfing a whole lot faster. You've got to be quick and do your thing at the same time. That's probably the main thing that helped me come back.

Beatrice Occhilupo: So, there we were, Mark back on tour. It was hard. Mark wanted to give up all the time. I kept saying 'No!', but he'd say, 'Oh, the judges have got something against me.' I suggested, 'Okay, let's write them a letter.' So we sat down and wrote them a letter. Mark lost a heat and said, 'That's it! We're going home! I just don't want to do it anymore.' I said, 'No! We're not giving up. You and me are going to do this together and we're going to get through it!' It was a team effort. He would get down, and I'd have to build him up. He was good, though. He stayed clean and didn't party, kept to himself, and we really concentrated on focusing. I was getting his mind really positive: 'You can do it! You can do it!'

Anyway, I forget where we were – France, I think – and Barton came up and said, 'You've got to change your style of surfing, mate. You've got to go fast.' As soon as Barton said that, Mark started changing his style of surfing and going faster and doing aerials and all that stuff. That's when he started getting better results.

Luke Egan: When he went on the 'QS, Beatrice came up and said to me, 'Would you look after him?' She couldn't travel everywhere with him because of Rainer and his schooling. So from there I pretty much had an adopted son who was older than me. And I always joke that that's what I call him, 'a son who's older than me' . . . It's hilarious. I just look about a minute forward into his life, like having a little kid around. It could be like that cord there, and I'd go, 'Occ, watch out for that cord', because I'd know he was going to trip over it and the computer would fall. It's pretty hilarious. He'd love it when he could do something for me, like, 'Gee, I helped you out there, Louie.' The score'd be like 1000 to 3, but he'd ham it up.

Mick Lowe: Growing up, Occy's always been one of my surfing idols. He was coming back when I was having my first dig on the 'QS, and it felt really strange. The whole world wanted him to requalify, and I was just this punk kid trying to get through heats. I remember Durban was about one foot, and I remember hassling the shit out of Occ. I came second and he came third, and I remember thinking, *this is one of my heroes, but I've still got to try and do my job.* I remember feeling pretty bad.

By Europe I was on the bubble, right on the cusp of qualifying. We went to Ericeira, Portugal, and I copped a really stiff decision by the judges. I was scored an interference that I just thought was totally the wrong call. I was so emotional that I stormed the judges' tower. Head judge Perry Hatchett told me, 'Get out, I'm judging', but I just unloaded on him: 'You guys don't want me to requalify, do you?' I really let my emotions fly in the tower – all the pent-up stress and tension just came pouring out – and I think I was better off for it. I don't know if I can say the same for poor old Perry.

Paul Sargeant: The judges made it really, really difficult for him. There were so many heats where Occy would lose by 0.1 or whatever – just ridiculous. And he was getting really, really frustrated, going, 'Sarge, they're not going to let me. They're not going to let me.' I went, 'Don't worry about it, just keep knocking on the door.' It was just a headspace that you didn't come back – when you're gone, you're gone. But, geez, they made it tough for him.

The thing that everyone was blown away with was how he'd sped up his surfing. You can't do that – but he did. He upped it by 30 per cent and somehow still kept that style, and that massive Raging Bull thing. It was really, really popular when it happened, but leading into it, nobody cared. It was Occy's private war, and he just kept relentlessly hammering away. I remember once he was in tears; he wanted to pull out halfway through that year. He said, 'I'm going home', and I said, 'No, you're not.' It was really, really heavy.

Renato Hickel (ASP judge): He was close to making the cut but not yet inside the fifteen to make the top forty-four, and he got a really close interference call in Portugal. He came to talk to me, crying, and it was tough. I said, 'Just because of one interference call doesn't mean you're not going to make the cut. It was an interference, you made a mistake and you've got to pick up and move on and focus on the next event.' And luckily he did make the cut and make it back on tour, and the

> rest is history. He was crying, saying, 'You guys don't want me to make the cut', and Beatrice came to talk to me as well. And we talked again over dinner, crossed paths at dinner, and he was calmer and we had a good chat. It was all positive.

After that we went to Hossegor, France, and Tony Seddon won it. I got second. It was only a two-star event, but I was really happy about that. These days, you wouldn't even count a two-star in your final points, but in those days there were only a couple of four- or five-star events, and second place in a two-star was a keeper. From there we went to Brazil and they gave me a seed, straight into the money round, which was an automatic result for me because that was a six-star. So I was looking good.

By the time I got to Hawaii at the end of the year, I was sitting about eighteenth or nineteenth, and there were a few surfers above me who had already qualified on the WCT, so people were telling me I had as good as qualified. But I wasn't taking anything for granted and wouldn't believe it until the final heat of the final event had been surfed and all the ratings had been finalised. I was watching all the events, doing all the equations. That was the best I ever got at maths in my whole life.

It came down to the last event at Sunset and, when it was finally official and I was definitely in, I was over the moon. There was a bit of a party that night, I can tell you . . .

That year was also the first time I rented the house at Rocky Point Lefts, which was my chosen spot on the North Shore for many years. My friend Randall Kim, who worked for Billabong in Hawaii, set it up for me. I remember walking into that house and seeing the view out the window of Rocky Lefts and just going, *oh yeah, this is it. I've finally found my spot.* I kept that place for years and had some great times. Taj Burrow and Joel Parkinson both stayed with us there over the years, and I could stroll out the back gate and surf my favourite spot at Rocky Lefts. I have so many great memories of staying in that house, but they're also tinged with sadness. It was around that time Randall and his wife, Carol, were shot dead by a neighbour during an argument outside their house in Milalani. It was such a tragic waste; they were such beautiful people who offered so much aloha to visiting surfers, and we were all devastated.

Richard Maurer: When he got back on the tour the second time, he said to me, 'I really want to do it for Rainer, because Rainer's only seen pictures of me surfing. He's never actually seen me winning contests or doing anything. I want to give him some inspiration. I just don't want him to see me on the lounge for the rest of my life. I want him to see me achieve something, and see if it rubs off on him.' And he went out and did it.

Bruce Irons: The first thing I remember about Occy is *Pump*, the Billabong movie *Pump*. We used to watch that over and over and over and over. That's still one of my favourite movies in the world . . . Reunion, French beachbreaks, Mundaka, that movie's sick. He's always been so radical, got such a cool style. And then I remember he came to Kauai when I was really young, and I was like, *wow, Occy's on Kauai.* Then we had a heat at Sunset. I used to stay at Brian Surratt's house, and he used to go to Brian's house a lot too. I was young, like thirteen, fourteen, staying at Brian's and I was in the X-cel Pro. I didn't know Occy, but we had a heat together. It was fucking one foot, two foot – there's no waves. He's paddled round me once or twice, whatever, grommet. I'm like, *fuck this, I'm not letting him go round me.* We had this paddle battle all the way up to Boneyards, fucking dry reef. And he's like, 'What the fuck are you doing? You wouldn't even be out here if it was six to eight feet.' I went, 'Fuck you.' He went, 'Fuck off.' And I ended up beating him, and the next day was six to eight feet, and I made the semis. I was like, *wow, my hero just shat on me.* And then a couple of years later we became friends. We always talk about that and laugh – 'My hero's hassling me.' He's Occy, he's everyone's hero.

1997 – THE SECOND COMING

Barton Lynch (from Jack McCoy's *The Occumentary*): To be able to come onto the tour at thirty-one with the maturity and the knowledge that you have, just through what you've lived, and then at the same time to have that youthful enthusiasm like you're nineteen again and that venom, that's the lethal combination, and to me he's just got unfinished business.

I won the first WQS event of the new year, the XXXX Classic at Point Cartwright on the Sunshine Coast. It wasn't a major event, but I realised with a bit of a shock that it was the first contest of any sort I'd won in five years. My first year back on the WCT felt really special, and I started strongly, riding a wave of goodwill from a lot of people. Everyone seemed stoked to see me back. There was a really warm acceptance of my comeback that made life easier.

I came third in my first event back, the Coke Classic at Narrabeen, losing to Kelly in the semis, who went on to beat Sunny in the final.

Kelly was the new benchmark on tour. In my absence, he had come along and raised the bar so high that everyone had to start surfing better. He definitely helped inspire my comeback. I was after nothing less than a world title, and if I wanted to win it, he was the guy I had to win it from. I followed up with a fifth at Bells, which was satisfying enough in itself, but my good mate Matt Hoy won it and the celebrations, as you'd expect, were epic. We all went back to the great local surfer Wayne Lynch's place, this beautiful beach house tucked away in the bush. Late that night, we all ended up in the teepee in his backyard, with a camp fire burning, people playing music, just a great vibe. I think that was why I did so well in the next event, a specialty one-off called the Skins.

We spent a long time at Bells that year, and I was really starting to feel in the groove of the place. When we heard of a new swell arriving right on cue for the Skins, a few days after the Rip Curl contest, we were so psyched. I love Bells, it's always somewhere I know I can do well. My boards were going beautifully – I had a perfect 6'5" Dahlberg channel-bottom that loved solid Bells, and I felt like I couldn't put a foot wrong on it. When the swell came, the winds were perfect offshores, and it was a ruler-edged six to eight feet.

The format was new to everyone, but I just seemed to get the hang of it straightaway. They were short heats and you could catch two waves, but you had to nominate your single scoring wave as soon as you kicked off, by raising both hands above your head to 'claim' it. I was stretching right out between heats, staying warm and loose and just psyched to go surfing. I had a strategy going where I'd always try and claim a score first, and then leave the guy out there hanging. It puts the pressure on. They know you've got a score but they don't know how good it is. They don't know whether to claim their first or second wave, and time's ticking away. Sometimes the other guy didn't even catch a wave. There were so many waves coming through, and I was just in the zone. I loved it.

Beatrice said the contest suited me so well because it combined my two favourite activities – surfing and gambling. And it's kind of true. You won $5000 every time you won a heat, and you stayed out until someone knocked you off. I won eleven straight heats over two days and won $55,000, plus a new Jeep Cherokee worth about $30,000.

I'll never forget jumping into that car after the presentation. They gave me the cheque for fifty-five grand and I jumped in my new car. There was a pretty good-sized crowd gathered, and I just dropped the clutch and kangaroo-hopped the whole way up the car park. I couldn't stop it, I was just going *rrrrr, rrrrr*, grinding the gears, and everyone was cracking up. I came out of the Bells car park and looked around, and I've got a fifty-five grand cheque in my hand and a new car. I just started laughing, and I didn't stop laughing the whole way back to Melbourne. I was just like, *is this for real?* That was such a good time. We went straight to the Crown Casino after that and stayed for a few days. I didn't cash that cheque, but we had a good time.

I even had Kelly on toast that day, which doesn't happen often. I'm the worst critic of my own surfing – people say how great I surfed that day and I look at it and go, 'It's not that good.' It's funny because you always have the best surfs when no-one's watching . . . I guess I pulled out the full bag of tricks that day, and every wave was different, which is probably why people were into it. The crowd was cheering like a footy match. The stands were still there from Easter. There wasn't the huge Easter crowd, but more of just the inner pro surfing crowd. The surfers had all hung around, and they were banging on the metal signs on the front of the stands and stamping their feet like it was a grand final. I loved the atmosphere, and it all came together those two days.

We used to stay at my friend Steve Perry's house back then, and over the years I've stayed there a few times. He has a place, the old Torquay library right in the main street, and it's this really quaint building. Then he got his place at Jan Juc, and he offered to have us stay with him there, but the old place was always our lucky house. I've always done well staying there.

Steve Perry: The old library he used to reckon was haunted. There was a weird neighbour up the road. He thought he was seeing ghosts, because she'd come knocking on the door at three in the morning. The year he won the Skins he stayed in that house. He stayed there for a couple of years; it was his lucky house. Then I'd built a new house at Boobs, and he stayed for five years at that house. You could sit upstairs and watch them taking off in the bowl at Bells.

The Skins, that was freaking amazing, in such classic Bells conditions. He was just unbeatable. It'd be four o'clock beer and chips, in bed at seven, and he'd be up at four. I have memories of really great times. He started the annual Easter egg hunt at our place. He'd be so excited, hiding the eggs in the garden, waiting for the kids to wake up. He's got the most beautiful, sweetest heart.

Kelly Slater: That display of surfing at Bells was the stuff of legend. It was probably still the best surfing I've seen. It was as if something magical was happening, something you only see the best-of-the-best do – and only once or twice in their careers.

Doug 'Claw' Warbrick (Rip Curl co-founder): He's one of the greatest surfers at Bells of all time. Bells and Occy have got this special synergy. It's a special thing and, when Bells was good, Occy came into his own, once it was five feet or bigger, offshore and walled-up and chunky. The angles he got going, the body english and power . . . they're pretty extreme, pretty remarkable.

Vince Lawder: Watching him at the Skins . . . that was amazing. He just had the style, and I think that's something a lot of the young kids should look at. A lot of kids these days try and mimic Joel and Mick, which is cool because it helps their surfing and they've seen them surf a lot. But the kids who really take it to a level above that are the ones who have their own unique style, and I think that's something Occ always had that set him apart from everyone.

Mick Fanning: The year at Bells, so many people talk about that. For me, that was my first year down at Bells and, seeing how good he was then, I felt so honoured just to be there. I was pumped . . . His bottom turn starts at the top of the wave. It's the perfect wave for him. That was insane.

Peter Wilson (photographer): He had this magic board, a 6'5" channel-bottom shaped by Rod Dahlberg. I had to do some shots for a Japanese magazine and Rod was saying, 'Don't show them the bottom of the board . . . They'll all want channels and they're too much work.'

Rod Dahlberg: I was his main shaper from about '95 to 2006. The '97 Skins, the 6'5" six-channel was the magic one. I shaped a lot of channels in my day, and you don't talk people into them, because they're a lot of work. If they want 'em, I'll do them. A lot of the pros rode channels after that. Kelly had channel-bottoms the next year at Bells.

Occ never got as many boards as most pros do. He wasn't a really heavy board slut. He gets confused if he gets too many. Occ would go, 'Give me three, and if I break one, make me another one quickly.' It was just a pleasure, just seeing your boards being surfed at that level. It really is the redeeming factor that lets you know you're on the right track. There's only one Occ, and there's not too many people who do turns like he does.

RUMBLE IN THE JUNGLE

That year we went to Grajagan, on the south-east tip of Java, and we got straight off the boat after the overnight trip from Bali into some of the best waves I've ever seen. The surf was eight feet, the tide filled in, and Speed Reef came alive. We all just went berserk. Some guys had never seen waves like it – sheet glass, drainpipe barrels just roaring down the reef. It was a feeding frenzy. Everyone got the barrels of their lives. Derek Ho ended up nailing himself and needing stitches. It was like that for days, dropping then picking up again.

I got a third, losing in the semis to Luke Egan, who was just in his element. That was one time I didn't mind losing too much, because Luke was untouchable in those waves and went on to win the thing. I was stoked for him. I was his caddy, and at times I couldn't help myself and ended up catching a couple. Luke was going, 'Stop it or you'll get me disqualified.' But it's hard to just sit and let perfect eight-foot barrels pass you by.

I actually paddled out of G-Land that year with my backpack on. At the end of the event there was a fast boat going straight back to Bali, which only took a couple of hours, or there was the all-night marathon by bemo and ferry. There was a party on in Kuta that night and I didn't want to do the all-nighter, so they picked up all our stuff before the final and stashed it on the fast boat. I went to the beach to watch the presentation and saw Luke get that beautiful carved wooden tiger. Then I literally paddled out of G-Land with my little backpack, jumped on the fast boat and got a ride back to Bali. That night I was back in the madness of Kuta, a few hours after riding perfect barrels out in the jungle. It was amazing.

> **Luke Egan:** He was waking up every morning and doing 200 sit-ups and 200 push-ups. G-Land in '97, when I won, every fucking morning in our hut I'd wake up to this *phew*, *phew*, *phew*, and he'd be doing sit-ups. As soon as he woke up he started doing sit-ups – just roll out of bed and do it.

By the time we got to Portugal, Kelly Slater had a solid lead in the world title, but I was sitting at number two and still in contention, which felt amazing in my first year back. It came down to a quarter-final with my old mate Shane Powell at Figueira da Foz. If I won, my slim world title chances remained alive. If I lost, Kelly had won his fifth world title. I spotted Kelly hiding in the bushes before my heat, trying to pretend he wasn't watching. I really put everything into it. I knew I had a lot of work to do to try and catch him, with only Brazil and Pipeline left. And everyone knows how good he is at Pipe. I really gave it my best shot, but Powelly won that one and Kelly clinched the title. I was right there to congratulate him afterwards, but was really keen to secure my number two spot.

The waves were pumping in Brazil for the next event and, lo and behold, Kelly and I again met in the final. There were some radical barrels during the event, and I remember Kelly scoring a 10 and being really on his game. The surf had dropped for the final, and it would have been interesting if the title had still been on the line. But Kelly was on a roll, and there wasn't much I could do to stop him. Still, my second place in the event strengthened my hold on the number two spot in the ratings.

With the '97 world title decided, Pipe became a bit of a contest for the locals, and two local legends met in the final: Michael Ho and Johnny Boy Gomes. Johnny was ruling out there and won the day, and I was stoked to see them get their due.

The ASP banquet was really emotional for me, and I gave a heartfelt speech, congratulating Kelly and apologising for all my wild behaviour during my dark days on tour. 'It's a beautiful world when people forgive,' I said, and I really meant it. I was so stoked to have been welcomed back into the fold, and it felt amazing to be standing in front of my peers as the runner-up for the world title.

DRIVEWAY FROM HELL

But while things seemed to be going my way in the water, I was no less accident prone on land. Our house at Bilambil had a radically steep driveway, which probably wasn't such a great thing given my track record with cars. Sure enough, one day my mate Steve, or 'Hambone' as we call him, came over and got stuck halfway down. It was wet – the driveway was always tricky to reverse down anyway – and he got wedged against a rock and couldn't get out. His wheels just kept spinning in the wet. I had a rental car at the time because my car was getting serviced. So I tried to tow him out with this rental car, but the rope kept breaking and the car wasn't powerful enough to shift his car. So I undid the rope and parked the hire car back at the top of the driveway while we considered our next move. But I must've not parked my car far enough up on the flats, because I heard this noise and turned around to see my car beginning to slowly roll down the drive. I was standing right in front of it, and I was going to try and stop it, but as it gathered speed I just went, *oh fuck, I so haven't got this covered*, and had to dive out of the way. It picked up speed fast as it got onto the steepest section, and I yelled out to Hambone, because he hadn't even seen it coming at this point. He was leaning under his car trying to undo the rope, and he looked up to see the hire car pelting towards him. It would have squashed him like a fly but, right before it got to him, it hit the side of the driveway and got air and landed flat on its roof in the garden, completely flattening it. It fully bounced, rolled again and landed back on its wheels at the bottom of the driveway.

It was completely written off, and I had to call the rental car company and try and explain what had happened. I said, 'You've got to come and check this out. I think the handbrake may have been faulty.' On the insurance forms they have a little area where you're supposed to do a drawing of how the accident happened, but my artistic skills couldn't really do justice to the reality. Who knows what they made of the claim form. But they probably just added it to the bulging Occhilupo file and bumped up my premium.

ROLLING IN IT

I loved living up there at Bilambil. I'd go up to the country club to play the pokies and started playing a bit of golf with my mates Blairy and Bing, and this guy called Richard Smith, who's the barber down at Tweed Heads. We'd play together every Wednesday and Saturday when I was home. I became a member and even won the C-grade championship, against this guy who was about ninety years old. I shot a 10 on the first hole and he thought he had me, but I came back, and he ran out of steam. He was a great old guy, but I forget his name. Bea was happy for me to go up to the club and put a few coins through the pokies. I was starting to make pretty good money again, and it was my release. But I always used to take more money than she thought, and I wasted a lot of money on those things. Those machines are such a trap, and I don't have any good stories about hitting the jackpot.

The clubhouse was about four fairways up from our house, and I used to cut across the golf course to get home. What money I did win I used to hide under trees on the golf course on the way home. Bea would say, 'Show me how much money you're going to take', and I'd show her a couple hundred bucks. But I'd have my little stashes under the trees from last time that I'd pick up on my way to the club. The only trouble was, sometimes I'd forget which trees I'd hidden the money under. People would be playing golf, just watching me rummaging around under the trees, wondering what I was up to. I reckon that's why the money went missing sometimes – because people would be looking for their balls and they'd find my stash.

It was a perfect downhill slope from the club all the way to my house, and if I'd had a really good night I'd just roll home, the way you do when you're a kid. I'd just lie down and roll all the way home. That might have been another reason why some of the money went missing . . .

FOR DAD

The next year I dropped down the ratings a bit to number seven, but I'd still been in contention for the title for most of the year, and there were some definite highlights for me. One was winning the Bells event and dedicating it to my father, Luciano. It was my first major contest win in twelve years, since the Newcastle event way back in '86, and I'd waited a long time to dedicate a win to Dad. So, for me, that win and honouring my father's memory was really emotional and a bit of a healing. Bells has been such a special place for me, and it was fitting that it happened there.

> **Occy's acceptance speech at Bells:** This is such a special moment for me, and this is such a special event. It's been such a long time, and I have a lot of people I'd like to thank who I owe this win to. I'd like to thank my wife, Beatrice, and my step-son, Rainer, who was caddying for me out there. He's been a lot of help to me and we've gotten really close over the last few years. I've been married for five years, and I'd like to thank my wife and my family for being there. I've been waiting a long time to win an event like this, Bells especially – it's really special.
>
> I'd like to commemorate this win to my father, Luciano Occhilupo, who passed away in 1990. I've been waiting a very long time and feel this is a good time to say that, because it's a special time for me.
>
> I'd also like to thank Rip Curl for having this event, it's always the best event and everyone treats the place really

well, because it's a national park and it's a real special place and I just love it. It means a lot to me to be a professional surfer and to be allowed to come here where the land's not built on. Being the Year of the Ocean, I want to give a lot back to the ocean, because we get so much from it. This is the place where the ocean meets Bells Beach, and there's some fantastic waves here.

I'd like to thank all the people that have been so good to me, everyone behind my comeback. I feel like I'm one of you watching me come back, because . . . it just doesn't feel like me, it feels like my brother or something. [*Crowd cracks up.*] It feels real good, so thanks.' [*He rings the bell; crowd goes nuts.*]

Danny Wills (August 1998, at a time when Wills is leading the ratings): I reckon Occy is the best surfer in the world at the moment. Everybody is good at WCT level. There's no leaks in it. Everybody rips, but he's definitely a hard man to beat. He's bullshit! It'd be great to see him do it. He got second last year, and he can only go one better. I wouldn't be spewin' – though I guess I would be . . . I'd rather see Occy win it ahead of any other person, just for the fact that he deserves it.

GOING HOME

In 1998 I also completed a pilgrimage to Italy, to see my father's homeland. And we even scored waves in the Mediterranean! Beatrice and her sister Naomi, Rainer and Sarge all came along for the journey, and the locals really took good care of us. They reckon they usually wait four months to get waves like that, and we walked straight into fun little three- or four-foot waves on the west coast, not far from Rome. I even got a little barrel on my last wave, and Rainer landed a couple of airs. I couldn't believe it. There were heaps of surfers there and every time we went for a surf a crowd would form. I remember looking at all the people, to see whether they looked like me, if any of them might have been distant relatives.

We saw all the sights, the girls lapped up the shopping, and it was amazing for me to walk down streets and visit places where my father might have been. I really wished I could speak Italian. When we were young, Dad really wanted all of us to learn his language, but back then you'd get paid out for being a wog, and we didn't want to know about it. But after going there I really wished I'd learnt Italian. It made me feel proud of my heritage, whereas as a kid I was never proud of it. It just felt like putting one more piece in the puzzle of who I was.

THE COOLY KIDS

But there was also a lot of sadness that year when two of the best young surfers in Coolangatta, Sean Fanning and Joel Green, were killed in a car accident. Rainer was really good friends with them and we were all devastated. The whole town was devastated. I always loved surfing with Sean; he was such a good surfer with a really nice style, and a goofy-footer to boot. It was just so heavy, a tragic accident. The girl driving, Bianca, goes out with Rainer now, and she's such a lovely girl and they're really in love. But it was a heavy time for the whole town.

Sean and Joel were part of a bunch of friends who called themselves the Cooly Kids, and we have an event in their honour every year. We all love that event, and it's always Joel or Mick or Dean who win it – I've made a few finals. It's a really special weekend. As Mick would say, 'It's all-time.' Mick wants to get a tattoo saying, 'What time is it? All-time.' We always go up to the surf club and have a beer before our heats and celebrate these two great young blokes who we all miss.

Chapter Fourteen

On a Mission

By 1999 I had a feeling of 'now or never' for my world title dreams. It was my third year back on the WCT and I was turning thirty-three, which was already older than most pro surfers when they retired and a lot older than any previous world champion. But the age thing never really bothered me too much. I felt good and the time off tour had kept me young, in body and spirit. I had a really good pre-season in '99, and did a lot of training – more training than I'd done in all my years on tour. I used to run on the beach at Fingal. I'd start on Monday morning and run about one kilometre in the soft sand, marking the distance with a stick. Each day I'd move the marker another half a kilometre. By the end of the week I was running about four kilometres in the soft sand, which is hard work, especially in summer. It was even harder when someone moved my marker – I just kept running and nearly ended up in Kingscliff before I realised.

The waves had been really good and I was surfing Snapper all the time, so I was as fit as I'd ever been. I got thrown a bit of a dummy when the first event was moved from Snapper half an hour south down to Cabarita, chasing swell. I hadn't been practising down there, so that threw a spanner in the works and I copped a seventeenth.

But I headed down to Bells feeling good, made the semis and had a great heat with Sunny in really good solid Bells. We both had a bunch of 8s and 9s, and he won, but that third put me back on track. The Coke contest was held in small waves at Manly and I suffered a dreaded thirty-third, so at that point the dream wasn't looking too good.

SOUTH PACIFIC BLESSING

I've always felt an affinity with Islander cultures, and I've always loved the waves and the people in those parts of the world. And that year the South Pacific leg really came to my rescue. It was the first time the Teahupoo contest in Tahiti had been a WCT event. I'd been there once before, but I'd never really surfed Teahupoo that much.

Luke Egan and I stayed with local surfer Manoa Drollet, and you could tell the waves were big that first night. It was washing right up under his house. You could hear the swell cracking on the outer reefs. Neither of us could sleep. The trials were on the next day, and we knew it would be big so we grabbed our seven-footers and figured we'd just paddle out in the channel and watch. As we were paddling out Johnny Boy Gomes, who was in the trials, came by on a jet ski and went right past us and yelled, 'DO SOMET'ING!', which is his favourite little saying. It was the perfect welcome to Teahupoo.

As soon as we got out there the wind went onshore and they called it off for the day. We weren't expecting to surf it, I didn't have a leash, and we looked at each other and went, 'What do we do?' And Louie said, 'Well, let's go try one.' I was like, *oh shit.* It was big, a solid eight to ten feet, and now it was messy with the onshore – not the ideal way to get to know the place. I was paddling into the line-up going, *I didn't expect this.* A big wide one came and I went for it, thinking that because it was a wide one it would be a good one just to feel it out. But it wrapped around at me, and I wasn't going to pull in because it was a bit onshore and not really barrelling. It just rolled me. I lost my board and snapped it and had to get someone on a ski to help me look for my board on the reef. And then I had to sit and watch for two hours as it glassed off and Louie just picked off one bomb after another.

But we had a great time there and got into a really nice rhythm. There was a little freshwater pool and waterfall near Manoa's house, and we'd stop for a swim every time we drove past. It gets so hot over there, and a waterfall makes your skin feel so clean and energises you. That was one of our little rituals that we had to observe every day, like one of the pieces in the puzzle. And we both did really well in the event. Luke organised a really good boat and a driver to take us out to the break every day, and this little Tahitian girl used to come out with us. She was our good luck charm. It was a really nice boat and we rented it for the duration, feeling like James Bond, zapping to and from the waves each day.

It was big for the early rounds, and I rang Bea just to tell her I loved her in case anything nasty happened. It felt that serious. I didn't want to freak her out, but I said something like 'I love you and someone could die here.' Just what she wanted to hear, I'm sure.

It was eight to ten feet. I didn't catch any of the massive sets but got some clean medium-sized barrels, like my old Pipe strategy, and beat Victor Ribas. Then the swell dropped and I beat Shane Beschen when it was small. It was predicted to come up huge again for the final day. It sounded so huge all night, and neither of us could sleep again. We got up really early in the morning on dark and drove along with the ocean on our right-hand side, trying to see the whitewater exploding on the reef somewhere out there in the greyness. You want it to be big, but not too big. Luke wanted it to be huge, because the bigger it got the better he went, but when it was too big I just found it an overload. I wanted it to be like six to eight, rather than eight to ten, to be honest.

We got there just as it was getting light, and I got a really good feeling. It was about six feet when we checked it, and I just went, *oh man, this could be my day.* It was perfect conditions. I didn't really want it to drop any more, but it dropped slowly through the day and I kept having really good heats. I had Manoa in one heat and he's one of the best surfers out there, but he doesn't know man-on-man too well. When you're really hungry and you've got a guy who doesn't know man-on-man, you know you can use it to your advantage. So I won that heat and found myself in the final with Damien Hobgood, but the waves were pretty bad by then, only two to three foot.

It started raining during the final and the clouds came over, but I felt like I'd built up enough momentum to keep powering away. I got one reasonable wave and did three good turns – there weren't really any barrels – and I scored an 8. Louie was in the channel, and he just roared at me, 'PADDLE, OCC!', because it was coming down to the wire. I looked at him and I couldn't paddle; I felt like I was in one of those dreams where someone's chasing you and you can't run. I was trying to paddle, but I wasn't going anywhere. I felt like I was so close to the finish line but I was paddling in slow motion. Luke was yelling, 'What are you doing?' And I went, 'I'm trying, I'm trying!'

Near the end of the final I got another good score and he didn't have much. I just thought, *oh my goodness . . .* Then the rain started pouring down, the hooter went, and I lifted my face to the sky and let the rain wash over me. It was one of the best feelings I've ever had in my life, sitting out in the ocean, in the rain, with those beautiful mountainous islands as a backdrop.

I remember coming in and walking to the presentation. I had to walk down this track where the trees kind of hang over and form a tunnel, and I could just see this clear blue sky at the end. That's why I went into the rest of the season with so much confidence. I felt like I was walking through a gateway to my world title. It felt like a really special day for me, like I'd been blessed by this beautiful island, its waves and people. I felt the most overwhelming sense of gratitude.

Luke Egan: I'm pretty structured when we travel. I hate mess, I hate drama, I hate fuck-ups. I'm always thinking that far ahead. We were like a machine, getting through airports, finding the way to new spots. We had a gnarly regime going. At 'Chopes it was the first year of a CT there, and all the guys were like, 'Fuck, how do we do this?' Everyone was paddling out with their quiver, with a backpack on their backs. I'm just hanging on the edge of the point, and this guy pulls up in this brand-new, twenty-foot, sick fishing boat. I just start talking to him, and I'm like, 'How much for the week?' And he goes, 'Five hundred bucks.' I go, 'Done – 24/7 you're ours, no-one else.' Occ and I pull up in this huge twenty-foot red fishing boat. All our boards are stacked up in the corner. Jake and all the boys are going, 'Where the fuck did you get this? What are you doing?' Even the event – we blew the event away before they had a lot of boats going. We kind of started that.

I made the quarters, Occy won it, and then they were all looking at the boys in the big red boat going, 'Fuck, you're just nailing us.' That contest was unreal. And if there wasn't any surf, he'd still take us fishing up the reef.

We got real good at things like that. I was running off the back of him. I was learning so much about surfing heats. He was helping me with my heats, and I was helping him with his heats, so I was sliding on his coat-tails. That's probably what I got out of it, ten more years on tour at that level. In my thirties I competed way better than in my twenties.

Japan was tiny that year, and I came up against a few of the young guys who are really good in small waves, but still managed a ninth. I went away happy, thinking, *that could help.* I wouldn't call it a roll, but things were definitely starting to come together. Fiji was up next, and that has become one of my favourite places in the world. It's so beautiful over there and the people have the nicest nature. They're so friendly, and if you're friendly to them, they make you feel like family. They're really sad when you have to leave and really excited each time you come back. The locals would come out in boats and cheer for me from the channel when I surfed. It was the sort of place that suited me perfectly.

I was staying in Bure One with Luke and Hoyo, and we were having the greatest time. So much funny stuff happened in Bure One. The surf was big for the early rounds, and I had a really good board and kept getting through. Then the swell dropped and I ended up having Victor Ribas in the final, who is deadly in small waves. The big days had been a real challenge, but facing off with Victor in small waves was just as much of a challenge. I'd had a few drinks the night before and had to take a couple of Panadol the next morning, which wasn't ideal preparation, but I found a few barrels and my board was going anywhere I wanted on those zippering little walls. I ended up winning it and was now officially on a roll, leading the ratings and absolutely ecstatic.

BURE ONE

The following interview was recorded on the balcony of the Rainbow Bay Surf Club during the 2007 Quiksilver Pro. As the sun set over the Gold Coast hinterland and several schooners of ice-cold Tooheys New were consumed, Occy and Matt Hoy reflected on their years sharing Bure One on Namotu Island during the Fiji event.

Matt Hoy: My two heroes, staying in a room with Mark Occhilupo and Luke Egan – I could not get two better blokes. Nothing much was going on, just skulldrags every afternoon . . .

Occy: And Matthew did take out the record for skulldrags. He did thirteen.

Tim Baker: What's in a skulldrag?

Occy: Every single thing they have at the bar. He has a strong constitution. [A skulldrag is actually: gin, vodka, triple sec, rum, orange juice and grenadine.]

Hoyo: I just went, 'I'm going to go for the record. I'm just going to sit here and go *boom* like, *hack, hack, hack*.'

Occy: So focused, so focused.

Hoyo: Good solid alcoholic drinks.

TB: Tell us about Bure One.

Hoyo: Bure One was fucking amazing. I got to hang with two of my heroes, Mark and Luke. It was just amazing times . . . Bure One was the most amazing place . . . Do you know where we are right now? Rainbow Bay Surf Club. The sunset's going to be amazing, the wind's offshore.

Occy: It's going to be so amazing.

Hoyo: You know what? Bure One and Namotu Island has got the most amazing sunset ever. It's probably the best bar in the world . . .

Occy: The kava night, Louie got caught up drinking kava with the boys way late . . . They make kava nights. We used to rock up with the local boys after drinking with our boys. And drinking kava, you've got to have thirty of them.

Hoyo: We were having the real kava. You get the numb teeth.

Occy: You've got to drink heaps of it, and you've got to have a toilet right close.

Hoyo: Fiji was the fucking best time.

TB: Does Fiji really feel like home for you?

Occy: Of course it feels like home, because I'm with Luke and Matt in a little grass shack on a little island – and, you know what, it feels like home.

Hoyo: They were the best times of my life, Bure One, hanging with my heroes. I came last, I got thirty-third every time I was there, and Occ and Luke won the contest. [Egan won it in 2000.]

After Fiji I was number one in the world, and it felt like I was officially going for the world title. I was just loving it. There's nothing better than looking at the ratings and seeing yourself up the top. It's such a good feeling. You carry that piece of paper with you all the time and just pull it out and have a look when you want to make yourself feel good. You're travelling around and you've got the ratings in your backpack; you're in transit for a few hours and you go, *think I might pull the ratings out and see where everyone's sitting. Oh look! I'm number one.*

I went home from Fiji and had a great break, did a lot of media but was loving it – I was just in my element.

> **Luke Egan:** After Fiji it started getting like, *okay, you're winning now.* But we were so entrenched in what we were doing that year that it didn't really change anything. We didn't even talk about it much. We were so entrenched. We were in our own bubble the whole year. I always had people asking me, 'Are you looking after him? Is he all right?' I'm like, 'Yeah, it's sweet. I'm enjoying it.' We didn't talk about it much. Probably the only thing we chatted about was, 'How good is it that

you're back and surfing?' But anyone like that, I don't talk about the past. I just look forward and talk about how good it is where you are now. It was all a way to a new life, back to the life that he had. I think he was really appreciative that he was able to get back there.

But just as I was starting to enjoy that number one spot, the wobbles set in. Jeffreys Bay is somewhere that I always think I should do well, yet results have eluded me for years since winning it way back in 1984. I always feel like I have better free-surfs than heats there. I copped another seventeenth, right when I needed a result to keep the momentum going, and left with my tail between my legs.

I went to Huntington fully psyched, ready to rekindle some of the glories of my youth. That place holds so many memories for me, but it just wasn't to be this time, and I walked away with a thirty-third, dark and gloomy. I could feel the pressure building.

There were a bunch of guys at my heels ready to challenge for the title: Taj Burrow, Victor Ribas and Mick Campbell. I knew I had to pull something out of the hat to keep the world title campaign on track. It's hard to keep your momentum up after a couple of wins, but I was determined to stop the slide.

Even though the waves were really small in Lacanau, I knuckled down and made the final. Timmy Curran beat me, but I was still really proud of myself. I'd dreamt of a good French leg, and a final was just what the doctor ordered. Yet every time I felt like I'd bought myself a bit of breathing space, I'd stumble again. A seventeenth in Hossegor took the wind out of my sails, as young Aussie Mick Lowe snuck up for a win. I was definitely starting to feel the nerves, but Mick was such a good mate – I couldn't help feeling stoked for him.

The trip down to Spain would prove fateful, one way or another. I could sense it. Mundaka's always been one of my favourite stops on tour. And the wave is just mind-boggling when it's on. We were expecting six-foot Mundaka for the final day, and I was so excited I could hardly sleep. I was up at five or six, and it doesn't even get light until seven, just peering into the darkness trying to see the waves, waiting for the sun to come up. I could hear the waves cracking against the cliff, and by the time the contest got going I was just about to jump out of my skin.

I beat CJ Hobgood in the semis and then met Guilherme Herdy in the final. By then the wind had come up onshore, so I changed my approach. Herdy was going up for a floater straightaway and losing the wave. I knew I had to get out in front of it on the open face before going for major manoeuvres, and not let the wave run away from me. It worked and victory has rarely tasted sweeter. At that point, I knew I was on track and just had to keep my head to achieve my dream.

BRAZILIAN SURPRISE

Going into Brazil, I never thought I was going to wrap up the world title there. There was a really big mix-up because someone said I had a large enough lead that I could clinch it in Brazil, but then I heard reports that I couldn't. I just tried to put it all out of my mind. I got through my first round against a local kid. It was a pretty tight heat, and as we came up the beach he put my hand up in the air, and the cameras came down to meet us. I had no idea what all the fuss was about. A reporter came up and told me that if Mick Campbell lost to Flavio Padaratz in the next heat, I would be world champion. You can see this moment on the news footage from the event. The look on my face says it all. I just went, *you're kidding me.*

I had to run away, because the cameras were everywhere. I went and tried to find a quiet place away from everything to watch the heat. It was so nuts. I had to watch from a distance, and I heard the crowd screaming. I was drinking a coconut, and I think someone put some vodka in it for me – I was that nervous. I didn't wake up that morning thinking I was going to win the world title; I didn't think it was possible. But as the heat drew to a close, and Mick was behind, the crowd started building around me, counting down the last few seconds. Then everyone just went mad. Brazil is an amazing place to win the world title, because the people are so passionate. It was all a blur of cheering and cameras flashing and reporters asking questions. It was all surreal. At one point, only a few years earlier, I was just worried that I wouldn't ever get fit again, let alone compete, and now I'd just won the world title.

At my lowest points, if you could have found a bookie to give you odds, I would have been a million-to-one to ever win a world title. I might have taken the title of Craziest Surfer on Tour or Fattest Bloke in Palm Beach, but the idea of me ever being world champion back then would have been laughable.

If there's one thing I'd like people to take from my world title win it's that anyone can do what they really want to do, if they set their mind to it. I have to admit, I was lucky. I had a lot of people helping me along the way and accepting my comeback. It's a beautiful world when people give you another chance.

The first person I wanted to tell was Beatrice. I woke her up at five in the morning, Australian time, and I left a message on the answering machine. I was all emotional, saying, 'Honey, I've won, it's all because of you, I've won.' And she rang me back and just thought I'd got through another heat, because no-one thought the world title was going to be decided that early on. She said, 'Are you drunk or what?' I said, 'No, honey, I've won – it's finished.'

I had a few beers that night, but I got a bit of sleep because I had to surf the next day. I was just so stoked, I couldn't even surf my heat. I lost to Peterson Rosa, and didn't mind a bit. He congratulated me beforehand, and that's when it really sank in and I felt like crying for the first time. It's also the first time I've lost a heat and had my hands in the air.

There was an amazing sense of satisfaction. All the hard work had paid off. I dedicated the win to my mum, and there's some news footage somewhere of a TV reporter telling her the news, and she was all stoked. It was great to see how much joy the win brought to so many people. I'd been tagged as the best surfer in the world never to win a world title, but I'd finally shaken that tag. I just couldn't have been any more stoked.

Luke Egan: That day crept up on us . . . He surfed in the morning and got through and we left. And then we went back to the beach to check it out. We just went to have some lunch, and then Renato was coming up to us, going, 'You better watch these next four heats. You could be world champion this afternoon. It could happen.' We were just drinking co-conuts, and all of a sudden it's all going down . . . I got a lot of satisfaction out of it. He'd given me that inspiration in '84. I had to repay him for what he'd given me.

Taj Burrow: It was my second year on tour. I was such a rookie and just stumbled into the whole thing and found myself in a race with him for the world title. It was pretty bizarre. Winning wasn't even on my mind. I was just thinking, *I'm just a kid and that's Occy and this is awesome – but I'm not going to win. How can I win?*

We were flying out of Brazil and someone gave me a fax from Kelly Slater, saying how proud he was of me. I read it and got a bit emotional.

I'd been bumped up to first class, but after the plane took off I went and sat down the back with Powelly, Beau, Lowey and Mick Campbell, and we drank the whole way. We were about two hours out of New Zealand, and the flight attendant comes up and goes, 'Don't you want to use your first-class seat?' I went, 'Oh, that's right, I forgot about that' and walked up there to a full bed and a chocolate on my pillow. So I jumped in and had a couple of hours' sleep. We got back on it at the airport lounge in New Zealand, but then I slept the whole way to Sydney, went straight to the Qantas Club and slept some more. I was having a dream about my mum, and she was going, 'Mark, Mark, wake up.' I opened my eyes and there was Mum. Somehow, they'd let her into the Qantas Club to see me while I was in transit. It was amazing.

I was starting to feel pretty fatigued after all the travel and celebrations, but the little sleep in Sydney and on the flight to Coolangatta left me feeling a bit better, which was just as well because I knew I had a big reception waiting for me. I didn't really know what to expect when we landed. I came down the stairs and there was a limousine waiting for me, pulled right up at the bottom. My feet didn't even touch the tarmac. Bea and Rainer were there and we drove to the press conference, past two fire engines with their hoses going over the top of us as a salute. It was such an incredible feeling to come home to this welcome as the new world champion. They had a similar reception for Mick Fanning when he came home from Brazil as world champ in 2007, but he didn't get the water canons because of water restrictions, so I'll always have that one over him!

The press conference was fun and the mayor of the Gold Coast was there. It was a great homecoming. When we'd finished the press conference and all my official duties, we got back in the limo and the driver poured us a glass of champagne. We drove from the airport back to Bilambil, clinking glasses and going, 'Mission accomplished.'

It was so nice to get back up to our home out in the country. My really good mate and neighbour Blairy and his wife were there to greet us, and it felt like time to unwind and celebrate all the hard work. I loved it at Bilambil, because no one goes up there unless they live there or they're invited. We were just kicking back when all these cars started arriving, and before we knew it the world title festivities were under way. It was really moving that so many close friends wanted to celebrate my achievement, and there was a magic mood in the air.

Kelly Slater: Occy is Australia's surfing pride, perhaps the greatest-ever surfer when he's on. I don't think people in America ever really realised how good he is. It's a magical comeback. I think it's truly the biggest thing in surfing. I have a huge amount of respect for what Occy's done. I'm truly amazed by it, and I hope the American fans and industry can respect that. I love to see great things in surfing. I want to see people rise up and reach their potential.

Blairy: I was working at the country club. I got to know him at the bar and playing golf. I got him into the golf scene. I used to be the head greenkeeper, and when I was mowing the fairways I would duck into his backyard and mow his lawn.

He used to get out there by himself in a golf buggy, and he'd come flying down and lock the brakes up and do 360s – I think he even rolled it once. I used to tell him, 'You can't do that while I'm here', and he'd go, 'That's why I do it – because when you're here I can't get in trouble.' He was pretty crazy in the golf buggies.

One time at Seagulls we bumped into that boxer Joe Bugner, and he gave us tickets to his fight there that night. But we were busy playing the pokies, so we gave them to this other guy. Then later the bloke we gave the tickets to went, 'They were calling for you. Joe was going, "We've got a world champion here. Come up, Occy."'

HAWAII AS THE CHAMP

It was really nice to go to Hawaii with all the pressure off. Only four years earlier, Beatrice and I had gone there almost as tourists, just so I could show her around, and I'd ended up in the final of the Pipe Masters. Now here I was coming back with the world title. I'd always felt right at home in Hawaii and received nothing but good wishes from all the locals. It was probably one of my best years there because, with the title already decided, everyone was in party mode all around me, but I just did my own thing. I wanted to stay really fit and focused, and just surfed, ate, had a few quiet beers, went to bed early and got up early and surfed again. I was on such a high that I didn't need to get on it with all the boys. I was really proud of myself and everything I'd achieved, and I even made the semifinals at Pipe.

It wasn't big Pipe, only about eight feet, and I was up against Kelly in the semis. It seemed like everything was going my way, and I finally had him combo-ed with only a few minutes left. I was so far in front I almost forgot I was in a heat, and I was sitting there cleaning my nails, going, *I can't believe the year I've had. I'm world champ, and I've got Kelly combo-ed at Pipe.* He caught a smaller one and got himself back in range, but he still needed a 10 or something and I had priority. Then a set came. There were mainly lefts, with only a few rights, but he faked me into thinking it was going to be a really good backdoor wave. It wasn't a big wave at all, but I looked at him paddling like crazy for it and thought, *I've got to stop him.* So I used my priority to take the wave and he pulled back, but it was nothing. I just took off and flicked out. I got caught inside and couldn't get out the back for a while so he paddled straight back and established priority.

As I was paddling back out I saw this set coming in and he paddled into it. I knew it was a 10 before he even took off. Sure enough, he got a really long, deep backdoor barrel and just squeezed out the doggy door and got the score: ten points. Kelly was into the final with Shane Wehner, which Kelly won, and it was yet another lesson: you can never count that guy out. But nothing was going to stop me enjoying that Hawaiian season.

Kelly Slater: I needed an 8.5 but was combo-ed just before that and got myself back in range. This little right came, and it was much easier to score on them, so I just made like I had to have that wave or my life was gonna end, but in a sneaky way, so he thought I was trying to hide it. He turned around and caught it, but it was just a block. I went over the next one and thought I saw this insane one coming, but it wasn't good at all, so I started laughing to myself that I didn't have *that* good of luck and just sat on my board waiting. There was under two minutes. I went over that one and then this perfect peak was there. I got so nervous, but it was a perfect one. I got a 10 on it to finish. He needed a high 9 I think after that. I remember hearing that all the Aussie guys were just so pissed off. I loved that. I don't remember Occy being so upset by it, and he was a really good sport.

I didn't have any big nights until the banquet night, and then I was ready to celebrate. The morning of the banquet I went for a surf and this guy dropped in on me and went over the falls. We popped up and I went, 'What the fuck . . . ?' And he just started screaming, 'Help me, help me!' and I realised he was in a pool of blood. His fin had stabbed him right in the main artery in the groin, and he was losing a lot of blood. I went into full action mode, ripped my legrope off, made sure he was secure on his board and just took him straight in on the whitewash. We got to the beach and I yelled to the tower, 'Call the ambulance!' The lifeguards came and put a tourniquet around his leg – it was touch and go but he survived. It was heavy. By the time I got the banquet that night I was ready for a drink. I gave what I thought was one of my better speeches, and I really enjoyed the feeling of being in Hawaii as world champion. There was a great mood in the air.

The banquet was a beautiful night. I was really in love with Beatrice, and there was a popular song on the radio called 'You

Are My Lady'. I heard it on the radio during my retirement year in Hawaii, and it still brings a tear to my eye. The late Peter Whittaker got them to play the song at the banquet as I was crowned world champion, and all the photographers started crowding around the stage and flashing their cameras in my face. I told them all to back off, that I wanted to have a moment with my wife, and to clear the dance floor because I wanted to have a dance with her. She was the one who really helped me win that world title, and it was a very special moment that I'll never forget. I went, 'No, no, no. This isn't a camera thing. This is between me and her.' So they all backed off and we did a slow waltz together.

Peter Whittaker was really prominent in the ASP at the time and held the show together through a lot of changes. Rabbit was thinking about going for the top job. Peter came to my place at Rocky Point after the banquet and we talked about it all. I really put in a good word for Rabbit because I wanted him to get the job, and he did. There was a feeling that everything was working out.

> **Brian Surratt:** When he won the world title, Maurice Cole called me and said, 'You have to show up . . .' I'm a full country guy, first of all, and for some reason a lot of the awards nights, Mr Rarick has them in the city. So I went and I'll never forget it, because Occy got up there and they gave him the mike and all these cameras are flashing at him and everything. And this guy doesn't fuck around. He got upset and said, 'Get the cameras out of my face, you've followed me all year long. Can I have my moment here, seriously?' He said, 'I want to have one dance with Bea.' He had me in tears. I'll never forget it: 'This is my moment, I'm going to have a dance with my wife.'
>
> It was so cool, so well put together. I was blown away. And then he had my whole family crying because he got the mike again, and he stood up there and gave a little speech

about how thankful he was, and he said, 'For the twenty years I've been coming to Hawaii, I want to introduce you to my Hawaiian parents.' And he introduced me and my wife at the time, my kids. He said, 'This is my Hawaiian family.' That's one of the things that really stuck out in my mind.

Rabbit Bartholomew: When he won both Teahupoo and Fiji, I thought that was quite a poignant moment in that he'd shown that he'd taken command of his life and taken command of his profession. He'd assumed his natural place, and right there at that time, I went, 'That's his destiny right there. He's going to win this world title.' From there on in, the whole year was a celebration. That was my first year as ASP president/CEO, and one thing I was quite concerned about was the Australianisation of the ASP. It happened by virtue of the fact that Australians tend to go to meetings and sit on committees. It's like a form of group therapy . . . And I was a bit concerned about that. Like last year when Mick Fanning and Stephanie Gilmore won the world titles, I went, *shit, they both come from Coolangatta – I'm glad that didn't happen in 1999.* But the fact was I had no qualms about it whatsoever, because Occy was such a universally loved person, and a universally acknowledged champion. I went, *no-one's going to call anything on this. It's perfect.*

Gerry Lopez: That was really pleasing for me, because to have gone through what he'd been through, he'd worked hard to finally get there. I really felt good for him. The contests never meant that much to guys from my generation, but I appreciated it just from watching the next generation – Michael and Derek Ho, that whole crew – and how important and how big the whole pro tour became. I can't say enough good things about him, and everyone was just so proud to know him and to see what he'd done. A lot of times people can become resentful of other people's success, but I think in Occy's case everyone was just so stoked for him. He's just the genuine article, a real person, that's him. What you see is what you get.

Richard Marsh: Surfing's such a cool sport, that side of it – everyone loves a good fight back. Everyone loves Occ on tour. He's so loved. The energy was behind him. Everyone was, like, driving him on, and that doesn't happen too much. Even the other competitors were willing him over the line. We were all really proud of him.

Gary Green: He used to do some radical shit. The hiatus gave him a chance to think about what he had and what he lost. When he won the world title, I was so stoked for him and everyone wanted him to win it. Even people outside of surfing were rooting for him. It gave a lot of sportsman inspiration. There was always that thing in a lot of sports: when you're thirty you're gone.

Rabbit Bartholomew: Occy's is just a wonderful story. He turned it around and blazed a new trail. There's not many that make it back . . . I challenge anyone to find another one in international sport, in the history of international sport, that's even close to it – top level, world champion, to get back to the top in a whole new era, from that far back. I don't think there's one. I'd like to see it. I'd like to see someone top that. George Foreman is one that I think is probably close, but he was a heavyweight champion, so he could be fat. When you look at it in retrospect, it's the modern-day Rip Van Winkle. It's the Rip Van Winkle story, because Rip Van Winkle slept for twenty years. Mark Occhilupo lay on the couch for seven years. That's a long time. It was a good rest. And it gave him longevity.

Dougall Walker: The thought was, *we've got to get him off the circuit.* The worst thing that could happen was to have him slogging around in forty-fifth place. But he proved us wrong. He completely broke all barriers. He kept going and going and going and getting better. We just didn't want him falling off the pace and being a journeyman, because we'd seen that a lot. We'd seen a lot of guys hang on too long, and what it does in any sport – especially surfing because it's so youth-oriented – the downturn overshadows the memory of the great surfing. There's no question that Michael Peterson was a great, great surfer, but if he had hung around another ten years, I don't know if he'd be remembered as so great. It's like the James Dean thing. But Occy fought through all that. It's amazing.

Steve Perry (Oakley sunglasses): The world title? Mark Occhilupo is so much bigger than that and so much more than that. The world title – to me it's not what Occ's about. He didn't need to win the world title for people to know how good he was. He's touched so many people in so many good ways. He's always giving money – gave money to Sea Shepherd when he first heard about them and stuck a Sea Shepherd sticker on his board. He's just so giving. He was one of the first to give money to SurfAid. He just wants everyone around him to be happy. They floated the company on Occy's back when he won the world title.

Chapter Fifteen

Joel Parkinson: We were pretty good mates, but we'd never surfed against each other. He's the world champ. My first event, I'm up against the world champ. It's the third round, lowest seed against highest.

It was perfect, small but a little bit south for Snapper – two, three foot. I hadn't been on tour and I didn't know anything about how good friends would flip a coin for priority, or play something like rock, paper, scissors. I didn't know anything. He walks down and he's got this mouthful of Barleygreen [a powdered dietary supplement], you know that green stuff? And with his head and this mouthful of green shit – he's like, 'Do you want to flip for priority?' The way he said it, with this green stuff all foaming up, and his lips all stuck together, I was just like, 'No, no thanks.' I regret it. I'd do it any day of the week now. I'd do it all day, but I didn't know what was going on. Flip for priority? Does that even happen? He thought I was being too cool for school. I just didn't know. Then we paddled out in the heat, and I just held my position. I always try and hold the inside at Snapper – you know, get a bit cocky at your home break. I was just trying to sit deep and I ended up getting the heat.

These days I'd flip for priority with any of my mates, and that's probably one of the best things he taught me, but I learnt the hard way. For a while after that we didn't talk because we were over each other. I didn't know what was going on, and he was off me because he thought I was a spoilt brat. We laugh about it now. He should have thought about it before he walked down with a mouthful of green stuff! I'm just a kid getting ready to surf against one of my heroes, and he walks down looking like Shrek. He can be really intimidating.

It was fantastic going on tour as the reigning world champ. I'd fulfilled my lifelong dream and felt no pressure. I just wanted to enjoy every moment of the tour, and that's exactly what I did. A few highlights stand out. I was so stoked to go back to Fiji that year. The local people had really embraced me, and Luke and Hoyo and I had a great vibe going in Bure One. I'd won the contest the year before, and the place is just about as close to paradise as you can get.

As it turned out, Luke and I ended up surfing against each other in the quarterfinals. The waves were perfect and we both had big scores. Hoyo had got knocked out earlier and had been caddying for both of us, so he didn't know who to cheer for. He was just cheering for Bure One in the end. I'd had a 9 and got another long barrel and just squeezed out the doggy door. I claimed it and got a 7. As soon as I claimed it, I turned around and Louie was sitting in the barrel for way longer than I was and did a huge hack at the end and scored a ten-point ride. I just went, *I'm toast.* And Luke went on to win the contest. He beat Guilherme Herdy in the final, and Hoyo and I were both caddying for him by that stage, though we ended up on the Namotu boat drinking beer. It was just as well he didn't need his spare board.

At the presentation that afternoon, Luke announced that he wanted to give his winner's trophy to Hoyo. He said, 'This might be the last contest I ever win, and I really want to give the trophy to my best mate, Matt Hoy.' I just broke down. Everyone was sobbing, it was really emotional.

> **Matt Hoy:** That heat that Luke and Occy had was the best heat I've ever seen in my life. I'd take Occ's board and sit on Occ's board, and then get Luke's board. I was going, 'Yeah, Occy. Yeah, Luke.' Then I was just going, 'Yeah, Bure One.' That day in my life, to see Bure One go up against each other, it was like a title fight. I didn't know who to go for. I'd change boards every time – 'Go, Occ. Go, Luke.' It was the most amazing heat; not *one* of the best – it's *the* best heat of surfing I've ever seen in my life.
>
> You know what he did that night? I was blind. I had a wig on. Occ said, 'You've got to take that shit off and come over to Tavarua.' I said, 'I'm not going over to that island. I hate that fucking island. Fuck that.' And he was going, 'No, listen, you have to come over to that island.' And Luke gave me his trophy. I was listening to the presentation, going, *what?* Everyone was sobbing, from the hierarchy of Quiksilver all the way down, they were bawling. I tried to put the trophy back in Luke's bag in the morning – 'I can't take that' and he said, 'No way.'

OP BOAT TRIP

I was really lucky to make it back on tour at a time when there were some amazing contests in incredible locations. I got invited to a specialty event called the Op Boat Trip, which was inspired by the Challenge events, taking a small group of surfers to a remote location and documenting the whole thing. It was more like a surf trip than a contest – me and a bunch of my best friends on a beautiful boat cruising the Mentawai Islands off the coast of Sumatra, Indonesia, and surfing mind-boggling waves.

There was Sunny Garcia, me, Andy and Bruce Irons, Shane Dorian and a few others, and we just had a ball. Because we were all friends, we decided to make a pact right from the start and split the prize money, whoever won. That took all the pressure off, and we just all relaxed and went surfing and enjoyed ourselves. It was about $30,000 first prize, and it was really stacked for the top place-getters, not much for the minor placings. We just went, 'Fuck it, we're all mates here – let's just split it', and it worked out to around eight grand each.

This maybe wasn't what the organisers had in mind, because they were after the drama of competition, but I guess we were on a different wavelength. For us, it was a break from the tour. We were all kind of over the guy directing the contest, barking orders at us all the time. We had one session at perfect Macaronis and, just to spin this guy out, we decided we'd all surf switch-foot for the session. There were about twenty cameras recording every wave and you could hear all the cameramen talking on the walkie-talkies, going, 'What the fuck are these guys doing?' We didn't ride one wave proper-stance the whole session, and the waves were cooking.

We had another memorable day at a place called Kanduis. We pulled up and it was heavy – a solid eight feet, top to bottom barrels, breaking hard and thick in super-shallow water. We were all tripping over each other to get out there. That was a great day. The best wave I got was one of the biggest sets of the day, and I spotted it from a mile away. It just seemed to come straight for me. I jagged it and got a long, deep barrel and scored a cover shot on *Surfer* magazine, which is always nice.

That trip was also special for introducing us to the work of SurfAid International, an aid group run by surfers that delivers medical aid to this really poor and remote part of Indonesia. While we're reclining in luxury on our charter boat, on shore children are dying from easily preventable diseases – and it's just too radical a situation not to do something to help. That's what Kiwi doctor and surfer Dave Jenkins decided when he visited on a surf trip and started SurfAid. They take a real grassroots, practical approach, distributing mosquito nets, running education programs and helping the local people to help themselves. I was so impressed by them and touched by the friendly locals who have welcomed surfers with open arms, I decided to do what I could to help too. I was honoured to be asked to become an ambassador for SurfAid, and I reckon every surfer who's ever visited the Mentawais, or anywhere in Indonesia, should do their bit to help.

> **Bruce Irons:** I remember going on those Op Boat Challenges, and that's when we became really good friends. He was about thirty-five then and he goes, 'I'm not retiring until you make the tour.' I made the tour and got to travel with him for four or five years. We had some sessions on the Op Boat Trip. Me and him and my brother and Shane-o, we were all hung-over surfing NoKandui, six feet with eight-footers, and that was the first time we all surfed together and it was one of the best surfs I've ever had.

> **Andy Irons:** We were on this little boat, with little quarters, and he got on with my brother. We'd just hang out and drink beers and talk story, and he'd tell these killer stories about his trips to Hawaii in the past. He was just really cool, really open with us. We surfed on his birthday at five-foot Macaronis. We were drinking beer in the line-up. It was the Occy birthday theme and he was getting all the waves he wanted. Every set that came, we were all, 'Occy birthday wave!' and he was just ripping. We had a big night that night, and the next day was, like, ten-foot NoKanduis. It was just pumping, six of us, getting barrelled every wave, like, ten-second barrels every wave.

Brazil's always radical, but it was especially radical in 2000, for all the wrong reasons. I'd made the final at Arpoador, this left-hand point off a headland in Rio, against a keen young Aussie rookie, Trent Munro. Trent was deadly on his backhand in small waves, and it should have been a great match-up. But, just before the final, I had been hanging out up the beach a bit when this local guy offered me a joint. We were in the middle of a crowded beach in the middle of a busy city, and I just went, 'No way, what are you doing?' But he kept pressing it on me. The next thing I knew, I was holding this joint, the guy had bolted, and a cop had grabbed me by the shoulder. I don't know if it was a sting or just rotten timing, but this cop insisted I was under arrest. A small crowd quickly formed as people tried to explain I was in the final and he had to let me go. Luckily, Sarge had seen all this go down and ran to get the mayor's son to sort it out, and he was eventually able to calm things and get me in the final.

But I was freaked out and was never going to be competitive in that final. The cops weren't stoked about missing out on their bust, and Sarge hatched a plan to get me off the beach as soon as possible. So as soon as the final was over, I ran straight to a waiting car and went back to our hotel. It was classic in Brazil – they used to pay us in cash, but they never wanted to give us cash on the beach because it was just too dangerous. There's a lot of crime in Rio, and it's not the place to be toting around a bag with US$30,000 cash. So they'd send these bagmen round to your hotel later with the money.

Trent came back to the hotel after the presentation – we were staying together – but I was still feeling a bit paranoid after the scene at the beach. There was a knock on the door and here's these two heavies in dark suits with a suitcase full of cash. They gave me fifteen grand and Trent thirty for winning, and between us we just had this great pile of money. It had been a completely surreal day, and I was glad to get on the plane home.

Paul Sargeant: One really radical time was when he nearly got busted in Brazil. We were talking and I said, 'Don't take him easy. Trent's a great surfer. He's got the power, just as much as you've got. That backhand in the small stuff is a weapon, mate.' And he goes, 'Oh, yeah, I'll be right.' I was standing talking to someone else, and I was aware of this scuffle fifteen or twenty seconds later, people pushing and shoving – ay, ay, ay. The second I turned around, Occy turned around and our eyes met, and it was the most terrified I've ever seen him look. And he was going, 'No mate, I'm in the final, I'm in the final.' This cop had him by the arm, and Occ was looking back over his shoulder at me with this look on his face. I sprinted up to the judges' tower, grabbed the guy who was the mayor's son, dragged him back and said, 'Look, you've got to get this sorted out.'

By this stage there were four cops there and all these Brazilian people going, 'No, no, he's in the contest.' He was nearly crying, it was full-on. And anyway, this guy, the mayor's son, sorted it out, and Occy went out and was just a shot duck. Trent won it easy – not taking anything away from Trent. But then halfway through the heat I ran alongside Occy on the beach after a wave, and I said, 'As soon as the heat's over, run straight up the beach at the southern end. There'll be a combi there with an open door waiting for you.' So that's what he did. We had this combi and just rushed him off. Trent had won and we did the presentation and I got in the car and went back to the hotel. I went up to Occ's room and said, 'You're out of here on the first plane. You're leaving your boards here, wear sunnies. This is what's happening.' And that's what we pulled off, went to the airport and put him on a plane home.

THE DIVORCE

Beatrice and I had been on such a mission together, and we'd been a winning combination. She'd helped me through my depression, really encouraged and believed in me, even when I doubted myself, and helped me fulfill my lifelong dream to become world champion. I owed her everything. But with our mission completed, we just seemed to drift apart. Maybe it had taken too much out of her and she couldn't just keep giving all the time, and I didn't blame her a bit. We'd also been trying to have children for a while without success, and I think that took a toll that perhaps neither of us fully recognised.

Somehow it just seemed like our journey together had come to a natural end. She was keen to travel to other places apart from the tour and was interested in importing exotic art and homewares. I was flying high, enjoying the tour as the new world champion. We had different paths to follow. It was sad the way it came to an end, and the divorce was heavy. I don't like fighting and just let her have whatever she wanted. My divorce lawyer couldn't believe it. She kept saying, 'Don't you want to keep something for yourself?' but I just wanted it over. I could never blame Bea or even hear a word against her, because who knows where I would have been without her.

> **Paul Sargeant:** It was pretty gnarly. He came home from Brazil to an empty house, and she'd just gone. She'd left his TV and the lounge, just the part of the lounge he sat on, and taken the rest. It was pretty shattering . . .

MEETING MAE

When I split up with Beatrice I went back to my usual single ways, going pretty mad. I'd already met Mae a bit earlier through Hambone, who ran the Mount Woodgee surf shop where she worked, but I was still married at the time and didn't think anything of it. But I did think something of it when I got divorced, and I said to Hambone, 'What's going on with that girl who works in your shop?' And he's like, 'Nah, nah, you've got to be kidding. She's too nice for you.' I'm like, 'Nah, come on, give me her number.' Eventually I wore him down and got her number.

I'd met another girl from Canada, who was working at the Calypso Tavern in Coolangatta, and she gave me her phone number. And it was like, *do I ring her or do I ring Mae?* That was definitely the best decision I ever made in my life, ringing Mae. So I called her and she was like, 'Yeah, sure, let's get together.' The first night we went to dinner with Nicky Wood and his partner, Wanda, at Burleigh. It was a really nice dinner, and we got to know each other a bit better and were almost holding hands under the table. I knew I really liked her straightaway.

The next time I saw her she read me some of her poems, and they were so beautiful. I started to appreciate the amazing depth behind her beauty. She'd stay over at my place and I'd stay over at her place, and pretty soon I asked her to move in with me. We'd really fallen in love, and my wild single days came to an end pretty quickly. When I'd come home from Brazil earlier that year, all the furniture was gone from my house. Beatrice had taken almost everything. I think she left the fridge and the TV. So we bought some new furniture and Mae created the most amazing home for us. She's such a beautiful homemaker.

Mae Occhilupo: We met for the first time tenpin bowling in 1999. I was working in a surf shop at the time and it was a retailers' night. I guess we just ended up bowling in the same lane. Everyone went out dancing after, and he was still in his bowling shoes. I actually pointed it out to him, like, 'You've still got your bowling shoes on.' He was kind of dancing, sliding around, being funny . . . We were just friends, I was going

Occy

out with someone and he was still with his wife, but there was a moment when we were bowling and we were high-fiving and it just felt like there wasn't anybody else there, but there were all these people around. That was probably what made me think, *oh, there's something there.*

It was a couple of years after that we got together. We'd see each other every now and again through mutual friends and have a talk. I wrote a poem for him, because he seemed really sad and he'd just won the world title. I like writing poems and I saw it the other day. It was just fitting for what he was going through at the time. When I'd broken up with my boyfriend and he'd gotten divorced, he asked me out on a date.

Our first date, he took me to the top of the water tower at Bilambil. We climbed up and sat up there, and then we played golf in the dark by the car headlights. He was trying to teach me how to play golf at night. The second date, he took me bodyboarding at Fingal, and I was getting smashed but felt safe. He tried to push me into barrels and things like that. He gave me all of himself. He didn't hold anything back. He really let me know him, everything, good and bad. He was quite childlike, so spontaneous. If there's something he liked doing, he'd just do it. You forget sometimes he's an adult. I think he just wants to have fun. He just doesn't like to get serious. But he can get serious, and he's very intelligent.

Dougall Walker: Back in 2001 things were a bit wobbly, I can't remember what happened, but we were going public or about to go public. There was a new emphasis on the board, and it wasn't just controlled by Gordon and myself. There was a real thing about, 'Well, what are we going to do with Occy?' And we came up with the ten-year contract, and that gave him security. He wasn't going to get as much per year, but it was a good thing for him and it was a good PR thing for us. By us doing that and allowing him to have other sponsors, we gave him the opportunity to extend his earning capacity.

THE ARRIVAL OF JAY BOY

Beatrice and I had never been able to have kids. I'd been to the doctor and he'd said there was only about a 1 per cent chance of me fathering a child, because I had a really low sperm count. There were things I could have done to try and improve it, but I'd never got around to it. So I didn't think there was much chance of me getting a woman pregnant. But I think Mae and I loved each other so much that it just happened. Mae announced one day that she thought she was pregnant, and I just couldn't believe it. I bought every pregnancy test under the sun, and made Mae take every one. When I was finally convinced, I was over the moon. I was happier than when I won the world title. Mae went into nesting mode and I started telling a few close friends, and everyone was so stoked for us.

Mae Occhilupo: I didn't have any expectations, because I knew he'd just gone through a divorce. But after a few months I realised I wanted to have his children more than anything. I knew he'd be a really good father and husband. We were both really surprised when I fell pregnant. I had to do six different pregnancy tests, all different brands, and it wasn't until I got the blood test that he said, 'Okay, I believe you.' He didn't think he could have children, but I was like, *why not?* He's so healthy. My mum always said we'd have children. It was unreal. I loved being pregnant with Jay.

Luke Egan: I'd always get these calls where I'd pick up the phone and he'd go, 'Oh Louie, you'll never guess what I've done.' And I'd be driving and I'd pull over and go, 'Okay, what's happened?' And it was always such a disaster . . . But then when he and Mae got together, he rang me and said, 'You'll never guess what I've done?' And I'm thinking, *what now?* And he told me Mae was pregnant. For once it was good news.

With a family on the way we needed a new car, because my beloved Jeep Wrangler that I won in the Skins at Bells had come to a sad demise. On my thirty-sixth birthday, Mae backed it into a pole and smashed in the rear. Later that night everyone ended up back at our place, and the next morning my mate Jye Gofton needed to borrow it. He ran into the back of someone and smashed in the front end. So it was double-ended, and a write-off, on my birthday! I loved that car. It even had a name: Tonka. But it was no biggy, I've never been materialistic when it comes to cars. But when I told my friend Mark Pripic that I needed a new car, he went, 'Wait till you see these new BMW four-wheel drives. You'll love them.' Just for the record, I was the first person in Coolangatta to get an X5. Now quite a few people have them, mainly friends of mine, but I started the trend.

This was a big step for me, because I don't exactly have a great track record with cars. I've always been a bit clumsy, and I'm really bad at reversing. When Mae was pregnant we went to BabyCo to get all the things for our baby – pram, cot, change table – and we were both so excited. Mae was heavily pregnant and it was pouring with rain, so I decided I should reverse up under the awning at the front of the shop so we wouldn't get wet loading everything into the car. As I was reversing I hit the gutter and my foot slipped off the break and onto the accelerator, and I drove straight through the front window of the shop. The car was wedged half in the shop, and the sales lady and Mae were like, 'What was that?' I just went, 'Oh well, at least no-one's going to get wet.'

The months rolled by and Mae kept getting bigger. I managed to finish second at the Quiksilver Pro at Snapper to Dean Morrison, just before Jay was born, which felt pretty amazing. Then one evening it was a full moon, still about a month before the due date. I was having a beer and Mae goes, 'Mark, I've got cramps.' And I go, 'You're sweet, bub, you're sweet.' I'm just watching the news having a beer, and she says, 'We'd better go to hospital and get it checked.' And I go, 'I'll just finish my beer and watch the end of the news.' She yells, 'MARK, GET IN THE CAR!' Those maternal instincts are pretty powerful when they kick in, let me tell you. So we get in the car and rush up to John Flynn Hospital. They put a monitor on her and go, 'Yeah, you're in labour.'

Mae's going into labour and it's a full moon. I'm freaking out, pacing up, down and around the room. And Mae's in the shower holding on to my fingers like she does when she goes to the dentist, but twenty times harder, and my fingers are numb. Mae's on the happy gas, and I'm on it with her. I'm really getting into the gas, and she's like, 'GIVE ME THAT! WE'RE NOT HERE FOR YOU TO GET HIGH!' Before we knew it, at three in the morning, little Jay pops out. I'll never forget it. I cut the cord and he opened his eyes just a touch and had a look at me. He almost looked a bit worried, like, *boy, are you going to be my dad?* It was the most amazing feeling ever.

We got a few hours' sleep and had him in bed with us, just holding him and cuddling him. Then I drove home to get some things for Mae, listening to music in the car, just so happy. I checked the surf at Duranbah, but I was too happy to go surfing. I couldn't do it – I just wanted to get back to the hospital. I went and got the things for Mae and rushed back.

That afternoon, Luke Egan and his partner, Natalie, came to visit, and Luke and I went for a surf then, and it was the happiest I've ever been in the surf. Then we met a few mates at Vikings, Currumbin surf club, had a few beers and wet the baby's head.

I was still so high on adrenalin when I walked back in the hospital, and little Jay was in an incubator because he had jaundice.

It doesn't set in until the first day, but they warned us this might happen because he was a month premature. I saw him in there and I was freaking out. Mae's like, 'It's all right, it's really normal', and I was crying, really emotional. But he was fine. We stayed in the hospital for a week, and they had the ultraviolet light on him to get rid of the jaundice.

There was one corner of the waiting room that caught the morning sun. I'd wake up every morning, take him out of the incubator and sit by the window and unwrap him, and just hold him in the sun, because I wanted him to have natural light. For the two hours the sun came in the window, I'd just sit there with him, holding him in the sun. The doctors and nurses said it was perfectly fine to do that.

After a week the jaundice went down, and they said we could take him home. It was so exciting taking baby Jay home. Mae had everything set up perfectly, and so we embarked on our life as a new little family. I so enjoyed waking up in the mornings and grabbing him and putting him in the car and driving down the hill to check the surf. I loved everything about it.

But not long after Jay was born, tragedy struck when our dear friend Mark Pripic was killed in a car accident. MP was the Oakley rep on the Gold Coast, and we had become really close. He was the sort of guy who was loved by everyone. His girlfriend, Angie, and Mae had become best friends, and they had a place up at Tomewin, in the hinterland, where we'd go and visit. MP had gone up to the property – he'd invited us but we couldn't make it – and this guy came past in a truck delivering gas bottles, because they didn't have electricity up there. He asked for directions, so MP just jumped in the back to show him the way to their neighbour's place. That's the kind of guy he was, always helping out. But the truck slipped off the side of this narrow, winding dirt road and rolled into a tree. The driver was thrown clear and only had a few scrapes, but MP was wedged in the back and died. It was radical. We got the call that night and none of us could believe it. It was such an extreme time, with the joy and celebration of our son's arrival, plus the grief of losing such a close friend.

Pretty soon our little family was on the road, travelling on tour together. We took Jay overseas, when he was about three months old, to Jeffreys Bay – a big trip for his first one. And we christened him on the beach at J-Bay. It was the first lay day of the contest, a beautiful day, and everyone got dressed up. A lot of my good friends were there. Luke became Jay's godfather and Sarge officiated. I dunked Jay's feet in the cold water, right in the keyhole where you paddle out, and he went, 'WAAAAAHHH!' Cheron put on a beautiful barbecue at her place . . . It was just a beautiful day. We took him everywhere with us on tour after that, and I loved competing with my family there. I'd kiss bubba for luck before a heat and come in and kiss him after a heat.

> **Paul Sargeant:** Jay's being 'dedicated' at Jeffreys seemed a predestined ceremony. According to Occ, Jay was conceived at J-Bay, and since Jeffreys was one of his favourite places on tour, if not *the* favourite place on tour, he reasoned there could be no better place to dedicate Jay to God's care. Occ also loves Cheron like a second mother, and so I think there was added significance in christening Jay there at the keyhole in front of Cheron's house. That I was honoured and chosen to officiate at the ceremony as the 'minister' stoked me big-time. Jay was not exactly too cooperative, and bawled most of the time, especially when I scooped some chilly J-Bay water out of the keyhole and anointed him with it.

Mae and I got married when Jay was about a year old, and the wedding was amazing. My old mate Dave Cantrell flew over from Hawaii for it, and Dave, Richie Maurer, Luke Egan and Brenden

Margieson and I all got ready together at my place. Mae was staying at a friend's place, and we all went out to Seagulls the night before, had way too many beers and then went for a surf in the morning. We got to D-bah and, you wouldn't believe it, Gordon Merchant was getting out of the water. We were all laughing and carrying on and he just went, 'What are you up to, boys?' and gave us a wry smile, as if to say, *this looks like trouble*. We all went for a quick surf, drove back up to Bilambil, got on the beers and got ready. We were in our suits and I was getting really nervous. Richie Maurer was being really funny, just to help put me at ease. We got to the church, St Monica's at Tugun, and I was waiting for Mae, meeting and greeting people. She was quite late, but when she finally arrived she looked so beautiful, I started crying.

Her favourite place is up at Springbrook, this beautiful rain-forest area in the Gold Coast hinterland, so after the ceremony the bridal party all piled into a limo and headed up there for photos.

We had to walk quite a way to get to our favourite spot, and someone was holding up Mae's dress but it was still getting a bit muddy. Everyone was going, 'What are you doing?' I kept saying, 'I promise you, it will be worth it.' It took about three hours to get up there and back, and we were really late for the reception. We took a few beers on the trek and had a bit of a glow by the time we got there. The reception was at Palazzo Versace, because that was where I proposed to Mae, and it was a lavish affair. I remember getting up and saying, 'Now every day is Mae-day', and everyone cracked up.

Gordon made a really special speech and said how proud he was of me, which made me feel really good, and we spent the night there in the most amazing suite. I remember checking out the next morning – it was the biggest credit card bill I'd ever seen in my life. It was our suite and the reception all in one. I put it all on Amex and had to sign a bill for fifty-four grand.

We got straight in a limo to the airport and flew up to Hayman

Island for a week for our honeymoon. Our timing was impeccable because there was a cyclone right off Hayman Island. We just bunkered down in our room while this radical storm raged all around us. But we still managed to have an incredible time. The weather finally cleared on the second-to-last day. We packed a picnic lunch and took a little dinghy over to our own private beach and had the most magical day.

When we came back home the cyclone had moved right off Coolangatta, and I had one of my best surfs ever. It was ten to twelve foot, breaking outside Snapper on the wide bank, and I was riding this 6'4" channel-bottom shaped by Ian Byrne, and it just went incredibly. I was feeling so proud about being married to Mae, and I felt like our union really had the ocean's blessing that day.

Mae fell pregnant again, almost as soon as she stopped breast-feeding Jay, but she had a miscarriage. We were down in Sydney, and Mae was playing with Jay when she fell off a swing. She started having really bad cramps on the way back to Cronulla, and I rushed her to the hospital at Carringbah, just across the road from the hospital where I was born. The nurse was really rude, and she said, 'You might miscarry, and expect some pain.' Mae was in a lot of pain that night, but it settled down and we flew home.

The next day it got worse – I've never seen anyone in so much pain. I went through every red light to rush her to John Flynn Hospital, where she miscarried. We were both really upset, but the doctor said, 'Don't worry, it's quite common – try again.' It took a little while, but she fell pregnant on Jay's third birthday. We were so stoked. It was a much shorter labour, and then little Jonah came into the world. Jay was so happy. He has been such a good big brother and shows so much affection to Johah.

I've never been happier since Mae and the boys came into my life. I feel like my life is finally all on track. I feel like life has meaning. I mean, life had meaning when I won the world title, but it *really* had a meaning when I met Mae and had the boys. I felt like I really had a purpose, and I've never ever been happier.

Jay's really into his skating and does little ollies. He's only three-foot high himself, and he can do a one-foot ollie. People say I should put him on a TV show. They're such beautiful babies; people say they could be in baby catalogues, but I'm not into that. They look a lot like their mum – which is lucky because Daddy's not the best-looking guy. But they've got my body, and Jay took to the water and the waves straightaway.

In his first Snapper contest he got a second, and he won the next one. He was so proud, and I was so proud of him. All the dads and mums push their kids into waves, and it's such a work-out pushing your kid through the whitewash. But it's easy to get a bit carried away with the whole competitive thing. One time, Jay had just caught a wave and I bodysurfed in to help him out the back again. I grabbed him by the arm and went, 'Come on, Jay, get back out there', and he's like, 'Daddy, don't force me.' And I slowed down and took a look around and went, *what am I doing? It's supposed to be* fun. It stopped me in my tracks.

I looked around and I could see another lady pushing her kid into waves with this look of total determination on her face. It was like a reflection, and I didn't like what I saw. It was heavy. The competitive instincts run deep in anyone who's played sport at an elite level, but Rabbit was really good at putting it into perspective for me. He said it's just a chance for the kids to have fun. If they're not having fun, there's no point. They've got plenty of time to get serious about it later in life, but it should be all about fun, at least until they're thirteen. Then they can decide for themselves if they want to take it seriously.

Rabbit Bartholomew: Jay came to a Snapper presentation night, and ever since then he's been like, 'Wow, how do you get one of those trophies? I really like that night when you give the trophies out.' And I went, 'Well, you'd better join the club and go in the under-7s with Keyo.' And last Sunday at the club championships we had the kids going in the little shorey on the beach. It just worked out unbelievably because I went up to get Occy to push Jay into some waves in his heat, and Occy was putting his contest jersey on, and they were both walking down the beach and going in their heat at the same time. And Occy was so stoked about that. He was going, 'I can't believe it. I'm going out the back and surfing a heat, and Jay's surfing a heat at the same time.' It was just a beautiful moment.

Chapter Sixteen

Once More With Feeling

I was really determined to keep my surfing at a high level and hold my position in those final few years on tour. Having a family also gave competing new meaning, as I wasn't just surfing for myself but providing for my family and our future. I never wanted to be the guy hanging on too long, getting his arse kicked, and I managed to do all right in my later years on tour – for an old bloke!

In 2004 I managed a quarterfinal finish in the first four events of the year, and was right up there in the ratings, but dropped off the pace a bit late in the year to finish twelfth, up from twentieth the year before, which felt nice to actually be climbing rather than dropping. My friends on tour were really supportive and seemed to love seeing me do well.

In 2005 I had a great heat with Bruce Irons at J-Bay. The waves were perfect and there'd been a long lead-up to the heat for about a week, waiting for waves. We knew we had each other, and we were trying to psych each other out, in a fun way. Our heat was in the middle of the day, everyone was watching, and I wanted to savour the occasion, take in the surroundings and really enjoy it. I didn't know at that point how much longer I'd be on tour, and to have a heat at perfect J-Bay with such a good friend, with all your peers watching, felt really special. If Bruce got the result, I was sweet with that.

I had a really good heat and found a nice, familiar rhythm out there, and most people seemed to think I'd won it – and I was pretty sure I did. But they gave it to Bruce. At that point I *did* get upset and had to go and have a word to the head judge, Perry Hatchett. Even Bruce was upset and was just about to put in a protest himself. It would have been the first time in ASP history that the guy who won a heat protested.

> **Bruce Irons:** Me and him had a heat at J-Bay, and we both had, like, 9s and 8s. I won the heat, just 'cause I got barrelled, but he should have won . . . Honestly, I never felt so bummed winning. It's the first time I felt bad winning a heat.

> **Joel Parkinson:** The heat with Bruce at J-Bay that time, he shouldn't have lost that heat. Bruce got a few little high-running barrels . . . but Occ's turns in that heat were fucking unbelievable. It was a lesson to every backside goofy-footer that *that's* the way you surf a point break.

I announced my retirement towards the end of 2005, but I ended the year in nineteenth place, well within the cut-off to requalify, and all my friends on tour set about convincing me to hang around. I didn't need too much persuasion, to be honest. The tour had become a second family to me, and now that I could bring my own family with me, that was really as good as it could get. The tour was like a favourite video game, and as long as I had credits I was going to keep on playing.

One heat at Bells in 2006 made my decision to stay on tour more than worthwhile. Andy Irons and I had a great quarterfinal in solid eight-foot waves, and I just found my old Bells rhythm. Andy was thinking it could be my last year on tour, and we were stoked to have a heat together. He said I could have priority, but the only problem was that this big set came as we were paddling out, and he got out and I didn't. And he was like, *well, if you're not out here you haven't got priority.* But we had a great heat, and then right at the end he had priority and I got dropped off by the jet ski right onto a bomb. This big set came and it broke out by the buoy. I didn't know where Andy was, but I went for the late take-off anyway, looking around going, *I don't even know where he is and he has priority.* I could easily have got an interference, but he had to duck-dive the wave. I asked him later, 'Could you have got that?' And he said, 'Nah, not even if I tried.' I dropped into it nice and clean, went straight into a bottom turn and just did three of the biggest turns I could do. The Dahlberg was feeling really nice, and when I kicked out, Andy was bowing to me. He is so nice, so respectful. Those guys have got such good manners, Bruce and Andy, and they always show me so much respect. It makes me feel really good.

> **Andy Irons:** When he got that wave, I was paddling out. I had priority and I could have tried to get it. I knew it was going to be a really good score, but I couldn't really slip it under Occ. Anyway, I would have got smashed trying to stand up. He ended up getting a 9.9 on it – smoked it. It was amazing that heat. That was a 10; I saw it later on video, I thought it was a 10 for sure. Before it I thought it was going to be like the Curren and Occy heat [in 1986]. I was having flashbacks, but he just smoked me, so when he came back out I just did the hail Occy thing to him and we were laughing . . . He definitely rose to the occasion and showed me how to surf Bells.

> **Kelly Slater:** His trademark is his backside bottom turn, off the top – it's the best in the business, nobody does it better.

I don't think anyone *will* better it. They're the best turns Occy's ever done, and they're maybe the best turns that will ever be done.

When I followed that up with a win at Margaret River, twenty-one years after I first won the event, I really felt I was surfing as good as ever. Margarets was only a WQS event, but it still felt amazing to stand on top of the winner's dais again. My good mate Jake Paterson and I got tangled up trying to split the peak out there, and he scored an interference, which gave me the win. It was a bit of a weird way to win, but I was still stoked.

The tour always threw up some other nice surprises too, in the people you meet and the situations you find yourself in. One Hawaiian season, Mae and I were having a drink at Lai Lai's at the Turtle Bay Hilton when I spotted the actor Morgan Freeman a couple of tables away. It was a bit of a role-reversal for me, because I'd always loved his acting and kept looking over and really wanted to say hello. Mae said, 'You've got to go', and I am a guy who will go. So I just went up and said, 'Hi, Morgan. My name's Mark. I'm here for the Triple Crown, and I really admire your work!' And he was like, 'Hi Mark, sit down, sit down and have a drink with us' in that deep, syrupy voice of his. Mae and I sat down with him for an hour at least and had a good old chat. He's got that aura about him, he's such a lovely man. He was interested in the surfing thing, but he didn't know who I was. I told him a few stories, and he was like, 'Wow, this guy's radical!'

A TESTING TIME

It always seemed liked 2007 was going to be a testing time. I knew my days on the tour were coming to an end – I couldn't keep going forever and sooner or later I was going to have to face life after pro surfing. But there were also some huge, unexpected challenges.

Beatrice and I hadn't kept in close touch since the divorce, but I was horrified to learn that she had been in a serious car accident and was in a coma in Townsville. It was hard to know what to do. Rainer and I had remained close, but Beatrice and I hadn't had anything to do with each other for a few years. One day I woke up and knew I had to go and see her. It was right before the Quiksilver Pro, and I woke up feeling really emotional about it and told Mae I had to see Bea. Mae was really good about it, and I flew up to Townsville. Rainer was there, and in a strange way it felt good having the three of us together again. We had been such a team. They say sometimes just hearing a certain person's voice can help bring someone out of a coma, and I felt like I had to give it a try. But at the same time I was scared because we hadn't exactly parted on the best terms, and I was worried she'd wake up and go, 'What are you doing here?' But her condition didn't change and I left with a heavy heart, feeling helpless and worried for Rainer and how he was going to cope. But he knew I was there for him.

Just before we left for Jeffreys Bay I received the news that Beatrice had passed away without coming out of her coma. I couldn't attend the funeral because I was heading off to South Africa and felt really torn. But I wrote a eulogy to be read out at the service, and she was very much on my mind. I still feel really fortunate that she came into my life. Rainer and I are still close and catch up whenever we can. He's a really good snowboarder and spends the whole season in the mountains. He still calls me 'Dad', and he'll always be a part of our family.

Mark's eulogy for Beatrice:

Dear Bea,
I just want to say thank you for giving and sharing with me some of the best years of my life. When we met I was at the bottom, and you took me to the top. You made me believe in myself and I will acknowledge that forever.

Rainer, I will always be there for you. I love you like my sons, which you are.

I'm sitting in the Qantas Club as I write this, on my way to Jeffreys Bay. I'd love to win it for you, Bea!

Everyone there, just remember Bea's beautiful smile and the advice she gave. Everyone get together and celebrate her life.

Love, Mark

I knew by mid-2007 that it was going to be my last year on tour. The results weren't coming, and I was starting to feel my age with a few niggling injuries. I was in California when I came to the realisation, the same place where I'd quit the tour for the first time nineteen years earlier. It has such significance for me, the scene of some of my greatest victories and some of my darkest, lowest points. It's such an extreme place – it can be heaven or hell, depending what's going on for you.

I had to fly to LA right before an event in Chile, the launch of a new book about Jeffreys Bay, published by Billabong. I was going to fly straight from Sydney to Santiago, but the LA detour turned it into a marathon – Sydney, LA, Miami, Brazil, Chile. I had a crook back at the time, and I just couldn't face sitting on planes that long, so I pulled out of the Chile event. I don't think it would have made any difference, even if I did well or went close to winning it. I still would have ended up where I did on the tour that year: last. You've got to laugh about that. But it just felt fateful being in California and making that decision. I was with Andy Irons, and we were having a few beers one night. He was like, 'Why aren't you coming?' And I said, 'I'm over it.' He said, 'Ah, sweet, do whatever you want. You can do whatever you want – you've earnt it.'

Andy's just such a fan – or not really a fan, but a supporter. At Bells the next year, when I was off tour, he started wearing his

Billabong sticker in the middle of the front of his board. I'm the only guy who has his sticker there, call it old-school or whatever. Everyone else has it up in the corner on an angle, as far up the nose as possible. I just knew he was doing it for me, like his own little tribute, like he was keeping my legacy alive on tour. It was only a little thing, but it surprised me how much it meant to me.

Even though I was struggling to get through a heat, I had a couple of moments in 2007. One was a great heat I had with Bede Durbidge, who was coming on strong on tour. We went at it hammer and tongs in France, and I ended up getting the heat. That was a really nice feeling – almost like winning a contest, given the year I was having.

But there were a couple of signs that year that maybe it was time to give up the world travel with a young family in tow. On the way back from Europe we found ourselves virtually stranded at Singapore's Changi Airport, lost in transit, so to speak. We'd just been through the full marathon, driving for five hours from Mundaka, Spain, to catch our flight from Bordeaux to London, and then on to Singapore. We were flying home early because I'd bombed out in the contest and we had no guarantee of a connecting flight out of Singapore back to Australia, but I figured we'd just try our luck and we'd be sweet.

Travelling with two young kids is challenging at the best of times, but when we got to Singapore the airline representative told us there was no way we could get on a flight that day. In fact, all the flights for the next week were completely overbooked. It looked like we were going to be stuck in Singapore for a week. All we could do was front up for each flight, hope there had been some cancellations and try to get on standby. But that involved actually hanging out at the airport and physically being there, ready to jump if a spot became available.

We got a hotel room at the airport, which you can book in six-hour blocks, and I kept walking back and forth to the airline counter for every flight to Australia to see if we could get on. We had no luck the first day and I was starting to get worried. The kids were beyond restless. There was so much waiting and walking back and forth that I thought I'd go crazy. The duty-free shop where they hand out little shots of Baileys were getting sick of the sight of me by the end, because I just kept walking back and forth and grabbing a shot of Baileys each time. They were like, 'Buy a bottle already!' Mae and I were ready to go on separate flights with a kid each, but finally on the second night we all got on a flight. I've never been so relieved to get home.

BRINGING THE WORLD TITLE BACK HOME

I really wanted to be there when Mick Fanning won the world title in 2007 – that was my main reason for going to Brazil – and I'm so glad I made it. As Australia's last world champion in '99, it felt important to pass on the torch after eight years without an Aussie world champ. And it felt fitting that he stitched up the title in Brazil, just like I did eight years earlier.

I went out early in the contest and sold one of my boards to this local guy for 200 real, the local currency. Then I noticed Joel was selling one of his boards for 800 real. I went, 'What's the story? That's a bit steep, isn't it?' And he went, 'Nah, that's like 200 bucks.' I'd got confused with the exchange rate and had just sold an almost-new board for fifty bucks Australian. The guy must have been stoked.

After Mick won, we had a big night and big day in Florianopolis before flying home. We took over the whole VIP area of this nightclub and went mad. The next morning Joel went down to the pool at our hotel, and most of the boys were already there drinking bloody marys. I slept till midday, and by the time I got down there they were about fifteen bloody marys ahead of me. It had been a huge twenty-four hours and we all just slept on the flight home. Rip

Occy

Curl team manager Gary Dunne wouldn't let us give Mick a drink on the plane. He kept saying, 'He's got a press conference when he gets home.' But in Sydney we managed to get him on the beers – you've got to have a few beers to celebrate a world title. On the flight from the Gold Coast to Sydney, Mick ordered eighteen Crown Lagers. The hostie thought he was joking.

That was such a highlight for me, coming home with Mick, with the world title. In a funny way, I felt like I was helping to bring the title home by making sure he made it back to Coolangatta in one piece. It gave the whole trip to Brazil meaning, even though I got knocked out first round. It's almost like you go off to battle and you have to bring your mates home alive. It's not really the same, but that's how it felt. We got him home.

Mick Fanning: In Brazil, he was so excited he jumped in the car and reversed into a tree and blew out the back window of a hatchback. We were in Auckland Airport and they were the first papers that we got to read. It had something about Mick Fanning winning the world title, and it goes, '1999 world champion and the last Australian to win, Mark Occhilupo, had a car accident on the way to the contest.' And he looked at everyone and goes, 'Oh, it was only a misdemeanour.' It does't sound that funny now, but it was at the time. Everything Occ says is funny. He could say he was going for a surf and it would be funny.

Bruce Irons: We decided, because it was Occy's last year, we're all going to go to Brazil: Joel, Occy and I. The waves sucked but we had a great time, all three of us. They have the contest on TV there, and me and Occ are watching it, drinking caiparinhas [a Brazilian cocktail] at, like, eleven in the morning. And Joel left his car for us. We were drinking and drinking, and Wardo comes up and goes, 'Tommy Whittaker just beat

Taj! Mick just won the world title, and he's out in the water in a heat with Joel.' We're like, 'Fuck, we've gotta go, we've gotta go!' We all rushed and jumped in Joel's car, Occy's driving, just so excited, and he reverses into a tree, BOOM, blows out the back window. We're like, 'What the fuck just happened?' We're laughing so hard. I was laughing because Occy did it, and because it was Joel's car.

Joel Parkinson: He's a fucking strong prick. In Brazil, me and Bruce Irons tried to gang up on him and throw him into the pool. Bruce had a new iPhone. I came from one side and Bruce came from the other, and he just twisted and threw me away from the pool and into the railing and threw Bruce into the pool all in one move. Bruce is in the pool with his iPhone, and I've landed over by these chairs. And we've both gone, 'Fuck, for an old prick, he's still got it.' He just fully Yoda-ed us.

THE LAST HURRAH IN HAWAII

I headed off to Hawaii with mixed feelings, excited as ever to be going back but with a bit of a heavy heart about my impending retirement. I really wanted to go out on a high note. I have to admit, my final event as a full-time pro surfer was a bit of an anticlimax. Pipe was small and shitty, and I lost in the second round, in the final minute of the heat, like I'd been doing a lot that year. But the send-off I got from everyone on the beach was amazing. And the party that night, first at Gerry's house at Pipe, and then at Waimea Falls, singing with Donovan Frankenreiter's band, was all-time. I'll never forget it and all the good wishes I got from everyone. There was a lot of hugging.

The farewell party at Gerry's house was almost an overload. There were so many people and so many friends there, and everyone was watching this special compilation video of me that Billabong had put together for the occasion. I just felt too much like the centre of attention and had to walk outside to get some air. But it was great at the same time and really special to have so many friends in one place to farewell me.

I really enjoyed my surfing in Hawaii after Pipe, even though it was small. I was riding my old beat-up four-fin a lot without a leash. I lost it on the rocks at Rocky Point, and it got even more beat up – they don't call it Rocky Point for nothing – but I really liked the feeling of surfing without a leash, with no pressure to perform. I don't think I'll be wearing a leash much from now on. It's kind of a hassle because there's lots of rocks on the beach at a lot of my favourite spots, and you've got to be really aware of where the rocks are, but it makes you pay more attention to the waves and the currents and how to hang on to your board.

I nearly put on a leash on my first surf after the event, as an official retiree. I actually did my little stretching routine, put the cord through the plug and thought about putting the leash on, but it felt so weird that I took it off and threw it on the steps. Mae walked down and said, 'What are you doing?' I said, 'I don't think I'm ever going to wear a leash again.' I feel freer without one, and now I feel like a free-surfer and I love it. When you don't wear a leash and you lose your board, you swim in, and you learn to bodysurf well. It keeps you fit and makes the surf more of an adventure.

I went stand-up paddling one day at Sunset, and Gerry Lopez was out there too, and I could imagine getting more into that. Even though I feel like a kook on the stand-up paddleboard, and I don't think that it's going to be my forte, it's a great thing to do on small days. I usually go out on my stand-up paddleboard at 4.30 in the morning, when no-one can see me. I had the fad bad for a while there – I loved it and was doing it every day – but I'm spending more time on my shortboard again now.

But cruising around with Gerry that day, I started to feel like I could stay on in Hawaii for longer. I was watching Rasta ride one of those traditional Hawaiian alai'a boards – just a thin, flat plank of wood that the first Hawaiian surfers rode way back when – and he surfed it so well. I could have watched him all day. I felt like it would be nice to stay in Hawaii and get into that all-round waterman thing. The waves were going to get good, and I could slip into that other role of the free-surfer. When the contest first started packing up, I was feeling a little bit depressed with it all over and the final event of my career well and truly finished. But then once it was all gone and there was no sign of it, and all the boys had gone home for Christmas, then it all felt new again. I like watching the place go back to normal after the contests, and I've always liked staying on after the tour leaves.

My last morning in Hawaii, as we were getting ready to leave for the airport, I locked our keys in the hire car. I couldn't believe it. I don't know how many times I've done that over the years. But in a sense it was the perfect way to end the season. I had to call Uncle Brian, and he had a friend who knew how to break into cars. This guy drives a tow truck and has to do it a lot. So Brian called him and he came and helped us out, and we made our flight in time. We were on the same flight as Michael Lowe and his family, which was perfect because our careers, at least the second half of my career, have kind of run in parallel. We both qualified and retired the same years, these two stumpy goofy-footers, and now here we were both flying home with our families to start our new lives. I know there's still a bit of uncertainty there, but it's going to be an interesting time, a new chapter.

I usually travel with Joel or Bruce and Andy. They're my favourite people to hang out with and I'm going to miss them, even though I'll still be on tour a bit here and there. I still get to hang out with the boys. We'll always remain close. Don't get me wrong, I miss the tour already, but the quality of surfing is getting so good and I am getting a bit older, so I think I left at the right time. You've got to know the right time, because it's just not a good look when you're getting really smoked by the kids. The only time I wasn't surfing good in my last year was when I had my niggling injuries and my stiff back played up. If I feel good, I think I can still mix it with the best. But as you get older you don't bounce back from injury like you used to, and you can't trust your body to perform under pressure, or it just goes all stiff on you and you're history.

The tour is such a rollercoaster ride, full of such extreme highs and lows, and it can be heavy. I'm losing those highs, which will be hard, but I won't have the lows, which will be nice. I'm looking forward to competing in the Masters events against all my old mates from the first half of my career – Pottz, Elko, Curren, Carroll, Barton, Damien – and I'm sure we'll have some great battles and all the old competitive instincts will come to the fore. But I just really want to keep my surfing at a high level and enjoy it, and it's good to have a reason to keep your edge sharp.

> **Mick Lowe:** Our lives have taken parallel paths. We've both got children now and are moving on to our next life stage. It was special for me the other day, to retire with Occ and have the presentation of the Australian rugby shirts from Mick [Fanning] . . . There's Occ and there's daylight. No-one else has really done what he's done. It's amazing. That's never going to die. That was what I aspired to and that's the way I tried to surf.

> **Bruce Irons:** Growing up with him as my hero and then having a paddle battle and him yelling at me, and then becoming one of my best friends and travelling together . . . I never imagined when I was a kid watching *Pump* that one day I'd be here, watching with all the boys carrying him up the beach when he

retires from the tour. It's trippy. It's going to suck without him. When I grew up, he was one of my heroes. There's no-one like him and there will never be anyone like him. I never, ever, in my wildest dreams thought I'd be on tour with him.

Joel Parkinson: He hangs out and acts just like one of your own-age mates, but then when you see a younger grommet, they look at him like a full elder, because that's what he is on the tour. We have those surfers' meetings, and they can be pretty rowdy, but when he talks a lot of people shut up and listen, because sometimes it's just a classic thing he's going to say or he tells you something great. He's got some good stuff to say. It will be really strange not having him there, especially at J-Bay. Every morning I'd get up to go to the contest, go see Occ and see what he's doing, because you know he's always up for the early.

Buddy McCray: He's still one of the most enthusiastic people I know. He just loves what he's doing and it shows. He's got a lot of natural ability. He's got a funny physique, but man does it work – so solid. It reminds me of some of those Italian statues chiselled in granite. That solid stature and that weight in his feet, there's no way he's going to fall off. I was just always so stoked to see the energy he has. He's so positive about it. He could go out in absolute ankle-snappers and still be full of enthusiasm, no matter what it was, or where it was.

Richard Marsh: I think there's that childlike thing, that man-child in him. I don't think many people could have done what he's done. The tour's quite a taxing environment, and he hasn't done that well in the last few years, either. The tour's the best job in the world when you're winning and the worst job in the world when you're losing, and to hang in there when you're not winning is really hard. I think everyone likes him so much, it's just home. It's just family. He's like the Don. I said, 'No wonder you're still doing it.' He said, 'Look at it – my family's here, why wouldn't I?'

It's going to be interesting. I know he'll do well. The tour teaches you really good life skills. You come off the tour pretty rounded with what you can do – you've just got to get the confidence to do it. I think that's what most of the boys face, to step out on your own, so I think he'll do really good. I just hope he steps up to the challenges. It's really good to do new things, but I'm sure he must be having the odd moment, drinking a beer, thinking, *what next?* I think he should go into the media, definitely.

LIFE AFTER THE TOUR

I still struggle sometimes dealing with the whole surf-star thing, and that's one thing I won't miss too much. Some days I wake up and I'm sweet, but other days I wake up and I deadset feel like I've got a magnet on me, because I get people coming up from everywhere. Just some days, everywhere you go, everyone goes, 'There's Occy.' It feels like you've got a massive sign on your head. It must be your aura. People just come up to you all day long, and I say to Mae, 'It's one of those days, I've got the magnet on me', and she laughs. Sometimes it's a good thing. If I'm on a trip somewhere in Australia and I go into some little country service station, and they go, 'Hey Occy, how you going?' It doesn't matter where we are, it feels like home.

I'm still not sure what I'm going to be doing. I had to host this international brand release for Billabong recently in front of 600 people at Twin Towns, Coolangatta. I was really nervous, and it was rubbing off on other people. I was introducing them and I was making them nervous. But I think I did all right. I enjoy that kind of stuff; I like trying to make people laugh, and usually I'm okay at it. I'm doing some stuff with Fuel TV, and that's good fun.

It's a weird thing, I've always loved working the till, from those days in the old G & S store as a grommet. Parko and I were doing a surf shop promo recently in Manly, and they had us working the tills. We put twenty bucks on it, to see who could sell the most. Joel sold $1200 worth of stuff in forty minutes. I did about $700. It was fun, and they can put your name in the computer so it spits your name out on the receipt – Occy or Parko. People loved it, they could show people their receipt and go, 'I bought this off Occy.' Maybe I'll run my own surf shop one day.

Luke Egan: It's hard. I've been through it and it's hard. You've just got to keep training as if you're in the events. After retirement, I just stopped everything, stopped training, had a surf here and there. And then after about six months I just woke up one day and went, *this is fucked, I've got to get back into training.* I train a lot. That's what I want to make him do, make him train. We go stand-up paddling, and he's left his paddle behind four or five times. People just know it's Occy's. Anyone else, it would get swiped, gone, but he just keeps getting it given back. Probably more than an ambassador, I'd like him to be an icon, because an icon can be whatever it wants to be and it doesn't have to change – ever.

Rabbit Bartholomew: It's a super-difficult transition. I'd have to say I've had a couple of moments with Occy where we've raised that subject. I think there's a lot of fear. I think there's been a lot of fear. I think that's what kept him on tour. If he felt a little bit more secure within himself, he may have left a year earlier, but I think he hung on and he's a little fearful of what happened last time, because he needs the motivation. He needs that 5 am dawn patrol. But I think there are several factors in his life now that will be of great assistance. One of those is Mae, and Mae is just such a beautiful human being, and she's such a fantastic support, and she's blessed his life – not only by herself, but by giving him two sons. And the fact that these two beautiful little guys are with him will be a great long-term motivation for him. And I think that's by far the most important factor.

He's going to go through some real sadness any moment now, because the reality of the tour leaving town without him is going to be a hard one, it's going to hit him hard, but there are things coming on stream. He's come back into club surfing now with his son. He'll always be a Cronulla boy, but he's loving competing with the Snapper boys, and he wants to be a part of the club scene, and his son wants to, so he'll do some representative surfing for the club. There's also the ASP World Masters that we're about to get going now, and he'll participate in that, and that will be a good thing because there's a world title on the line. And so there'll be those reasons to do some more surfing and give some purpose to his surfing. There's lots of things going round in his head right now. He said something to me that made me realise there's still some concern. He went out one morning and said he felt like he was surfing as good as he ever has, and then he went, 'But what for? What does it matter?' He couldn't see a point to maintaining that level of surfing, and that concerned me.

It's funny looking back over my career and how it evolved. There was a day at the Beaurepaires in '83 when I surfed through the trials and made the main event, and it was at Elouera and it was about eight to ten foot. It was really hard to get out the back, but I was superfit then, and I powered out the back and got this right-hander and did one of the biggest backhand turns I'd ever done in my life. They showed it on the TV news in the highlights, and I went straight out of the bottom, straight into the lip and straight back down again and just landed it perfectly. And I felt like that's what I really wanted to do – just do the biggest turn I possibly could and blow everyone away. I don't think I even got through the heat, but that wasn't the point. That was the kind of surfing I wanted to do.

But when it got small, there were a lot of guys who could just surf a smarter heat and smoke me. I had to learn that contest repertoire, that it's not all about big barrels and big turns – sometimes you've got to play the game. But maybe I learnt it too well, because when all the new-school crew came along in the second half of my career busting airs and reverses, suddenly I was the three-to-the-beach guy, and I was like, *what happened there?* Hopefully not too many people think of me too much like that, but I do a bit. Sure, my big turns helped keep me on tour for as long as I did, and they suited the new tour in good waves. But I had to learn to surf smart heats and change my surfing to get through. Now the kind of thing that's been knocking me down the ratings is the aerial surfing, and I've gone from new school to old school.

People ask me if I miss the tour, and of course I do. I used to love turning up at a new event. You've got new luck, a new hotel, a new car, all new things. And whatever path you take, if you're feeling positive, you stick to that line. If you lose that feeling, you lose. Then you hate it, and you're on the first plane out of there. Life's perfect as long as you're winning heats. Even second sometimes can do your head in. When you win, you've won, you've done the puzzle, the whole puzzle. From the time you get off the plane and get in the hire car, to the time you fly home, you've put the last piece in there. People always say it was the old tour that brought me undone, because there were so many events, but I loved it. I like it better now, but back then it was just more puzzles to do. When you're young, you just want to do puzzles. I guess I'm going to have to find other puzzles to do to keep life interesting.

Mae Occhilupo: I don't think I really quite grasped it, what he was saying goodbye to, but I think he's been preparing himself for it. It's been like a two- or three-year retirement. He just hasn't been ready. About five or six years ago, when we first started dating, before the kids came, he used to say, 'I could give up surfing and go and live in Jamaica. Would you come with me?' And I said, 'Of course.' He said, 'I really want to take up singing', and I said, 'Let's do it.' I think we're going to try and go to the Caribbean and feel it out. He's got a great voice, and he's got so much feeling. There're a few times when he's had me in tears. He would serenade me and get the guitar out.

One thing I've really come to believe is that the ocean heals us. If I'd been some other sort of sportsman or musician or something, and had reached such a low ebb in my life, I don't know if I would have ever made it back. But it was surfing and coming back to the ocean that really helped me heal my life. I think of the ocean as my friend. Every time I see a piece of rubbish in the ocean I put it in my wetsuit, and every time I see rubbish on the beach I pick it up. Whenever I greet the ocean I always take one step into it and two steps back when a wave hits me, just in respect. I really respect the ocean, and I think it kind of knows that. I feel like I've lived a big part of my life in the ocean, and it's like we know each other pretty well.

There are times in Hawaii when it's really big and angry, and you can't help but go, 'Okay, you're in control.' But for me the ocean's in control whether it's one foot or ten foot. It writes the script. It writes the script for everyday living. Every time I go surfing I come in happy, no matter what. It's a spiritual thing. I've had so many incredible experiences in the ocean, and it feels like it just delivers to you exactly what you need at that point in your life. Sometimes you see or hear things in the ocean right when you need to. You might hear a backwash slap together, and that might scare you a little bit, and wake you up to pay attention. It can humble you if you get cocky. Or it just totally glasses off for you and gives you a magical session when you most need it. I had one this morning – the sun came up and it was so still and it was such a beautiful sunrise, and I was just in awe of my good fortune to be a surfer and to be in the ocean. That happens for me a lot of mornings. People who don't surf can only imagine how special it is to be a surfer. You can be feeling so low and the surf makes you feel so special, whether it's seeing that sunrise or that sunset, or some wildlife in the ocean. So many special moments happen in the ocean; it just draws you back, no matter what. I think it's irresistible.

The ocean is such a special thing, it's got be treasured and respected. That's why I am such a fan of people like Dave Rastovich and Captain Paul Watson from Sea Shepherd, and anyone who's on that program to help save the oceans. That's why I want to work for SurfAid and Sea Shepherd and be an ambassador for them. I wear the Sea Shepherd stickers on my boards, and I'll do whatever SurfAid wants me to do to promote their work. I feel like I want to give back, because the ocean's given me so much, not even materially, but spiritually. If you've had that much enjoyment out of the ocean, it's only natural that you want to give back. And really, what you are giving back is to the kids growing up now – my children and everyone else's children, who are all the ocean's children.

They reckon all life came from the ocean – maybe that's why we all want to keep going back there. People sometimes say to me, 'I hadn't surfed for so long and you got me back in the water.' I always say, 'I don't think I got you back in the water, I think the water got you back in the water.'

Afterword

It's about 9 pm on the Fijian island resort of Namotu, and most of the Australian pro surfers on hand for the Globe Fiji Pro are gathered about the bar, playing a noisy video game called Guitar Hero. It's a layday in competition, and the boys are letting their hair down. I step outside to get some air and take in the night sky. In the shadows, on the outskirts of the pool area, I notice a group of Fijians sitting on a grass mat, conducting their own quiet kava session. One tangle of sun-bleached hair stands out amongst circle. I wander over, hover in the shadows, uncertain if I should intrude on this private moment. The Fijians seem to sense my presence, wriggle along and indicate a place for me in the circle. Occ is pushing the hair back off his face and grinning like a Cheshire cat. 'I don't know how many nights I've had with these guys, drinking kava till three in the morning, laughing our heads off,' he tells me later.

At a glance, you could be excused for thinking Occ is on the kind of mad bender that brought him unstuck in his youth. He seems to be always at the bar, belting the karaoke until there are only a few stragglers left, pouring his heart into each tune, tearing at his clothing like some tortured pop starlet. But look more closely and there are subtle, telltale signs of a growing maturity, the wisdom of experience. He is drinking water between beers for a start, so when everyone else is legless late in the night, Occ is still cruising. If he has a big night, it's more often on the kava than the booze, a mild sedative that seems to have few short-term side effects. He's on the early boat out to Cloudbreak almost every day, pre-dawn. There are

295

long, leisurely naps in the afternoon, and one civilised cocktail on dusk. This is a man who has refined his lifestyle over many years and, after exploring all sorts of extremes, has found his own kind of happy equilibrium.

A couple of nights later, the locals hold a full-blown traditional kava ceremony in Occy's honour. Sereanna, the head lady among the staff, who was working here when Occ won the event in his world title year in '99, stands to say a few words. Occ's almost in tears from the outset, trying to hug her before she's even finished her speech. I'm trying to commit it to memory, figuring this is one moment not to reach for the pen and notepad, or recorder, and just take it in. So I can't tell you word for word what this stately grandmother said that night. But it was along the lines of how much they've enjoyed having him stay over the years, how they've always followed his career. How proud they were of him. Every time they'd see him in a magazine or video, they'd all go, 'Hey, there's Occy!'

They'd been told he was retiring and, because they weren't sure when he'd be back, they wanted to wish him good luck in the future with his family. I asked Sereanna later why the Fijians seemed so fond of Occ, why they connected with him? 'He has a big heart,' Sereanna told me. 'He mingles with us. He's just different.' The feeling's definitely mutual, and you get the sense that there are few places in the world Occ feels more at home, more in his element than as popularly elected Emperor of this fine empire – with three gourmet meals a day, comfortable beachfront quarters, world-famous bar, great fishing and ridiculous waves. It's what you might dream up as a school boy surf fantasy.

At one stage, Occy is sitting at the bar, watching Parko fish for shark off the beach around dusk. Suddenly, he announces he has a clear line of sight from the bar to the water and that, therefore, it should be theoretically possible to fish from the bar itself. He becomes gripped by an urgent need to prove his theory, wanders down the beach and heckles Parko until he gives over his rod and becomes his willing assistant in this mad endeavour. Sure enough, to his word, Occ takes his place at the bar, rod in hand, watching his line bobbing in the wind-ruffled South Pacific surf, a potent 'Skulldrag' cocktail to his left, karaoke microphone to his right. Ready for anything.

As I write this, the stories keep coming in. I can't turn them off. I have had to admit defeat and confess I cannot collect and transcribe every Occy anecdote in the world. There are simply too many. There's a great old Australian film called *Man of Flowers*, and in it this eccentric, philosophical postman makes the observation that the Queen Mother has met around a million people in her life, and every one of them will treasure the memory to their grave. 'Now, if one old lady can spread so much joy, well, the potential for human happiness is boundless,' he theorises boldly. It's a bit like that with Occ. There are probably thousands of people spread around the planet who count themselves as dear friends of his. I could never get to them all. But among those I did get to, without fail, their spirits lifted at the mere mention of his name, eyes sparkled, reminiscences flooded in. The times people have shared with Occ always seem to be among their most treasured memories.

I meet his old golfing mate Bing at the Tugun bowls club over dinner, and he tells me the story about one of Occ's birthday celebrations at the Gold Coast Casino, how he had a big win, about ten grand, and stashed it in his room so he wouldn't blow it. Ingeniously, he stuffed the chips in the bar fridge and returned to the casino floor, safe in the knowledge that his winnings were secure. He was driving home the next day when the casino rang him. They'd found something in his room. His heart skipped a beat. *What sort of something?* 'Forget it,' he said. 'Whatever it is, keep it.'

'I think you're going to want this,' the casino man said. 'It's probably best if you come see for yourself.' Occ pulled a reluctant U-turn and reported back to the casino reception. 'This yours?' the casino man asked, holding up ten grand in chips. 'I'd completely forgotten about it,' Occ marvels, even still.

I guess what I'm trying to say is, this biography, *no* biography, can really be an exhaustive account of everything that has happened in someone's life, especially not Occ's. At best, this is hopefully a fairly representative cross-section of what is an expanding body of work. Even as I write, there are new chapters being lived: wildcard visits to J-Bay, Mundaka, a promo trip back to the ancestral home of Italy – conveniently enough, now one of Billabong's fastest growing new markets. It's an evolving, writhing, twisting beast. One thing I've learnt too: there are multiple versions of the truth. Where there were discrepancies, I've gone with Occ's version of events, tried to be faithful to my subject. Others will have other versions. There are some I couldn't get to, tried and failed, or just ran out of time. I've had to admit to myself, you can never really finish a book like this. There's new material to add every time you think you've written an ending. And that's as it should be. Occ's alive and well, after all, still being paid to go surfing, beautiful family to enjoy, new opportunities arising.

My abiding image of the Man from all this is a story he told over beers at the Namotu bar, about driving to Brisbane Airport for his flight to Fiji. Occy has always had unusual ways of transporting surfboards. This is a man, remember, who used to check in at airports with his prized Rusty completely 'naked', without any sort of boardbag or covering, because he figured the baggage handlers would take care of it if they saw how fragile it was. Genius! This time, Occ secured his two large coffin boardbags to his luxury four-wheel drive with a couple of legropes. 'They've got a bit of give in them,' he explained, 'so the boards kind of lift up a few inches above the roofracks.'

By some intuitive understanding of aerodynamics, Occy calculates the correct tension on the leggie to allow the boards to rise not more than a few inches off the racks at high speed. This transforms the load into an efficient spoiler, Occy explained, the boardbags suspended in a kind of delicate equilibrium that kept them secure. The sight, however, of this wild-haired, big-jawed man hurtling down the freeway, boardbags aero-planing a few inches above the car, proved so alarming to fellow motorists that there were nearly several accidents. Every passing driver would gesticulate wildly at Occ as they drove past, indicating the imminent loss of his cargo. Occ would wave back and try and reassure them that he had it covered. 'Nah, it's sweet,' he'd insist. One fellow was so concerned that he wound down his window and start screaming at Occ to pull over. He pulled alongside and recognised the driver, just as his sunglasses blew off in the wind. Then he started demanding Occy's glasses as compensation for the loss of his own. Occy told him, 'No way', and just kept on driving.

Mick Fanning and Joel Parkinson just happened to draw up on the whole mad scene on their own way to the airport. 'Check out this clown with his boards coming off,' they laughed to each other. Then they too pulled alongside and realised who was driving. Occ just waved to them all regally and kept on his way.

'The leggies are looped through the handles, so they can't ever completely come off,' he reasoned.

That's the kind of journey it's been – Occy's merry Mr Magoo parade through life, happily oblivious to the carnage he so often seems to leave in his wake. I can see him now, driving happily on, while the world protests his defiance of the natural laws of physics, decorum, endurance. Almost, but never quite, losing his load. It's an incredible high-wire act, and he's entranced us all for a couple of decades now. I reckon Occ's earnt his retirement, though he doesn't look like slowing down any time soon.

Tributes

Gerry Lopez: That's what surfing is – overcoming adversity. Like getting caught inside, especially on a big day: you either give up or you keep paddling. And I guess that's what you could say about Occy: no matter what, he kept paddling, and made it back outside. He not only did that, but he got the best wave of the set.

Rabbit Bartholomew: Occy's a shining example of everything I believe in about pro surfing. It goes back to when Mrs Peterson told me, 'Rabbit, you're nineteen – if you don't do it this year, you never will.' She got it into my head. And Nat and Midget and those guys had all been world champions at eighteen. By the time they were twenty-two or twenty-four, they were off doing their other things. Twenty-five was very old, and then came my era. One thing that always upset me – and it really influenced my thinking at ASP –when I came to the Stubbies ranked number one, one of the judges made a statement, saying, 'The worst thing for surfing right now would be if Rabbit won the world title, because he's old, he's thirty years old.' And that really stuck with me, and I said, I will wipe out that attitude, because this sport is an individual sport and everybody should be able to develop and blossom at different times. And it shouldn't be dictated to you by some parameters.

I think you can surf to your late thirties as a pro, especially in good waves, all you want is that it's fair. Everybody's got to be able to run their own race, and surfing's not a contact sport, it's a sport where if you work at it you can surf at a very high level for a long time. And if your hunger and desire is there, and you're not burnt out, you should be able to go a fair way. And Occy's record-breaking longevity was exactly what I was talking about. And others will do it, and I think that's a great thing. It's not like rugby league where your injuries really do catch up with you in your mid-thirties. If you've got natural attributes . . . And Occy had the rest, but he had the natural attributes in that he could maintain his power base without any work. And I think that served him well. His attitude was childlike, and that served him really well, because who enjoys life more than a grommet? It's the ultimate. We all try to stay there, but he actually did.

Andy Irons: He definitely mentored me and gave me some great advice. I used to really get upset about what magazines would write and really dwell on them. It was never anything positive, and it used to spin me out. And he said, 'Don't even read them anymore . . . Just look at the pictures.' So, for a year when me and Kelly were going head to head, I didn't even read them. It really helped – it just helped me relax.

Dougall Walker: Every new generation of grommets that have come through have been able to relate to Occy. He has a very disarming personality. Occy's been in some pretty wild situations over the years. Considering how aggressively he surfs, I've never seen any aggression in his personality. For instance, he's had many opportunities to get into fights over the years, given the places he's been and the people he's been with, but in all those years I can never, ever recall any physical violence. It might not sound that astonishing but, given what he's been through, that's a pretty amazing circumstance, and a lot of his peers can't say the same.

Rabbit Bartholomew: What about the legions of teenagers that love him? That's a hard nut to crack. It's very difficult to move out of your box, generationally, but he has done that as well. I think it's a combination of things. He's a very sociable guy and just a very lovable human being, at once very down to earth and yet a little bit out there . . . and that childlike quality as well. People see the natural stoke of the guy, and they relate to his 'grommetishness', the passion of a young guy who loves something so much that he's just completely ensconced in it. And I think Occy likes people, and he embraces people. He holds court at Mundaka in that circle of life, and people love that. There will be no-one sitting there this time. And he was the rock, he was the catalyst. In Hawaii his best friend is Brian Surratt, and he's really adored by a lot of people over there. At Namotu he'll have a beer with the best of them; he'll have a little dance with the Fijian ladies; he'll drink a bit of kava – and they love that. And the same here; this is his adopted home now and we love him.

Gary Green: It's amazing the youthfulness he's kept given how hard he's gone. He used to act pretty naive, but he's a lot smarter than he let's on. He plays dumb because then there's no expectation on him.

Andy Irons: He's just classic. Everyday's funny with him. His laugh's all-time and he's just a kid. He loves karaoke; he loves to sing; he's just a professional entertainer in surfing, and I think he likes to do the same on land – put on a good show. And any time he's got the karaoke on, he does some really good Bob Marley songs. Any time we're hanging out, there's always something good happening. It's always fun. I always look forward to seeing him. If he's ever anywhere near, I always make the effort to go find him and hang out.

It's rare, I think, to have one of your heroes as such a close friend. Me and my brother, we're probably the luckiest guys in the world to have a hero who likes to hang out with you. He gives me a call every once in a while, and it's like the best thing in the world. It's a real friendship. For him being such a nice guy to us, it just means the world to us.

Joel Parkinson: You see when he gets on a wave he generates speed through his turns, and a lot of guys try to do that now because of him. Only a handful of the top guys generate speed through the momentum of pressure on the water through your board, know what I mean? I try and do it, try and get that whole body momentum and pressure, like a slingshot effect almost. That's why he's so good at the points – six-foot J-Bay, howling offshore, I'd hate to have a heat against him. You'd probably pick forty other guys in the contest before you'd pick him. And fifteen years from now he'd probably still be able to go out there and do it.

Nick Carroll: Occy was always a hero of little kids; the little kids always wanted to know about Occy. Even when he was in his mid to late teens and started to shine, he was always a favourite of the little kids. We surveyed a high school class recently about their surf heroes, and Occy was right up there. There's something essentially childlike that people can't help but connect with, partly because they feel like they've left part of that behind, and it's nice to be reconnected with it. That guy is one of the smartest readers of a contest heat in the sport's history, maybe even better than Kelly. People think he's all goofy, but when it comes to surfing heats you couldn't find a smarter guy. When it comes to the ins and outs of heats, and what can go wrong or right . . .

That's why guys like Andy look at him like a guru. And also because he was a train wreck, and some of them think they could become train wrecks. He gives them all heart. We could all be potential train wrecks. Sometimes you think they're all hanging on to things by a thread . . . There's that vulnerability, people want to protect him.

Tom Carroll: That guy is awesome. When I see him watching a heat, I always want to hear what he's got to say. I think he'd be an awesome coach, one of the best ones you could ever find. If he could develop trust in the competitor, he would be an awesome coach. Because he's so analytical – he's very good at breaking stuff down and keeping it simple. He has a very tuned intellect; he's tuned in because he's so sensitive. He's a really sensitive soul, there's no doubt about it. A twenty- to thirty-minute heat, he's so highly tuned into breaking it down. I learn something every time I hear him do it, because I'm hopeless.

Rusty Preisendorfer: Aside from his absolutely freakish talent, Occy is a character, almost nerdish or oddball. He believed he was a rock star, but Occy was more like a seal or an otter in the sense that he was capable of functioning for brief periods on dry land, a little awkward and out of place, but once he slipped back into the water he was completely in his element. Occy is always upbeat and rarely, if ever, had a negative thing to say about anything or anybody. He just went about his business of blowing minds.

Tom Carroll: By going down so hard in the late 80s and early 90s, by actually letting go of himself and fully falling apart, he was able to give himself longevity. It's almost contradictory to how we think it works. It's like the Buddhist teachings about birth and death – something has to die for new birth to happen, and that happens inside us too. Occy was the ultimate example of that. One thing about Occy, he can bring to light action and involvement without ego; he can come along in that space, and the vulnerability he shows is so attractive and so magnetic. It's a really special and blessed kind of state to be in. It just keeps on shining. He doesn't hang onto anything; he's just there.

Paul Sargeant: You can't explain it – the only thing I can put it down to is God's blessed him with this incredible favour from people. Everybody gives him favour, whatever he wants, whenever he wants it. People just love him. What they see is someone who they perceive as innocent, incredibly talented, humorous, and at the same time has just retained this incredible naivety that humours people. He's like everyone's little cuddly toy.

John Howitt: Anyone who's got these kinds of talents, they're complicated. In having those talents they also have weaknesses. To get to as low as he did and come back and win the world title, it just shows how strong he is.

Luke Egan: It's been a big journey, and he feels pretty humble that he got through. I think he looks at his kids and goes, *I want them to grow up like me, but oooh, there's some shit there I'd like them to miss out on.* He worries about that . . .

We're going to turn into old blokes together. We've already got it all planned. We're already sorted. All we've got to do is just stay alive. We both live in Coolangatta; we both hang out together – it's all set up. We've just got to hang in there, and we're going to be doing exactly what we're doing now for the rest of our lives.

Acknowledgements

There are too many people who are owed thanks for the coming together of this book to list here. But what the heck, I'm going to try anyway. Mark's mother, Pam, was generous and gracious in sharing the family history, photos and reference material. Pam has written her own heart-felt account of her son's life, a remarkable document of Mark's career, extracts from which appear throughout this book. It would have been much the poorer without her help. Mark's sisters Shan, Alex and Fleur were all helpful and welcoming and beam with pride for their brother. Special thanks to Paul Sargeant for his incredible archive of photos and memories, and additional research. Sarge's interview with Beatrice, before she was killed tragically in a car accident in 2007, was the only surviving testimony to her life with Mark, and her pivotal role in his comeback. It was eerie to hear her voice from the grave, and it seemed especially important to honour her role in Mark's story. It was great to see Rainer too, now grown into a man, and the bond he and Occy still share. Mark's wife, Mae, was incredibly understanding and accommodating to make time for the research for this book, another in a long list of duties that Occy's post-tour life now involves. Sons Jay and Jonah are adorable, and two of the best young travellers I've ever come across.

Craig Wilken was a valuable assistant researcher, scouring through piles of old *Tracks* magazines for Occy references, and thanks to his family too for their understanding.

Renato Hickel, from ASP, provided invaluable help, specifically, every heat draw from Occ's career on disk. It would have been almost impossible to verify dates and events without it. This disk did, however, cause it's share of grief. Burnt on a PC, my Apple stubbornly refused to open it. Eventually, Occy suggested getting them printed out so he could hold the heat draws in his hands, like he did at surf contests over the years, and all those old names from the various eras of his career brought the memories flooding back.

Brandon Van Over has been a patient, diligent and enthusiastic editor, and Alison Urquhart and Jane Burridge have been my twin pillars of support in the sometimes baffling world of publishing. Many thanks. Everyone at Random House has been hugely behind this project from the start, and I thank them all for their energy and enthusiasm.

Everyone who granted me an interview for this book has helped keep me going, injected new excitement, humour, warmth and drama to spur me on when the interminable grind of transcribing and editing nearly proved too much. The staff and management of Namotu Island Resort, Scott and Mandy, Sereanna, Charlie and everyone else at Namotu treated us like kings during our stay and made the final stages of this project more pleasure than pain. Brian Robbins at Globe was an out and out champion in finding room for me on Namotu during the Globe Fiji Pro, providing the perfect setting in which to complete our research. Thanks to everyone at Billabong for their support, especially Luke Egan, Talon Clemow and Andrew Flitton. And special thanks to Bree Andrews at International Sports Management for all her help, particularly managing Mark's time to make sure we spent as long as we needed on this book.

Most of all, I'd like to thank Mark, for somehow coming through this wild ride, with spirit, humour and talent in tact, with one hell of a story to tell and a willingness to share it. It's been an honour to help facilitate this documenting of Mark's life. I wish he and his lovely family well in the new chapters ahead, yet to be written.

To all my sponsors, past and present; everyone at Billabong around the world – especially Derek O'Neill, Andrew Flitton, Paul Naude, Cheron Kraak, Graham Stapelberg, Reid Pinder, Craig Sage. Everyone at Globe, especially Brian Robbins. JS Industries, Hoven sunglasses, Skoda Auto and Corona. My management: Bree Andrews, Michael Searle and everyone at International Sports Management.

Tim, thank you for your time and patience and your hard work in making this project a reality. We had some great moments along this journey, whether in Hawaii, Fiji, Angourie, or just sitting on top of D-bah hill and watching the surf. Mate, I couldn't have done this without you.

And thanks to everyone I've forgotten – anyone who's ever given me a wave, shaped me a board, cooked me a meal, given me a bed for the night, driven me up or down the coast, or hooted me in the water.

And biggest thanks of all to the best thing that's ever happened to me – Mae, Jay and Jonah.

– Mark Occhilupo

About the Author

Tim Baker is a former editor of *Tracks and Surfing Life* magazines and the author of four books on surfing, including *Bustin' Down the Door* and *High Surf*. He has twice received the Australian Surfing Hall of Fame Media/Culture Award and been nominated for the CUB Australian Sports Writing Awards. His work has appeared in *Rolling Stone, GQ, The Sydney Morning Herald, The Australian Financial Review, The Bulletin, Playboy, Inside Sport* and *Alpha*, as well as surfing magazines around the world. He is currently a senior contributor to *Surfing World, The Surfer's Journal, The Surfer's Path* and US *Surfer* and *Surfing* magazines.

He lives in Currumbin, Queensland, with his wife, Kirsten, and children, Vivi and Alex.

To find out more go to: www.bytimbaker.com

The co-authors on location, deep in their research.
(Photo: Steve Sherman)